A Musical Journey Across

Three Centuries,

Four Countries,

and a Half-Dozen Revolutions

Chasing Chopin

Annik LaFarge

SIMON & SCHUSTER PAPERBACKS

NEW YORK   LONDON   TORONTO   SYDNEY   NEW DELHI

Simon & Schuster Paperbacks
An Imprint of Simon & Schuster, Inc.
1230 Avenue of the Americas
New York, NY 10020

First Simon & Schuster trade paperback edition August 2021

SIMON & SCHUSTER and colophon are registered trademarks of Simon & Schuster, Inc.

For information about special discounts for bulk purchases, please contact Simon & Schuster Special Sales at 1-866-506-1949 or business@simonandschuster.com.

The Simon & Schuster Speakers Bureau can bring authors to your live event. For more information or to book an event, contact the Simon & Schuster Speakers Bureau at 1-866-248-3049 or visit our website at www.simonspeakers.com.

Interior design by Carly Loman
Transcription and music graphic on the dedication page © 2020 by Oliver Kwapis (BMI)

Manufactured in the United States of America

10 9 8 7 6 5 4 3 2 1

The Library of Congress has cataloged the hardcover edition as follows:
Names: LaFarge, Annik, author.
Title: Chasing Chopin : a musical journey across three centuries, four countries, and a half-dozen revolutions / by Annik LaFarge
Description: New York : Simon & Schuster, 2020. | Includes bibliographical references.
Identifiers: LCCN 2019049711 | ISBN 9781501188718 (hardcover) | ISBN 9781501188732 (ebook)
Subjects: LCSH: Chopin, Frédéric, 1810–1849. | Chopin, Frédéric, 1810–1849. Sonatas, piano, no. 2, op. 35, B♭ minor.
Classification: LCC ML410.C54 L195 2020 | DDC 786.2092—dc23
LC record available at https://lccn.loc.gov/2019049711

ISBN 978-1-5011-8871-8
ISBN 978-1-5011-8872-5 (pbk)
ISBN 978-1-5011-8873-2 (ebook)

for Ann

Contents

Dancing About Architecture

Almost immediately after I began working on this book, I stumbled on an old cliché that will resonate with anyone who has ever tried to explain in words what a piece of music means to them: *Writing about music is like dancing about architecture.*

No one seems to know who said it first, but the statement stuck around because it so perfectly captures the challenge. Music is an abstract art form, one that exists in time, is defined by mathematics, and is written in a complex language that consists of symbols, numbers, a horizontal grid, and emotion-laden words in (usually) Italian. If I were getting ready to tell you a story about a work of art, I would insert— probably right below this sentence—an image. That would give you an immediate context for what comes next, something to hold in your mind as you read about the people, places, and events, as well as the joys and sorrows, that animate my subject. But musical notation in the pages of a book like this, one that attempts to tell a human story about the creative process, would be useless to all but the most expert of readers. So to help bridge the gap between words and music I built a companion website that makes it easy to find and listen to the works of Chopin, as well as the many other composers who become relevant in the story, from J. S. Bach to Cole Porter.

The site, which lives at www.whychopin.com, is accessible in any Web browser and is organized more like a book than a traditional website. Each chapter of *Chasing Chopin* has a section, or web page, where links to recordings (along with basic information like the title of a piece, its opus number and date of composition) are listed in the order in which they appear in the text, along with the page number for easy reference. Sometimes there are two links for a single work, so a reader can hear the same piece of music as it's played on both a modern Steinway and a nineteenth-century pianoforte. This is because I spend a good deal of time talking about the pianos that were available during Chopin's lifetime, and the many differences between them and the instrument we know today—things that actually affect the way we perceive the music. This allows a reader to experience what is the closest we can come to a nineteenth-century soundscape, when recording technology didn't exist, and compare it to the sound a modern artist might produce at Carnegie Hall or on National Public Radio. There are also links to a wide variety of interpretations of Chopin's work in jazz, modern song, and popular culture, along with photography and video from my travels; scholarly and popular resources; and more.

One of the first links on WhyChopin.com is to a recording of the funeral march from Chopin's Opus 35 Sonata, whose composition story constitutes the narrative arc of this book. What you hear first is the familiar dirge—*dum dum da dum*—written in the key of B-flat minor. Then comes the surprising and beautiful major-key interlude (in D flat), which is in turn followed by an inexorable return of the minor-key dirge. It's this modulation, the striking progression from minor to major to minor, that I would illustrate with an image if I could. It's at the heart of the story I'm about to tell, and is what astonished me the first time I heard the sonata, and inspired me to learn more about the man who conceived it and the circumstances in which he wrote and lived. Even if you know absolutely nothing about music, I think you will hear what captivated me in this startling, original statement about death and life.

Of course the website is not necessary; it's just a tool, something that might enhance a reader's experience by making it easy to access the best, and in some cases inaccessible, recordings. Beyond a few observations in the opening pages about the two sections of the funeral march, there's very little technical or theoretical stuff in the pages ahead; it's mostly, in effect, a love story, one that connects humans to one another, and all of us to art. But if you do come across a term that feels foreign or confusing, my advice is to just skip over it and keep reading. Or, better yet, get up and dance about it.

INTRODUCTION

Bull's-eye

Music is often the language we speak when we speak about death. My father was a poet and playwright, but when he became so ill it was clear the end was near, it was music that was on his mind, not words. The only request he made was that, after he died, we let his body remain on the hospital bed in his room and fill the house with music for twenty-four hours before the undertaker came. It was Bach's Suites for Unaccompanied Cello that he requested, and so someone in the family who had a basic level of technical expertise figured out how to put the six suites, played by Pablo Casals, into a continuous loop. All day and all night, as people came and went, slept and wept, talked and laughed, the music of Johann Sebastian Bach permeated every room of the house, offering a kind of structure to those many minutes and hours of our collective grief. It also, and this came to me as I sat on the stairs leading up to my father's bedroom that crisp, sunny, late October morning, served to connect us, not just to him but to each other. Music, unlike poetry, requires other humans to animate it from the page. Whether you play for one person or many, it is at some level an affair of the community, something we do together to bring a bit of beauty and meaning into our lives. It also reminds us, especially at times around death and dying, of what connects us. This is because music needs both a player *and* a street, the one who brings it to life and the cohort that participates through listening. Once launched, whether on a stage or in a Rhode Island farmhouse, it becomes a kind of adhesive, knitting together disparate people for the brief passage of its duration, accompanying us in our attempt to accept things that are, perhaps, beyond understanding.

I thought about all this many years later, when death once again beckoned from afar. It was January 2017, and I had flown to Chicago to say goodbye to a dear friend who was in the final stages of ovarian cancer. Slowly and with great difficulty she walked me through every floor of the house, just a few blocks from Wrigley Field, that she and her husband had built in the early days of their marriage. Then we sat by the fire and talked about our work together—I had been the editor of her first book—and the new project she was working on with her daughter, which they completed in the days before she died. I had never said goodbye to someone so young—she was in her early fifties—and when I left the house, was so rattled I got hopelessly lost trying to navigate the unfamiliar streets of Chicago's Northwest side. It was cold, rainy, and getting dark. With several hours to kill before my overnight train departed Union Station, I hailed a cab and headed to a jazz club. My feet were wet, I was feeling exhausted and sad, drinking bourbon alone at my table near the stage, listening to a group called the Andy Brown Quartet. Then, in the middle of a swinging tune, the pianist suddenly started riffing on Chopin's funeral march. This was surprising enough, but what startled me most was the expression on the faces of the band members: they were all smiling, leaning into a dirge now animated by a bebop lilt, in what looked like a mode of joy. They passed the melody around from one to another:

piano threw it to guitar, who played with it for a while, then handed it over to bass. Meanwhile the famous rhythm was being tapped out on cymbals by the drummer. Finally it was returned to the pianist, who fooled around a bit more with Chopin and then returned to the song that had kicked it all off.

I've long felt a special attachment to Chopin's funeral march, and can remember with perfect clarity the first time I heard it, back in 1998, in the Polish Consulate on Madison Avenue, a Beaux Arts mansion built in the early years of the twentieth century. The Polish government bought the house in 1973 and soon began hosting concerts in its spacious, ornate rooms. I had begun taking piano lessons a few years earlier and was in the process of falling deeply in love with Chopin's music, when I learned that an upcoming recital would include his Second Piano Sonata, known as Opus 35, a major work by my favorite composer that I didn't yet know. Or, at any rate, *thought* I didn't know.

The sonata begins almost with a sigh and then it rampages. It takes Chopin just a few seconds to move from the heavy, slow, ponderous tempo of *grave* to a more restless, tumultuous, *agitato*. Throughout the first movement he throws out themes, varies and restates them, kicks the mood around from stormy to meditative; now heroic, then impatient, then back again. The second movement is a scherzo—a word that comes from the Italian for "to joke"—and it also modulates in mood, tempo, and spirit, going from un-danceable madness to what sounds, for a moment or two, almost like a polonaise, the quintessential Polish national dance. The opening section of this movement always appears in my mind's eye as a parabola, a perfectly symmetrical pattern that creates, in real time, a mirror image of itself. Climbing and falling in a sinuous, wave-like figure, Chopin's melody is so visceral you can practically *see* it. Then, suddenly, it breaks into a gorgeous, dreamy section that recalls Chopin's most enchanting nocturnes, before turning back to the rapid-fire, volcanic eruptions of the opening section, now pounded out in dark octaves. Again he hurls at us juxtapositions of gloom against joy, agitation against meditative calm. The Scherzo ends with a gradual slowdown; Chopin first marks the score *lento*—simply slow—and then *smorzando*: "dying away." It ends in a puff of sound.

Then comes the third movement, music everyone knows, even those who don't know a thing about Chopin: the world's most famous funeral march. *Aha,* I thought, *so that's where this comes from.* It starts with the groaning tones of the familiar melody, emerging from silence in the death-haunted key of B-flat minor. The heroic drama that follows comes from dense chords played in stark juxtapositions of loud and soft, long pauses, and the vast expanse between notes: a low B flat that scales four octaves as it climbs to a high F, a distance of fifty-four keys, almost two-thirds of the entire keyboard. A rumbling trill in the left hand sounds like a bell slowly tolling; the steady marchlike rhythm—*dum dum da dum*—evokes a military drum. There are times in the first half of the funeral march where the music seems to be going in both directions, up and down, at the same time. But the key to its power resides in that little word, *half.* The march comes to an end, and then, without asking the performer to pause, Chopin suddenly modulates into a new, now major, key: D flat, which in music theory is the tonal relative of B-flat minor. What that means is they have the same key signature, which determines which notes are flats and sharps, yet despite this existential similarity they strike very different moods. They are related, but in an almost Jekyll and Hyde way. Cole Porter captures this complexity in his song "Ev'ry Time We Say Goodbye," which is about two lovers parting: "There's no love song finer / But how strange the change from major to minor." It's a change we feel in our souls.

What follows Chopin's funeral dirge is one of the most perfectly beautiful pieces of music I had ever heard. It is hopeful, sweet, beckoning; a grown-up lullaby in which Chopin now says to the listener: *It's all right, I never left. I am here with you still. Remember me in joy.* You don't need to know a thing about harmony or music theory to actually *feel* how the movement from B-flat minor to D-flat major makes cosmic sense. The music has resolved itself in a way that simply feels natural. The *Trio*, as this middle section is called, goes on for less than thirty measures—it's just a single page in the score—tracing a path through its new tonality and assuredly leading the way out of the somber, bone-crushing chords of the funeral march that set the stage for it. We have been taken to an entirely new place, where the mood is brighter, gentler, dare I say happier. But then, again, Chopin pulls the rug out from under us. With the *Trio* over, he asks the performer for a tiny pause and then the deep, hollow, minor-key tones of the funeral march are back, inevitable in their steady, relentless pulse. In just ten minutes or less Chopin has bookended the entire human experience in music, taking us from lullaby to lament.

It was in this moment that I experienced a sense of awe. The paradox of this movement, the rampant joy that has been smuggled into the heart of a death march, arrived for me with a shock of recognition. It seemed daring but also fundamentally true, that our experience of death should be animated, not haunted, by a force of beauty. Of life. That this can happen through a change in harmony is the magic of music and also the special genius of Chopin. The effect is something I can best describe by quoting cognitive scientist Douglas Hofstadter, who made a deep study of Chopin's work and concluded with the observation that "he hits some kind of bull's-eye in my soul." It wasn't until much later that I learned Chopin was doing something truly innovative with a time-tested, familiar genre—something that had never been done before with such power and deliberation. The old musical cliché, it turns out, had a much deeper story to tell, one based in a kind of emotional counterpoint that only music—and, for many of us, *mostly Chopin*—can conjure.

Chopin brings his sonata to a close in a notorious, knuckle-breaking finale, a wisp and whorl of sound he deploys to complete the picture. If the third movement of his sonata is the most famous, the fourth is the most controversial. Modern scholars have described this last bit as "poised on the brink of atonality"; it reveals a composer who is looking deep into the future. Robert Schumann, a contemporary and fellow composer, didn't find much to like throughout Opus 35, but he declared the fourth movement to be "more mockery than music." He was offended by it, felt that a genius—or, in his words, "a sphinx"—was laughing in our face. We have sat through some twenty minutes of music so far, and the last movement, intended by Chopin to be played fast (he marked it *presto*), lasts for just over a minute. It consists of a rapid-fire series of notes madly running up and down the keyboard, creating a wave of rising and falling harmonies and dissonances. Luckily we have Chopin's own account of what he was doing here; to a friend he wrote: "The left hand and the right hand gossip in unison after the March." It has all come down to this: two friends nattering away, talking over each other, gossiping about the acquaintance who has passed away. Finally, the whole piece closes in one loud, fortissimo chord in B-flat minor—home at last.

What struck me in the Polish Consulate that evening was hearing a piece of music that was so familiar but also so new. And so unorthodox: a funeral march that speaks the language of life as well as death. Intrigued, I went to a music store the next day and purchased the score for Opus 35. The entire piece was (and remains) too difficult for me to play, but my fingers were capable of mastering the march and *Trio*. Now I could lift the hood on this music and pick apart the mechanisms that make it work: little dissonances and key changes that alter and define the mood, that stake out the emotional territory Chopin wants to lead us through. In effect he does the same thing with the mechanics of his trade that a writer does with hers. I remember one especially powerful tribute to the novelist Toni Morrison that expressed this miracle of craft. "For all the astonishing edifices she built," Wesley Morris wrote after her death in 2019, "the woman knew what to do with a brick." When Chopin tweaks a single note in his funeral march—when an E flat becomes, one measure later, an E natural, traversing that smallest interval that exists on a piano keyboard but encompassing what is, for the listener, a universe of emotion—he is doing something with a brick.

I played the piece every day for a year or so, until it slowly got buried under a pile of new music. And then, twenty years later, on the night train heading home from that jazz club in Chicago, I began Googling. Chopin's funeral march was appropriated by many musicians in the century after it was published. It all started with Erik Satie, who wrote the melody into his weird 1913 piano composition *Embryons desséchés* ("Dessicated Embryos"), a satirical contemplation of decaying crustaceans: sea cucumbers, tiny shrimp, and the fourteen-legged wood lice. Later there was Duke Ellington's "Black and Tan Fantasy," a tune so popular it was incorporated into a short film in 1929. The movie tells the story of a young beauty, a brilliant dancer with a heart condition, who sacrifices herself for music, dancing on stage until she collapses, all so her band can land a big contract. On her deathbed she asks to hear the "Black and Tan Fantasy," and the quotation from Chopin's melody occurs just as she takes her last breath. As my train rumbled east through the night, I found more tributes: Cab Calloway rocking the Cotton Club with "The Man from Harlem," whose lyrics are introduced by Chopin's march; Felix Arndt's "Desecration Rag," which quotes it at the end; and a funky flute solo in the middle of the 1975 *Oratorium* by a Dutch experimental musician named Willem Breuker. I also learned that jazz musicians particularly love Chopin, a tradition kick-started by a young Polish pianist named Mieczysław Kosz. He, like Chopin, experienced severe illness and died young (he fell out a window at the age of twenty-nine in what was probably a suicide). Born in extreme poverty, he went blind before the age of thirteen, but his misfortune led him to a special school that nurtured an exceptional talent. Largely self-taught (also like Chopin), he was twenty-three in the late 1960s when, during a jazz festival, his trio riffed on one of Chopin's preludes in a set that included works by Kosz's other two favorite composers, Bill Evans and Miles Davis. It's still considered one of the greatest moments in Polish jazz history. It would be another twenty years before a conservatory-trained Pole, Andrzej Jagodziński, and his jazz trio put out an entire album devoted to Chopin and found a large, enthusiastic audience. "Chopin simply conquered our minds," Jagodziński later said. Five albums followed, including a 2008 recording of the Opus 35 Sonata with its iconic funeral march. In the hands of these jazz musicians the language of the march is still there, but it's been rhythmically transformed into a new vernacular, and ends in a long drum solo without a single piano note. Jagodziński in effect takes the genre back full circle to Henry Purcell's 1695 founding tribute to Queen Mary, which is considered the first true funeral march ever written and was composed for muffled drums and a few trumpets.

Back in New York I sent an email through the website of Andy's, the Chicago club, to ask if someone in the band would talk to me about their use of Chopin's funeral march the night I had been there. Why, in the middle of a boisterous jazz tune, did the band suddenly change key—and centuries—to quote Frédéric Chopin? Not long after, I heard from Jeremy Kahn, the pianist. Over the course of several messages he shared a story about his wife, who had been living with the same cancer as the friend I had visited before arriving at Andy's. At the time of my visit his wife was just weeks away from her own death. He talked about the practice of improvisation, and how tunes often take on a life of their own on the bandstand, sometimes veering off because a beautiful woman walks by, or because a particular harmony from one song just happens to fit in with another. But this time, the evening of my visit, he confessed there was "at least a hint of gallows humor" at work, a musical defense mechanism against the impending loss of this woman to whom he had been married for twenty-nine years. What had jolted me that evening—the way the band members joined in, taking this very old, very sad tune and collectively upending it with a loving smile—had been done in support of their mate. The left hand, as it were, gossiping with the right. It all suddenly seemed quite Chopinesque.

Having experienced the power of this music in two very different settings—one formal (the glitzy consulate), the other intimate (a dusky jazz club)—I set out to investigate the Opus 35 Sonata and learn everything I could about the forces that were at work in Chopin's life when he composed it. It took him three years to complete the entire thing, between 1837 and 1840, and this aspect of *time* in his composition hovers over the whole sonata. The decade in which he wrote it was a uniquely vibrant historical moment, one marked by extraordinary technological and artistic innovation, when artists of every sort—painters, writers, musicians, photographers, choreographers—were forging new creative pathways. Chopin is both at the very heart of this world and an outsider from it, and it's that contradiction that I found so intriguing. I wanted to find the man who inhabited both worlds, whose work continues to have such relevance and poignancy in our own. He was born into a time of transition, a bridge period between the Enlightenment, with its emphasis on reason, logic, and the precise observation of the natural world and universe, and the Romantic era's fascination with the wild extremes of human emotion amid the powerful, chaotic forces of nature. By the time he arrived in Paris in 1831, at the age of twenty-one, this new world was in full flower and sparking experimentation everywhere: on the opera and theater stages, in the fiction pages of newspapers and journals, in concert halls, salons, museums, and even France's great churches and cathedrals. Chopin rides the tide of all these energies but also stands, in many ways, beyond them, an artist powerfully linked to classical traditions who was, at the same time, busy forging a truly modernist vision.

As I began researching his life and times, I realized that the story of Opus 35 contains all the crucial threads—musical, political, social, personal—in Chopin's life: his self-exile from Poland, and the way he conjured his homeland in his music; the emerging technology of the piano, which enabled his unique tone and voice; his complex relationship with the writer George Sand; how he developed an innovative approach as a teacher that informs piano lessons to this day; his artistic relationship with other composers, which featured a deep reverence for J. S. Bach, cool respect for Beethoven, and all-out dislike for the music of Hector Berlioz, all of whom play a role in the Opus 35 story; his ill health and untimely death, after which the sonata was played for the first time in an actual funeral and then, finally, took on a life of its own in popular culture. This book arose from a humble desire to restore the full narrative of Chopin's funeral march and in the process tell a larger story about music: how it comes into the world, and how it pulls us, generation after generation, along with it.

Introduction

The Chopin I encountered along the way is a somewhat different figure than is commonly portrayed. The literature about him supports an unsympathetic view of his character: a snob, a dandy who was obsessed with fine clothes and aristocratic ways, a man who didn't read books or show much interest in the works of other artists, melancholy, short-tempered, and (perhaps) anti-Semitic. I saw all those qualities as I read and dug deeper in the massive global library of scholarship, criticism, and journalism about his life and work. Even so, another person inexorably emerged in my pages: an unrelentingly independent spirit, a celebrity who shunned the limelight, an artist who coaxed large meanings from the smallest forms, an innovator who created a new musical language, a spiritually generous teacher, a mimic with a playful, roguish sense of humor, a loyal—if demanding—friend. Moreover, and I think this last thought gets at the unique power of his music and story, Chopin was creatively monogamous. While other composers were catching fire in these early, heady days of the Industrial Revolution, as instruments were getting louder and concert halls and orchestras growing ever bigger, Chopin remained true to the piano. For him it was capable of everything. He wrote a handful of orchestral works, but virtually his entire output was created for the piano alone—even, many scholars (and my own teacher) argue, his concertos, which are themselves vehicles for a soloist. This puts all of us who play and love the piano in a direct, unmediated relationship with him, our access to his ideas and unique sound immediate and ever-present, always right there at the keyboard. Chopin does for us today precisely what he did for his students back in the 1830s: encourages the development of *our own* voice as we engage with his work. The French writer André Gide, who, like Douglas Hofstadter, made a lifelong project of interrogating this man and his music, put it well when he wrote: "Chopin proposes, supposes, insinuates, seduces, persuades; he almost never asserts." It's tempting to observe that his music is a tonic to our uniquely tortured, narcissistic, bloviating modern age, but Gide published those words in France in the years preceding World War II. Chopin is, like Shakespeare, a needed artist in every age. One difference is that he speaks so directly, even physically, to us: from notations he left on a page, through the ligaments in our hands and fingers, to that incantatory machine that sits in our home, the one that contains in its very name, *pianoforte*—soft and loud—an entire universe, and which reached its full potential during the years when Chopin began writing music.

If my project is preoccupied with time, and the relatively long period during which Chopin composed Opus 35, it's equally concerned with place. I traveled many miles to experience the diverse environments where he worked on his sonata, from Paris and Majorca to George Sand's beloved hamlet of Nohant in central France. But there were other places closer to home that help unfurl the larger story, like the remarkable Frederick Collection of historic pianos in tiny Ashburnham, Massachusetts. Here you not only meet instruments from the 1790s to the 1920s, but you can *play* them. You can cast yourself back in time to the soundscape of nineteenth-century Europe, a time when countries had their own distinct sounds, and keyboards from Vienna, Leipzig, London, and Paris all sounded different, each to each. The collection includes an 1845 Pleyel, the same model Chopin owned in his Paris studio during the last decade of his life, and getting to know the distinct character of this particular instrument, and how it differed from other brands he knew and loved, is a crucial step in understanding Chopin himself.

I also made an enlightening visit to the Morgan Library in my hometown of New York, where I was allowed to examine the original manuscript of a handwritten, never completed, how-to book Chopin drafted in the 1840s. From the dozen or so pages saved after his death emerge fascinating insights into his teaching philosophy as well as his unorthodox approach to technique, which he based on his own observations of human anatomy. In Paris I visited historic sites like the Montmartre home of painter Ary Scheffer, built in 1830, which has preserved the salon where Chopin spent many evenings at the piano in the company of other artists and writers. At the Polish Library across town, which sits on the banks of the Seine across from Notre-Dame, I came within inches of a plaster cast of his left hand, made after his death. You can't truly appreciate the superhuman feat Chopin accomplished at the keyboard, or the ontology of his teaching technique, until you see up close the slenderness, the delicacy, the smallness of this hand. A contemporary and fellow pianist/composer described his amazement at watching it suddenly "expand and cover a third of the keyboard . . . like the opening of the mouth of a serpent which is going swallow a rabbit whole. In fact, Chopin seemed to be made of rubber." He wasn't, of course; he just developed techniques that allowed his physical mechanism to behave that way, and then he taught them to his students, who carried them forward, generation after generation, so that I could encounter them from my own teacher in a small music school in midtown Manhattan.

There were musical excursions too, including a rousing concert of works by French composers at the Church of the Madeleine in Paris, where I went to hear for myself the organ that was played during Chopin's funeral in 1849. Once home in New York, the associate music director at St. John the Divine, America's largest cathedral, invited me into the organ loft for an illuminating conversation about the improvisational musical culture in churches of nineteenth-century Paris. During the course of my research I also met with concert artists, including Yuan Sheng, a Chinese pianist who recorded much of Chopin's work on the Frederick's 1845 Pleyel and is also a highly respected interpreter of Johann Sebastian Bach, whose work was profoundly important to Chopin. Backstage at Carnegie Hall I met Nobuyuki Tsujii, a young Japanese pianist whose pilgrimage to the medieval charterhouse in Majorca where Chopin worked on Opus 35 deepened my understanding of this place and its enduring role in his living legacy. As a counterpoint to the sonically diverse, historic instruments in Ashburnham, I took a long, trippy tour through the Steinway factory in Queens, a sprawling, multilevel production line where some two hundred workers assemble more than twelve thousand parts into the much more homogenous yet booming instrument we hear today under the fingers of every type of piano artist, from classical and jazz to rock and country. There were other side journeys and conversations, concerts, ballets, festivals, competitions, encounters with cartoons, animé productions, and video games, each of which shone its own beam of light on the question I started with: What's behind this music and why does it resonate so powerfully today? And what does Chopin uniquely reveal to us about the challenges, and ambiguities, of our lives?

The funeral march presents a funny paradox: it's Chopin's most recognizable work but also his least truly known. Virtually everyone is familiar with—and can hum without even thinking about it—the dirge. For folks in my parents' generation it was the soundtrack of JFK's funeral procession in 1963; for those in mine it was an omen that foretold something *really* bad was about to happen: for example, the execution of Sylvester the Cat in the old Looney Tunes cartoon. *Pray for the dead and the dead shall pray for you.* Wait a beat. *Simply because they have nothing else to do!* Howl with laughter. But behind this music is a fascinating story of innovation and creative independence, featuring an artist who took three years to assemble a work that, within weeks of his own death, was misappropriated and then, for centuries, basically misunderstood. Yet it continues to exert its haunting power, lurking there on the bandstand at a jazz club, showing up when we least expect it, stimulating, perhaps, a smile of recognition when the full story unfolds. In Chopin's time, Opus 35 was brutally and colorfully attacked, and it took almost a hundred years for the critical tide to turn. But there were those who, like his friend and student Wilhelm von Lenz, understood exactly what Chopin was doing. Lenz was in the room when Chopin played the work, and of this unconventional, two-part funeral march he observed: "It is a touchstone for recognizing whether the performer is a poet or merely a pianist; whether he can tell a story or merely play the piano."

Readers familiar with Chopin's life and works, whether professional musicians or curious music lovers, will find familiar stories here, but also, I think, some illuminations. My perspective is quite different from that of the musicologist, concert pianist, or even professional biographer, and so are the emphases I've chosen to make in this relatively short and narrowly focused book. For example, I decided to look more deeply into the backstory of the Marquis de Custine, a fascinating character in Chopin's orbit whose story helps illustrate the social climate of the 1830s and 1840s, both its liberations and oppressions. All writers discuss George Sand and her works, but my inner English major emerged to make a close reading of books that others have largely (or entirely) ignored, like *The Seven Strings of the Lyre*, which is about music, and *Gabriel*, which is about gender identity. These figures in Chopin's world dramatize a quintessential characteristic of the Romantic spirit: the tendency of its artists to relentlessly interrogate reality and establish their own voice in a culture that didn't always want to hear it. I discovered a boldness, a kind of intellectual gumption, in the way the Romantics responded to the world around them, and it has genuine resonance for us today. In her 1831 preface to *Frankenstein* Mary Shelley reminds us that invention "does not consist in creating out of the void, but out of chaos." Making sense of the extraordinary changes swirling around them, from industry, science and technology, to the rules governing society and gender, was the project they took on, and I found in their example much to be inspired by.

In the end, virtually every experience I had while researching this book, whether in churches, study centers, recital halls, libraries, museums, websites, or wide open landscapes, was in one way or another a lesson about *listening*. If Chopin offers anything to a modern reader, it is how to attend in a more perceptive, intimate, even holistic way; how to practice a form of observation that takes in two opposing ideas or emotions at once, and embrace that inherent tension as a fact of nature. He is also, it can be said, the one whose arrow never fails to hit the bull's-eye. In the pages ahead I will use the story of when, how, and where Chopin composed his unorthodox, iconic, and oddly inspiring funeral march, as a way of exploring why. That question—the gnarly *why?*—is especially hard to answer when it comes to music. For my father, the works of J. S. Bach, particularly the cello suites, revealed some aspect of the universe that simply made sense to him. This came from the constant, and familiar, flux of tension and resolution he heard in the harmonies; the miracle of all those multiple voices that somehow come together to form a single, fluid line; the embrace of contrast and ambiguity—a cheerful, bouncy gigue suddenly gives way to a sad, brooding sarabande—that are such a familiar, if unpredictable, force in any life.

Why Chopin? As I followed the trail of his sonata through the terrain of politics, romance, and patriotism, into the teacher's studio and through varied foreign landscapes, the story of his life in music became something of an antidote to the culture of virtuosity, celebrity, and noise that today envelops us. For all the distance between his world and ours, the nature of the tumult that existed then is not so different from what we experience today. Chopin is, I discovered, an unexpected torchbearer who keeps showing up in surprising—and, for me, most welcome—ways. My project is, I confess, somewhat unorthodox in that it combines various tactics of investigation—biography, travel reporting, a tiny bit of musicology, detours through literature and art history, conversations with experts and professional musicians—in an attempt to illuminate those aspects of Chopin's aesthetics and genius that resonate so meaningfully today. But as I think you will come to see in the pages ahead: if anyone ever encouraged an independent mind and iconoclastic approach, it was he.

ONE

In a Word, Poland

"All the contemporary assaults upon society date from the
partition of Poland. The partition of Poland is a theorem of which
all the present political crimes are corollaries. . . . When you
examine the list of modern treasons, that appears first of all."

VICTOR HUGO, *Les Miserables*

One morning in 2010, the official "Year of Chopin," a young Polish
entrepreneur woke up with an idea that was crazy but wonderful:
Frédéric Chopin could return from the grave and save the world from
itself. As a creator of video games he had all the tools to make it happen, and that day Zbigniew Dębicki, known as Zibi to friends, put
his team to work. Artists and animators worked with writers and pro-
grammers to develop a storyline and graphic landscape. Musicians selected, then remixed, a dozen compositions—polonaises, nocturnes,
mazurkas, waltzes, études, songs—into mashups with contemporary
formats: reggae, rap, country, rock, and chiptune, a form of synthe-
sized electronic music. The game opens with an animation in black-
and-white as Chopin, dressed in tailcoat and cravat, awakens in his

grave at Père Lachaise. Moments later the graphics turn to color as the confused composer passes through the cemetery gates into noisy, twenty-first-century Paris, where he is greeted by three Muses. They present him with special artifacts, including his own grand piano (now pocket-size) and a magical horse-drawn carriage that will take him home to Poland. This is the game's ultimate goal, for while Chopin's body was buried in Paris, his heart was removed after he died in 1849 and smuggled by his sister across a heavily guarded border into Warsaw, where it was eventually interred in the pillar of a Catholic church.

The title of Zibi's game is *Frederic: The Resurrection of Music*, and its premise is that the world has lost its collective soul, thanks to the greed and creative bankruptcy of modern content creators for whom music is just one bullet point in a marketing strategy designed to craft brand image and sell product. We are all surrounded by this soulless stuff, and only one man can save us. The gamer's task is to escape the mind-numbing stereotypes of contemporary commercial music; Chopin's is to finally return to his homeland. Along the way the two of you must engage in a series of musical duels against all manner of opponents, from a Jamaican Rasta man to a New York City gang-banger, until finally you come face-to-face with Mastermind X, the evil worldwide producer who owns every musician and cares only about money and power. The funeral march from Opus 35 appears in a country-western-techno remix when Chopin finds himself in a deserted cowboy town, forced to duel with the local sheriff at high noon.

The game's interface is a piano keyboard, and during each battle musical notes fly fast and furious toward the gamer, whose job is to hit them with the cursor as they land on the keyboard, thereby gaining points. It's clear that whoever designed this game was a pianist, because basic keyboard technique—skills I learned once I had mastered scales and arpeggios—serve the player well by netting higher points. The more musical you are, it turns out, the better you will perform against the bad guys. For example: if you hit a flying note in just the right spot on the key, which on a real piano would elicit a highly coveted rich, singing tone, you'll get a 10 instead of a 7. Artfully sliding your finger from one key to another—a technique scholars cite as one of Chopin's keyboard innovations—gains even more points. The *Help* section includes a tip that will resonate with any musician, reminding us that "the key to success is not faith in your eyes but *your ears.*" If I had a dotted quarter note for every time my teacher told me to make better use of my ears at the keyboard, I could write a symphony. . . .

Frederic is one of a handful of Chopin video games available today on multiple platforms, from Nintendo to iPhone, but it's the only one that puts music at the center of play. And it's not just about melodies

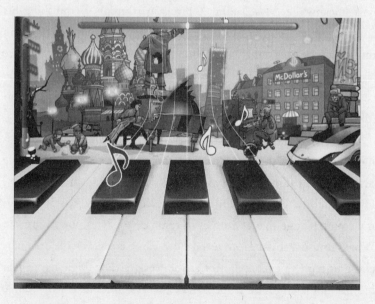

The gamer's keyboard in *Frederic: The Resurrection of Music.*

and techniques; it's also *ideas* that animate the experience, beginning with Chopin's painful self-exile from his homeland, a theme that's introduced in the opening moments back in Père Lachaise. Thinking there were worse (or certainly more predictable) ways of exploring Chopin's Polish roots, I emailed Zibi to see if he would speak with me. Most of all I wanted to know why, at the dawn of the twenty-first century, a young software developer would choose Frédéric Chopin, of all people, as an international superhero.

Frederic is hard to master if you're over fifteen, but it's strangely addictive, and because I wanted to find out what happens in the end, I was highly motivated to complete all the duels. Chopin does make it home to Poland, but there's an interesting twist that Zibi explained to me via Skype from his home in Gdańsk. "First," he promised, "you will fail against Mastermind X in the final duel. Every player does, it's built into the game." Your loss creates a sense of doom and unhappiness; meanwhile, Mastermind X revels in triumph, brandishing his contracts. But then the Muses return and tell you that *this time* you must play the music that comes from your own heart. Finally, in one last duel, you and Frederic defeat Mastermind X. He gives back the contracts, frees the musicians, and disappears forever. The art of soulful music has been saved, and Chopin is home at last.

These themes of homelessness, yearning, and redemption through music are among the key threads in the story of Chopin, and since his death have formed the basis of his long, enduring cultural legacy. His music *and* his life, Zibi told me, "tell a very hard story about my country," one that continues to resonate today in powerful ways. What's unusual about *Frederic* the video game is the way the designers chose to represent Chopin: not as the weak, sickly, tragic figure that has become a common trope but as a clever superman with nimble strength, artistic independence, and vanquishing power. "It's crazy, I know," Zibi kept saying during our conversation, the idea that Chopin is a musical zombie and my iPad a magical piano. But what better way to bust up the musical and cultural stereotypes of our times than by reanimating old forms and creating unexpected surprises? After all, that's what Chopin himself did.

The "very hard story" of Poland is often told through music, a tradition that predates Chopin by many centuries. You can experience it for yourself any day in Kraków's main market square, where, if you hang around for at least an hour, you'll hear a trumpet call sounding from the top of the fourteenth-century St. Mary's Basilica. Actually, you'll hear it four times: a plaintive melody that ends as abruptly as it begins, mid-note. Look up at the tower and you'll see the bell of a trumpet emerging, first from a window facing west, toward Wawel Castle in honor of Poland's kings and heroes, and then three more times as the trumpeter makes his way around the points of the compass. Down below, tourists flock with cell phones and wave to the tower. Usually the trumpeter—a member of Kraków's fire brigade in dress uniform—waves back. The call is made every hour on the hour, seven days a week, 365 days a year.

The melody the bugler plays is known as the *Hejnał Mariacki*; it consists of just thirty-three notes, but it's never played through to the end; the final cadence is always cut off in a sharp, unmelodious way. The reason for the broken note dates to a legend from the thirteenth century, when the cupola of St. Mary's was a watchtower manned around the clock by a guardian with a bugle. Every morning he woke the residents of Kraków with his call; throughout the day he alerted them to the opening and closing of the city's gates, signaling the arrival of an important visitor, and his job was also to warn the community of fire and foreign invasion. In 1241 an army of Mongol warriors known as "the scourge of God" rode from the steppes of Central Asia into modern-day Poland, where they razed village after village, killing all or most of the inhabitants. Before they reached the gates of Kraków, so the legend goes, the bugler atop St. Mary's sounded the alert, blowing his horn until an enemy arrow pierced him through the throat and stopped his call mid-note. His warning allowed many of the town burghers to escape without harm, and in tribute to the fallen musician the survivors endowed a city fund to pay a trumpeter full-time. The first mention of an hourly bugle call comes from the mid-fifteenth century, and the playing of the *Hejnał* with the broken note has endured since sometime in the seventeenth. In 1927 Polish Radio began broadcasting the noon call and claims it to be "the longest running serial broadcast on Earth," one that sounded through the years of Nazi occupation in World War II, the fall of Communism under the Solidarity movement in the 1980s, and the rise of a new right-wing party, Law and Justice, that assumed power in 2015. It is still, as historian Norman Davies observed, a reminder to millions of listeners "both of the ancient pedigree of Polish culture and of Poland's exposed location . . . one of the few active mementoes of Genghis Khan, and the irruption of his horsemen into the heart of Europe."

The story of Poland, poignantly and symbolically preserved in the lacerated tune of the *Hejnał Mariacki*, is animated by a paradox: the juxtaposition of enlightened ideals against violence, subjugation, and oppression. "This country," Davies wrote in his two-volume national history, "seems to be inseparable from the catastrophes and crises on which, paradoxically, it thrives. Poland is permanently on the brink of collapse. But somehow, Poland has never failed to revive . . . and to flourish." His observation frames a story of some seven centuries of invasion, occupation, and partition that begins in the thirteenth century when the Golden Horde descended from the east. In the fourteenth and fifteenth centuries the Poles were repeatedly attacked by Crimean Tatars and Teutonic knights; the sixteenth and seventeenth centuries brought the subduing armies of Russia, Sweden, and the Ottoman Empire. But in the eighteenth century a fresh threat emerged that would prove far more devastating—and enduring—than any barbarian horde: its own neighbors. In 1772 a troika of new power in Europe set its sights on Poland and carved the country into three parts to be shared among them. Over the next two decades this coalition of Russia, Austria, and Prussia (roughly today's Germany) executed two further partitions, varying the configuration of borders until finally, in 1795, Poland was literally erased from the map and its name banned from official use. This condition of statelessness lasted for the greater part of its modern history, until 1918, when the establishment of a "New Poland" became one of president Woodrow Wilson's Fourteen Points in peace negotiations to end World War I. Then, with a stroke of a pen, the country finally resumed its place on the map of Europe. Davies observes that while other nations—he cites India, America, and Africa—during this period were attacked, occupied, pillaged, or stripped of territorial possessions by foreign entities, the Polish partitions were different and without precedent in modern history. Poland was "annihilated . . . in cold blood," he writes, "the victim of political vivisection—by mutilation, amputation, and in the end total dismemberment." In 1793 Irish statesman Edmund Burke reflected what many in the capitals of Britain, Europe, and America took to be Poland's political reality when he said: "With respect to us, Poland might be . . . considered a country on the moon."

There is, however, another side to the story of victimhood that came to be known as "captive Poland," one that tapped into a larger narrative that had taken hold in the early nineteenth century. Even as it was under constant attack by foreign enemies, as far back as the sixteenth century Poland practiced a kind of liberal humanism that even today seems fragile around the world. The idea of a parliament, an assembly of members drawn from the community, took root there in 1454; a century later, religious freedom was engraved into the Confederation of Warsaw. "We swear to each other," the document reads, "that we who differ in matters of religion will keep the peace among ourselves, and neither shed blood on account of differences of Faith, or kinds of church, nor punish one another by confiscation of goods, deprivation of honor, imprisonment, exile." The nobility *elected* its kings in an elaborate ceremony that took place on horseback in a meadow. They retained for themselves the right to control military finances and declarations of war and taxation, and all it took was one member's vote to overrule any decision made by the king. Baked into the political consciousness of Poland's "Noble Democracy" was the right of citizens—*noble* ones, that is—to resist. It was in Poland in May 1791 that the first constitution in Europe was written and adopted; this is astonishing because at the time its people lived in a fractured country carved up by a "Satanic Trinity" of foreign autocrats. Even then, stateless and oppressed, the Poles produced a document that poet Czesław Miłosz called a "landmark [on] the road to a new type of democracy." It guaranteed freedom of the press, religious tolerance, personal liberty, and, perhaps most important of all, the right of peasants to acquire land. What Miłosz describes as Poland's "abnormal" history gave rise to an idealistic notion of citizenship and individual freedom—values that put many Poles in sympathy with the French in the years following their revolution. It was precisely those values that posed an unacceptable threat to the Habsburgs, Hohenzollerns, and Romanovs who had claimed Poland's lands for their collective empires. It was only four years after Poland adopted its unprecedented, progressive, enlightened constitution that the final partition of 1795 wiped the country off the map of Europe. No longer a nation, Davies writes, "Poland was now an Idea."

For the generation that followed, which included Chopin and his equally famous compatriot, the poet Adam Mickiewicz, the Romantic ideal of the homeland developed from all this violence and loss. It's so ingrained in the Polish character that the country's own national anthem, composed two years after the final partition, begins with the lines "Poland has not yet perished, as long as we live." This strange, oddly disheartening amalgam of verb tenses suggests that patriotism is a perpetual fight to a death that never quite arrives. For Mickiewicz, these words signify that "people who have in them what indeed constitutes nationality are able to extend the existence of their nation regardless of the political circumstances of that existence, and may even pursue its re-creation." What he meant is that even if their country was controlled by foreign invaders, as so often was the case, the *idea* of Poland constituted the nation itself in the hearts of its own people, and that idea could live on, no matter what. When a friend of Chopin's wrote that "through his music he imparted Poland; he composed Poland," this is what, I believe, he was expressing: that Chopin's music manifested the juxtaposition of tragedy and hope that both define and animate the history and spirit of the Polish people. What's extraordinary is how enduring this legacy turned out to be.

The decisive moment in Chopin's story, and that of Poland during the first half of the nineteenth century, came in 1830, when he was twenty years old and a spark of independence flew in Warsaw. The year before, Nicholas I of Russia had crowned himself King of Poland, disregarding the national constitution and parliament. The czar's brother and factotum, Grand Duke Constantine, unleashed his secret police, abolished press freedoms, imposed taxes, closed Vilnius

University, and deported Mickiewicz, the country's most famous poet. The final insult was a Russian scheme to use Poland's army against the people of France to suppress their July Revolution, which deposed the last Bourbon monarch and put Louis Philippe—the "citizen king"—on the throne. On November 29, 1830, a cadet at the Warsaw officers' school led a group of co-conspirators in an attack on Constantine's palace. The grand duke managed to escape (according to one historian he scurried off in women's clothing), but the failed rebellion launched six months of unrest and turmoil.

Chopin had left Warsaw three weeks before the November Uprising for a European sojourn of music and adventure, traveling through Dresden, Vienna, Salzburg, and Munich, going to the opera and immersing himself in the local musical life. It being his first long-term trip abroad, a group of friends sent him off with a silver cup filled with earth they had collected in Żelazowa Wola, the small town where Chopin was born, thus allowing him to carry a bit of the beloved homeland away with him on his travels. When the uprising began, Chopin's friends rushed home to join the fight, but insisted he remain in exile and use his music to give voice to Poland's struggle. Traveling the Continent, keeping in touch with friends and family through a regular stream of letters, he went to parties, dinners, plays, and operas. Then, as he wrote to a friend, he would return home around midnight, sit down, "play the piano, have a good cry, read, look at things, have a laugh, get into bed, blow out my candle and always dream about you all."

The November Uprising lasted less than a year, and in September 1831 the Russians brought the hammer down in Warsaw. From Stuttgart Chopin learned there was hand-to-hand fighting in the streets, including in the cemetery where his younger sister Emilia had been buried after suffering a massive tubercular hemorrhage at age fourteen. Being separated from his family was, for Chopin, a type of death. Only a month after he left home, he described himself as "a corpse" and began using the metaphor of the crypt to convey his melancholia. "Graves behind me and beneath me, everywhere," he wrote to a friend; "a gloomy harmony arose within me." In Stuttgart, his separation anxiety developed into a morbid, fantastical obsession with death. He imagined his family butchered, the woman he loved in the hands of the Muscovites . . . "seizing her, strangling her, murdering, killing." In his notebook Chopin wondered: "is a corpse any worse than I? A corpse . . . knows nothing of father, mother or sisters . . . it cannot speak its own language to those around it." He was voiceless, homeless, and alone, "beyond ten frontiers" from friends and family, and to make matters worse his passport had expired and there was no safe way back to Poland. Stuttgart was an abyss; "I pour out my grief on the piano," he confided to his diary. It was during this time, as he faced his first Christmas alone, that he likely began composing the harrowing B-minor Scherzo op. 20, a work that begins with a piercing cry at the top of the keyboard followed by an anguished growl at the bottom. It then proceeds on a frenzied, anxious journey until suddenly, and surprisingly, the music devolves into a melody known and loved by all Poles, the Christmas carol "*Lulajże Jezuniu*" ("Hush Little Jesus"), only to be rudely interrupted again by the tonal lacerations that began the piece. The scherzo concludes with the repetition, nine times in a row, of a single dissonant chord, a piece of musical language that always elicits in me the same tragic pain I experience when King Lear exclaims, over and over, the word *Howl!* after discovering the hanged body of Cordelia.

This early work contains Chopin's musical signature: a collision of worlds fueled by the polar opposites of mood, tempo, melody, and emotional shadowing he would later deploy with such power in the funeral march of Opus 35. During this period he experimented in many genres, taking, for example, the mazurka, a lively, traditional Polish national dance, and reimagining it with startling rhythms and chromatically induced inner conflict. Leonard Bernstein loved these pieces, especially the op. 17, no. 4 Mazurka in A minor, because Chopin put him in "a bliss of ambiguities." In études, short practice pieces traditionally designed to explore different aspects of performance technique, Chopin experimented with tones, harmonies, and syncopations that would, a century later, become standard features of modern jazz. He also took a salon genre, the nocturne, and repurposed it. An early example is the otherworldly op. 15, no. 3 in G minor, composed in the early years of the 1830s. It begins in one style, that of another Polish folk dance, the kujawiak, and then, after passing through a dark, sometimes jagged melody, he pauses, almost like a novelist reaching a chapter break, and changes the voice of the piece entirely, moving into a chorale, a form of plainchant one might hear in a church service. Then, before sending it off to his publisher, he slapped onto this strange-sounding work the label "Nocturne," a brand-new genre pioneered by an Irish composer, John Field, which Chopin undertook to reinvent in his own voice and style.

These were startling creations, works that threw listeners into an unfamiliar musical landscape. For scholar Jim Samson it was this sojourn, far from home and with news trickling in week by week of the worsening situation in Poland, that saw Chopin's now unmistakable tone journey from a post-Classical to a Romantic idiom. Responding to the turmoil at home, he "renovated" the old forms, mixing styles and bending genres, using a new kind of musical language to disrupt a listener's expectations and tell a different kind of story. Exiled from his homeland, wandering through Europe trying to decide where to settle, Chopin began developing the voice that would come to define his music deep into the future. He arrived in Paris in the autumn of 1831, just weeks after the uprising had been brutally put down, and virtually overnight became the poetic embodiment of "captive Poland." It would be just a few years later when the story of the failed revolution and Chopin's poignant separation from family and friends crept into his writing and, without his planning it, formed the basis of what would become his most famous composition. For not only is a love of homeland deeply embedded in the funeral march; it's where it all started.

The earliest clue in the composition story of Opus 35 turns up in an unlikely place: an auction house on Madison Avenue in New York City. It was a Tuesday in March 1969 when the Parke-Bernet Galleries held a sale of "Important Autographs and Manuscripts" that was noteworthy for its scope and variety: rare original documents spanning three centuries, authored by notable figures in politics, science, and the arts. Just a partial list includes Alexander Hamilton, Napoleon Bonaparte, Clarence Darrow, Henry David Thoreau, Queen Victoria, Washington Irving, Charles Dickens, John James Audubon, the abolitionist John Brown, items from twenty-three American presidents (including a letter from Thomas Jefferson stating "I am out of wine"), and a handwritten manuscript by John Steinbeck. Also included was a musical fragment in the hand of Frédéric Chopin, a manuscript consisting of just eight measures with no title except the notation *Lento cantabile*: an instruction to the performer to play slowly, in a singing style. (The word comes from the Italian verb *cantare*, to sing.) It's the melody of the *Trio*, the major-key lullaby that breaks up the two statements of the minor-key march—the music that so startled me when I first heard it in the Polish Consulate. This is the sweet, nocturne-like tune that invites you to forget, at least for a moment, the heavy, violent dirge that precedes and follows it.

Little is known about the Parke-Bernet fragment, which immediately disappeared into private hands after being acquired at the auction for $1,500, but the best guess of scholars is that Chopin inscribed the music into someone's autograph album. These were popular in the nineteenth century: large, blank books bound in leather that friends (and the occasional celebrity) would "autograph" with a poem, drawing, musical sketch, or personal greeting. Some of these albums apparently had pages with music staves that made it easy to dash off short compositions, and Chopin was known to have inscribed his music into the albums of friends and admirers. Once, for fellow composer Ignaz Moscheles, he wrote out eight measures from the celebrated refrain of the 17th Prelude from op. 28, popularly known as "Castle Clock" for the low A flat that is intoned eleven times in a row, like a tolling bell. There's something touching in this gesture: one great musician copy-

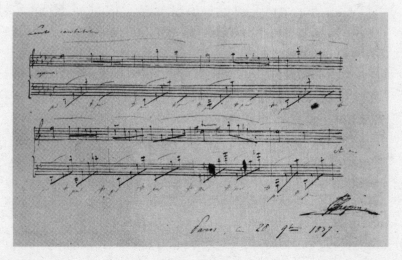

Lento cantabile fragment.

ing a famous lick for another. In the case of the *Lento cantabile* fragment there's an intriguing clue about Chopin's intentions, and reason to believe he attached great sentimental value to that lovely, portentous melody. It's right there in the date near his signature, November 27: the eve of the November Uprising in Warsaw six years earlier.

No one knows who the recipient of the *Trio* fragment was, but given the anniversary it seems likely it was a fellow Pole living in exile in Paris, part of "the Great Migration" from postrevolutionary Poland. What's poignant about the discovery of the fragment is it suggests that the roots of Chopin's funeral march—one of the saddest pieces of music ever written—were put down in the soil of patriotism and hope, not death and loss. He built the minor-key march around this beautiful, major-key melody; it was the seed from which the larger composition grew. Yet all this is lost in the austere ceremonies and pop culture vignettes where the march is so frequently evoked and riffed on, because when we hear those iconic bass chords tolling a new death—be it of Joseph Stalin, Winston Churchill, or Sylvester the Cat—we are hearing only the half of it, the part Russian pianist Anton Rubinstein famously described as "night winds sweeping over churchyard graves." Outside of the concert hall where the entire work—both statements of the funeral march bracketing the *Trio*—is played as written, most of us never knew there was another, juxtaposing reality embedded in Chopin's contemplation of death. Like so much about the story of the man himself, his most famous melody became a stereotype of sorrow, tragedy, illness, and death, abrogated in the public sphere so it could serve a heroic purpose that, as we'll see, Chopin never intended for it.

Love of country may have been inscribed into the original melody of the *Trio*, but there was another ache in Chopin's heart at the time he composed these lines: rejection by his sweetheart, Maria Wodzińska. She was seventeen when he (then twenty-six) proposed marriage, after they had spent much of the summer of 1836 together. By this time Chopin was a famous musician, but rumors of his ill health had circulated widely. Maria's mother, the Countess Teresa, seems to have been torn between these two realities. Frédéric's celebrity was attractive to her for many reasons, not the least of which was his access to *more* celebrities. In 1835 she wrote to him: "Forgive me, dear Mr. Fryderyk, if I ask you to obtain for me a collection of the autographs of the famous people among whom (quite rightly!) you live: Poles, Frenchmen, Germans, etc.—it's all the same to me—even a bearded Jew, such as we see at home, provided that he is worthy of it. I shall be immensely grateful." Whether Chopin complied is unknown, but in the end Maria's parents settled on a slow form of torture for the poor man. Nervous about their daughter's future happiness, they sat on his marriage proposal and prevented Maria from replying. Chopin, trying to make the best of it, joked in a letter to a friend that Maria's father, after all, considered him just "a street musician." He returned to Paris to wait, but the silence was agonizing. The following summer, with still no reply to his proposal, he made a trip to London, hoping a change of scenery would ease his mind. In salons he kept a low profile, going around town under cover as "Mr. Fritz," but the moment he sat down at a piano everyone knew who it was. Just before his return to Paris in July 1837 he had his answer: Maria declined. Chopin gathered together all her letters, placed them in an envelope, scrawled across it "My Sorrow," and secreted the package in his apartment, where it was discovered after his death. It was just a few months after he received Maria's breezy, final epistle ("Goodbye, remember us") that Chopin, recovering from a broken heart and with the anniversary of Poland's political upheaval in mind, copied out the melody for the *Trio*.

The literature about Maria Wodzińska is thin, and it's hard to get a real sense of her. She was not without talent, both as an amateur pianist and artist (she painted one of the surviving and most evocative portraits of Chopin), but history has not been kind to her. Her own niece described Maria as having had a "passive nature," being without "energy and independence . . . and easy to influence." Édouard Ganche, an early twentieth-century Chopin biographer, dismissed her pretty much altogether: "It is useless to incriminate [her] conduct," he wrote. "She was a girl of seventeen years old, without will, without courage." Maria is interesting in the story of these years not because she was Chopin's last Polish love and callously broke his heart, but for the way she prepares us for what's to come: another liaison that will have, in the end, a much greater consequence, with an artist who was, in the words of her prolific rival and friend Honoré de Balzac, anything but passive: she was a "lioness." These very different women—the traditional Polish family friend and France's notorious, cigar-smoking, cross-dressing, writer (Ivan Turgenev: "What a brave man she was!")—represent two animating forces in Chopin's life that intersected around the time he began working on Opus 35. The first would largely be forgotten; the second became the stuff of legend that still, hundreds of years later, captivates modern imaginations.

Chopin met George Sand the year he proposed to Maria, but it was not an auspicious beginning. "What an unattractive person La Sand is," he commented to a friend after their introduction in late 1836. "There is something about her which positively repels me." (Maybe it was what Balzac also described as her "double chin, like a canon of the church.") Then he asked the question that was on so many minds at the time: "Is she really a woman?" But when they met again two years later, it was love at second sight. The situation, however, was complicated, and in classic Sand style she treated the question of an affair with the exotic Polish exile as she would a new writing project, casting it in a sweeping, contemporary theme that was especially dear to both of their hearts: nationhood. It was a subject that came naturally to her. Sand's autobiography, *Story of My Life*, was so huge it took a team of sixty-five translators five years to produce the entire thing in English; she becomes so immersed in the role her family played in the history of France that it takes twenty-one chapters to get to her own birth. Sand's memoir has been read by scholars not just as the life of a singular woman but as the story of a century of French history and the birth of the modern nation.

So when Sand wrote a letter that was immense even by her own standards—more than five thousand words—to Chopin's closest friend to solicit advice about what course their relationship should take, it was perfectly fitting she would cast the drama in terms of patriotism. In the aftermath of revolutions in America, France, Poland, Belgium, Italy, and Switzerland, the idea of citizenship, of national belonging, was the most powerful metaphor she could reach for when it came to articulating the project of human love. Someone once said of George Sand that "her work is an immense legal plea, advanced by an indefatigable lawyer," and her June 1838 letter to Albert (Wojciech) Grzymała, a Polish statesman and banker variously described as a brother and father figure to Chopin, is worthy of the Cour de Cassation, France's highest court. She begins with the reality on the ground: she is involved with another man ("as good as married") and Chopin is still in love with "this childhood friend . . . this *young lady*." After a peroration on chastity and her own honorable intentions she goes all-out Cleopatra, casting their love in a language for the ages. "I have no wish to steal anyone from anyone, unless it be prisoners from their jailers, victims from their executioners, Poland from Russia." She commands Grzymała to "tell me whether it is some

Russia whose memory haunts our boy," in which case she would, like the avenging sorceress in a popular opera, muster her "allurements" and "save him from surrendering." But: "if it is a *Poland*, let him go on," because "Nothing is so precious as a fatherland, and a man who has one already must not make unto himself a new one." If that were the case, she goes on, "I shall represent for him an *Italy* . . . a land that one dreams of, longs for or regrets . . . which one visits and enjoys on spring days but where one cannot remain permanently."

Like almost everything Sand wrote, this masterful letter is about many things at once, including a worldview about love and marriage that was well ahead of its time and had been developing for many years. She had articulated her notion of true love in a letter to a girl-hood friend ten years earlier, explaining it could only occur "when the heart, the mind, and the body understand and embrace each other." It was rare, she admitted—"This happens once every thousand years"—but it became her lifelong project. She had begun working out these ideas in her first novel, *Indiana* (1832), a highly unconventional portrait of an unhappy woman trapped in a crippling marriage Sand describes as a form of slavery: "the chain beneath which my life has been shattered and my youth spoiled." Now, instead of shackling herself and her companion to a traditional union defined by laws of the state—"a graveyard for this artist soul" she said to Gryzmała, no doubt speaking for them both—she puts forth a vision of ideal love that eschews "the bonds of everyday life" and favors a true friendship based on "chaste passion and gentle poetry." Sand was famous for her gender-bending liberation—dressing like a man, earning money by the pen like a man—but at this moment in her life, when she met Chopin, she was focused on something more complex: a penetrating contemplation of what gender really meant—for women *and* for men. She would refine and develop this theme in *Gabriel*, the novel she commenced writing just after the love affair with Chopin began, but it's here, in the "frightful letter" (her words) that she begins working out her ideas about friendship between the genders, exploring a radical notion that people should be able to love in "different ways." She outwardly wrestles with "this question of possession" that defined relations between men and women and seeks a richer, more enlightened path, one that was unmoored from physical and sexual burdens. She herself, Sand confides to Chopin's mentor, had known many varieties of love: that of an artist, a woman, sister, mother, nun (from her Catholic school days), and poet. She believed that the heart can—and ideally should—be large enough to contain two different but simultaneous loves: one "for the *body* of life while the other is the *soul*." Sand is well known for innovating in her work as a writer; here, at this early stage in her relationship with Chopin, she was, it seems, ready to improvise on a whole new style of friendship. There's no record of a reply from Albert Gryzmała, but within some number of days following Sand's epic letter she and Chopin consummated their love.

In the end Sand did not have to become Italy in the contest of nations, but her famous letter anticipated the way future generations would come to associate Chopin with an enlightened ideal of patriotism, a phenomenon that becomes manifestly evident every hundred years as the world pauses to commemorate his birth. If the second centennial "Year of Chopin" in 2010 inspired young entrepreneurs to resurrect him as a superhero in high-tech video games, it was the first that paved the way by solidifying forever the idea that "Chopin composed Poland." It was Ignacy Jan Paderewski, himself one of the world's most famous pianists, who opened the Chopin Centenary Festival in the Polish town of Lemberg in October 1910. Like every Pole of his generation, Paderewski had grown up under authoritarian rule; even now, when he was fifty, the region was still under Austrian control. We have suffered "thunderbolt after thunderbolt," he told the crowd, and the whole shattered nation "quivers, not with fear but with dismay." Why then, he asked, "should the spirit of our country have expressed itself so clearly in Chopin, above all others?" For Paderewski, the answer was in the music, and to explain how his compositions personified the embattled nation he cited Chopin's innovative use of rhythm, fixating on his signature technique of *tempo rubato*. Franz Liszt had dubbed this the "rule of irregularity": a rhythm flexible enough to depart from the unforgiving metronome, but which always accelerates just a bit to make up for lost time. This strategy of "stolen time" (the term derives from the Italian verb *rubare*, to steal) accounts for the often improvisatory sound of Chopin's works, because the performer has some discretion to liberate notes from the mathematics that govern a piece of music, which are set out in the little fraction known as a time signature at the beginning of each work. Rubato is permission to, at least temporarily, thwart time, to put your *own signature* on a phrase, and it was in this gesture that Paderewski located the historic fighting spirit of the Polish people. To his countrymen in Lemberg he said: "This music which eludes metrical discipline, rejects the fetters of rhythmic rule, and refuses submission to the metronome as if it were the yoke of some hated government: this music bids us hear, know, and realize that our nation, our land, the whole of Poland, lives, feels, and moves, in *Tempo Rubato*." How do we endure through our tragic journey? Paderewski asked his fellow Poles. "Chopin best of all can tell us."

Paderewski's story took an improbable turn eight years later, in what I think of as an *only in Poland* phenomenon: in 1918 he abandoned the concert hall and became prime minister of his newly freed country. It's hard to grasp how astonishing this is, but if you're an

American living in the twenty-first century, imagine Yo-Yo Ma giving a stirring speech about how George Gershwin "composed America" through his use of melodic chromaticism, unexpected rhythms, and wanderings into remote harmonic territories (and yes, using that highly technical language) and then, a decade later, becoming president of the country. The sensitive musician as supreme leader; it's something unimaginable—unless, apparently, you are Polish.

After Paderewski's speech there was much more suffering ahead, beginning with the German invasion of Poland in 1939, which led to a ban on Chopin's music in his homeland. Paderewski died in New York in 1941; his body was taken to Washington, DC, and transported by a horse-drawn caisson and military honor guard to Arlington National Cemetery, where it was temporarily entombed in the vault of USS *Maine* Monument. "He may lie there until Poland is free," Franklin Delano Roosevelt proclaimed. In 1992, after the fall of Communism, Paderewski's body was finally returned to Warsaw. All but his heart, that is; it was the pianist-statesman's wish that it remain in America forever, and to this day the organ is interred in a shrine at the Our Lady of Czestochowa Cemetery in Doylestown, Pennsylvania.

The "very hard story" of Poland continues in the twenty-first century under the far-right Law and Justice Party, with its nationalist vision of "Poland first." Since assuming power in 2015, the government has acted to seize control of the country's public media; attempted to overhaul the judicial system and neutralize the highest court by imposing age restrictions on justices; curbed public gatherings; imposed restrictions on freedom of speech; and launched a nationwide initiative in schools committed to "patriotic education." A leading Polish intellectual described the party's philosophy in stark, if haunting, terms. Law and Justice, he said, "offered a meaning [and] their meaning was: 'We'll make Poland great again.'" Even so, the ruling party could be counted on to use the language of music and Frédéric Chopin when, in 2018, it kicked off a year of events designed to commemorate a century of independence. In opening remarks before a concert in Warsaw on February 24—the day that, two hundred years earlier, an eight-year-old Chopin first performed in public with an orchestra—Law and Justice president Andrzej Duda said that without Chopin it was highly likely Poland would have remained under the yoke of its autocratic neighbors. Unlike Paderewski, he offered no concrete examples, musical or otherwise, but ended by stating that "it was thanks to his music that Poland re-emerged on the world map in 1918."

This is how Chopin became, over the course of two centuries, inextricably embedded in the patriotic imagination of his country, in both its historic struggles and contemporary culture wars. Most of the landscape he knew in Warsaw was destroyed by German bombs in World War II, and during those years of twentieth-century strife there were many attempts made to censure his music, remove his name from repertoires, musical publications, and radio programs. Even monuments erected to commemorate his work were destroyed, including the most famous, which depicts Chopin underneath a willow tree, a symbol of Polishness. It was restored in 1958 and placed in a Warsaw park, where every weekend during the summer a piano is set next to the statue and an artist performs Chopin's music to a large, diverse crowd. In recent years city officials went even further in their effort to fill the air with Chopin by installing "musical benches" that, at the touch of a button, play a famous work. New smartphone apps hit the market regularly, enabling users to do everything from take a selfie with Chopin in places where he once hung out to providing geo-tagged locations with relevant background and history. But while technology, monuments, and media programming come and go, one thing never changes in this remarkable country, with its long, poignant, ever-present history. As a Polish journalist put it in 1995, as the entire country was fixated on the prestigious International Chopin Piano Competition being broadcast live on national television and radio: "Poles are born with Chopin in their souls. Chopin for us is everything that surrounds us, everything we would like to express, but for which there are no words."

TWO

Pianopolis

Unable to return to his homeland after months of peregrinations through Europe's capital cities, Chopin finally arrived in Paris in the fall of 1831. France at this moment was recovering from its own revolution: the "Three Glorious Days" of July 1830 that put Louis Phillipe on the throne. This was a liberal revolt by French citizens against Charles X, who had issued a series of repressive ordinances suspending freedom of the press and limiting voting rights, among other things. It was the social revolution that, four months later, sparked Poland's November Uprising by angry young cadets who didn't want to fight with the Russians against the French. By this time Paris, which Chopin chose for his new home, was the nexus of a love affair between two countries. The French intelligentsia enthusiastically welcomed a wave of Polish émigrés—artists, poets, political thinkers—who streamed into their capital. As a people these refugees from "captive Poland" were considered exotic (vaguely Oriental), fearless (descendants of warriors who fought off Genghis Khan and Tamerlane), and tragic (having been wiped off the map of Europe, they were geopolitically homeless). Like their French brethren, the Poles had presented arms to advance a treasured, newly modern ideal of citizenship. Victor Hugo's *Les Misérables* culminates with a riot in 1832; as the battle heats up, a young French rebel stands on the barricades, draws his sword, and cries "Poland for ever!"

Chopin was astounded by what he discovered in Paris, a city of contrasts and unbridled energy. To one friend he wrote: "You find here the greatest splendor, the greatest filthiness, the greatest virtue and the greatest vice." To another he marveled, "Paris is whatever you care to make of it. You can enjoy yourself, get bored, laugh, cry, do anything you like, and no one takes any notice because thousands here are doing exactly the same. Everyone goes his own way." Louis Phillipe would be France's last king; his reign, which spanned almost exactly the years Chopin spent in Paris, marked a period of transition from the Old World to the New—the *ancien régime* to a more modern, constitutional, liberal system, albeit still a monarchy. But the existential change went way beyond politics; it was a time of newness and experimentation in everything: science, social and intellectual life, art, music, literature, industry. Paris in the decade of the 1830s has been called "the capital of the nineteenth century;" it was teeming with scientists and entrepreneurs developing a new generation of machines uniquely suited to the Romantic zeitgeist. This was no longer the "clockwork universe" of the Enlightenment, governed by levers, gears, and universal laws that allowed scientists to measure, describe, and quantify the natural world. The Romantic machines were designed instead for self-expression. Among the most transformative was the steam-powered printing press, which allowed people in every corner of society to experience in their own homes, via mass-produced, affordable novels, the strange Gothic worlds of Goethe (whose *The Sorrows of Young Werther* many consider the literary spark that set off the Romantic era), Victor Hugo, Mary Shelley,

E. T. A. Hoffman, Ann Radcliffe, Alexandre Dumas, Walter Scott, and, of course, George Sand. In 1823 there was one cylindrical steam press in France; by 1830 there were thirty. Inventors understood the disruptive power of their technologies; one entrepreneur, Pierre Leroux, cast his invention of a new keyboard printing press, dubbed the "pianotype," as an "instrument in service to the ideal [that could] reorganize society." He dared to imagine a day when writers would all have their own printing presses and "we will set the human spirit free." As printing capacity grew, the publishing business soared: journals and newspapers popped up everywhere, including specialty publications dedicated to music, literature, art, and politics. There was even a dedicated columnist whose beat was the emerging field of popular science itself.

Over the course of the 1830s other machines arrived that would connect people and ideas in even more dynamic ways, like the first steam-powered railroad, which opened in 1837 and linked Versailles with the capital city. In Paris the following year Samuel Morse demonstrated his telegraph, an event one observer predicted would, within ten years, cause far-flung nations to "be literally wired together." By the middle of the decade art and science were so conjoined that Honoré de Balzac used the occasion of a comet over Paris to coauthor a vaudeville play he claimed had been written entirely by steam power. (Looking back on all this from the screen of one's iPad, the concept of Chopin's magic piano in *Frederic: The Resurrection of Music*, doesn't seem so crazy after all. . . .)

The machines of the Romantics were designed to transform, create, and manipulate human emotion and experience. Only weeks after he arrived in Paris, Chopin got a dramatic introduction to this new era in, of all places, the opera house. Giacomo Meyerbeer's *Robert le Diable* premiered in November 1831 and had all the narrative and scenic hallmarks of the new Romanticism: a battle for the soul of the devil's son, villainous knights, a forest cave where the spirits of hell commune, a magical tree branch, and, at the end, a chorus of ghostly nuns who rise from their tomb in a ruined cloister and perform a strange, sensual dance. But the production also introduced innovations in staging that audiences had never experienced before, like trapdoors and "speaking trumpets" that eerily amplified voices of a demon chorus hidden below stage. A diorama inspired by Louis Daguerre employed gas lamps covered in foil to create never-before-seen illusions of depth and color. These were punctuated by exploding fireballs made by throwing resin dust on moss spores over an exposed flame. Overhead lighting produced perhaps the first realistic representation of a moonlit stage, and the dancing nuns wore skintight costumes with little veils attached that made them seem otherworldly and ethereal—and from which the ballerina's tutu would later evolve. Chopin was as impressed by the theatrical razzle-dazzle as he was by the sonic aura that enveloped the audience, thanks to the unprecedented use of a church organ on stage. It was so loud, he wrote in a letter, it "practically drowns the whole orchestra," and yet it "enchants and amazes. . . . If ever magnificence was seen in a theater, I doubt whether it has reached the level of splendor shown in *Robert le Diable*. It is a masterpiece of the modern school." Many years later a professor in a real modern school, the University of Pennsylvania, would put this event in context for a twentieth-century audience: "*Robert* was to grand opera what Michael Jackson's *Thriller* was to MTV: by taking phenomenal technologies to unprecedented heights, it showed subsequent artists what a new audiovisual medium could achieve."

For Chopin, the most important machine was a musical one, and it too was developing through new technology and industrial steam power into an instrument that could achieve the ultimate ideal of self-expression in ways no keyboard instrument ever had. The story of the piano begins around 1700 with the man credited as its inventor, Bartolomeo Cristofori. Originally a maker of harpsichords, clavichords, and spinets, Cristofori was offered a position in 1688 to care for a large collection of fine musical instruments at the palace of Grand Prince Ferdinando de' Medici in Florence. He served under the protection of the prince and was paid a monthly stipend—an arrangement no prior instrument maker had ever enjoyed. Like other early keyboard makers, Cristofori was more than just a skilled woodworker: he was a sophisticated polymath well versed in performance practice, mathematics, engineering, and materials science. He was also, to his core, deeply musical, and imagined a soundscape that didn't exist in the late seventeenth century: keyboard music that could range from soft to loud. Violins could do it, so could trumpets and wind instruments—all the voices of the orchestra, in fact. But the harpsichord, because its strings are plucked instead of struck, has just one volume, one tonal color, in its portfolio of sound. No matter how hard you hit the key, the result is the same. Cristofori's great idea was to change the mechanism and deploy a hammer against a string. His first technical innovation was the *escapement*, a concept watchmakers had been using for many years to transfer energy and regulate the movement of gears or a pendulum in a timepiece. In a pianoforte—the instrument that plays soft (*piano*) and loud (*forte*)—an escapement allows the hammer, once it has struck the string, to fall back immediately, thereby allowing the string to resonate. This hammer also allowed the string to be hit harder than it could on a clavichord, thereby generating a bigger sound. Cristofori's other innovation was a device that served as a "check" on the hammer, allowing it to rapidly return to its home position without bouncing off (and therefore reanimating) the string after it had been struck, which meant it could now strike—and elicit tones—in rapid succession. Cristofori also innovated with raw materials, beginning with the soundboard, the soul of the instrument. Music may be the most difficult phenomenon to pick apart and explain, but at its heart beats a simple truth: it's all about vibration. Cristofori understood that the physics of vibrating waves participate in the production of tone—science that had been around at least as far back as Pythagoras's experiments in the sixth century BCE to measure numerical distances between musical intervals. This is the project that, according to legend, Pythagoras undertook after hearing various pitches made by a blacksmith pounding on his anvils. Cristofori took the soundboard of his pianoforte and isolated it from rest of the instrument, thereby allowing it to vibrate more freely and produce a greater volume. He added more tension to the equation with thicker strings, which he put at a higher tension than had previously been used on harpsichords, permitting both the metal *and* wood to vibrate even more.

Today there are three remaining pianofortes by Cristofori, one of which is at the Metropolitan Museum of Art in New York. Very old things make us see—and, it turns out, *hear*—our own world in a new way, which is what happened to me when I visited Cristofori's machine at the Met. This delicate, three-hundred-year-old instrument quite simply changed the world of music by allowing a keyboard player to capture a new universe of emotional color. It's surprisingly small, with just fifty-four keys and slender, workmanlike legs. Nearby you can press a button on a screen and watch a video of Dongsok Shin, a specialist in early keyboards, playing on the 1720 Cristofori, which the museum claims to be the oldest surviving piano in the world, the first piece of music ever written specifically for the piano: a suite of twelve sonatas by Lodovico Giustini, composed in 1732. In his score Giustini included the notations *forte* and *piano* to indicate changes in dynamics, which illustrates the unique thing the brand-new instrument could do: get loud, then get soft. As Shin plays, you can see the revolutionary action at work behind his fingers: hammers hitting strings. You can hear the change in dynamics as he varies the weight of his fingers on the keys, moving from loud to soft and back again. It's the sound of the future.

After Cristofori, piano makers puzzled over ways to further enhance the instrument's capacity to sing. One crucial development arose not for the hands but the feet: a pedal for the right foot that could sustain tones across many octaves, and another for the left that could dampen just a portion of that tone, producing a change in volume. In 1826 a Frenchman, Jean-Henri Pape, took out a patent for hammers made of felt, which replaced the tanned deer leather that was previously used. Leather can become brittle with age, producing a hard, dry tone. Pape's soft, pliable felt made the sound rounder, richer, and longer-lived because it allowed the string to develop its vibration more gradually. Another innovation was the double-escapement, invented by Sébastien Érard in 1821. Érard built on Cristofori's technology by allowing a note to be repeated even if the key had not yet returned to its maximum vertical position. This meant notes could be repeated *very* rapidly—single ones as well as chords and octaves—introducing new textures and complexity to the sounds a piano could summon. Meanwhile, in steam-powered factories that were being built all over Europe during these early years of the Industrial Revolution, manufacturers installed metal plates and eventually full cast-iron frames inside wooden piano cases, which allowed the resounding parts of the instrument and its strings to grow yet larger in size and power. And as it grew physically, the piano also developed a greater capacity for expressing nuances of emotion. For Chopin, who derived his greatest pleasure from Italian bel canto opera, it was the paragon of instruments, capable of imitating all the attributes and techniques of the human voice—the deep, vibrating sonorities of individual notes and, with its pedals and repeating mechanical action, the phrasing, breathing patterns, and long, beautiful lines a soprano could carry and decorate. You find evidence of this on the page too: in Chopin's earliest compositions, going back to his op. 2, the Italian word for singing, *cantabile*, shows up as a direction for the pianist. It's perhaps no coincidence that the first person to write about Cristofori's invention—Scipione Maffei, who in 1711 also pioneered the language to describe it, *piano e forte*—referred to a crucial part of the mechanism as a "movable tongue." From the very beginning, it seems, the instrument was humanized, and it was the "singing tone" that composers and listeners would prize above all else.

By the early nineteenth century the piano world had bifurcated, leaving composers and pianists with two options: the light-actioned Viennese-style versus the heavier English pianos. Chopin's favorite instrument—and the primary one on which he composed Opus 35—was a Pleyel, which he deemed "the last word in perfection." Its inventor, Ignaz Pleyel, was the twenty-fourth child of a poor schoolmaster living in a small town outside Vienna. A friend and student of Haydn, he moved in 1783 to France, where he worked as a church composer. His association with the church, combined with his status as a foreigner, caused him to be brought before the Committee of Public Safety under the Terror, where Pleyel was accused of being a Royalist collaborator. Spared from the guillotine (his strategy: write compositions for the new republic), he settled in Paris and became a music publisher. In 1807 he began making pianos, but rather than using Érard's double escapement, which provided more leverage and therefore greater power, he finessed and improved on the single escapement action. This created a more direct contact between hammer and string, granting the pianist a more precise control. What was lost in power potential was gained in emotional delicacy. Pleyel also experimented with the veneering of the soundboard, which is often described as the soul of the instrument, seeking through chemistry to find "a sound with a basically dark hue, capable of as much nuance in color as in dynamic range." The result was what Franz Liszt described as its "silvery and slightly veiled sonority." It was these qualities of precision and nuance that Chopin prized in his Pleyel. He once warned a student against what he called the "dangers" of Pleyel's French rival, Érard, whose piano was so solid and robust that it made no difference whether you "thump it and bash it" or tap its keys lightly because "the sound is always beautiful and the ear doesn't ask for anything more." For Chopin, such an instrument was a "perfidious traitor" to a real artist because it made it too easy to achieve a beautiful sound. "When I feel out of sorts," he famously said, "I play on an Érard piano, where I easily find a ready-made tone. But when I feel in good form and strong enough to achieve my own individual sound, I need a Pleyel." This was the instrument for "the enunciation of my inmost thoughts." His loyalty to the family and its brand was unfailing; not only did he dedicate his Preludes, op. 28 to Camille Pleyel (whose father, Ignaz, died just a month before Chopin's arrival in Paris), but he wholeheartedly promoted the pianos for the rest of his life and then, for another 164 years, from the grave. Until 2013, when the successors to the original House of Pleyel finally ceased manufacturing pianos, the company used Chopin's endorsement in all its marketing materials.

Nowadays it's possible to experience firsthand what Chopin meant in his endorsement; you just have to drive to a small town in Massachusetts and be prepared to lose yourself to another era. Unlike virtually all other world-class collections of musical instruments, the Frederick Collection of Historic Pianos in Ashburnham is filled with keyboard instruments you can actually play. It's the perfect place—and the only one in the United States—to learn in a dynamic way how the piano evolved: how it learned to sing, what the difference is between an Érard and a Pleyel, and why this matters in the story of Chopin. The married couple that runs the collection for students, pianists, researchers, and writers, Patricia and Edmund Michael Frederick, started purchasing old pianos in 1976. Today their collection consists of twenty-six grands and a Study Center filled with historic books, recordings, and sheet music that occupies a handsome brick building built in the 1890s.

On my first visit, Pat and Mike moved me through the rooms of their collection, the two of them taking turns playing pieces by the great composers on the type and period pianos they used when composing their works: a Debussy prelude played on a 1907 Blüthner grand; a Brahms waltz on an 1871 Streicher; Beethoven's op. 27 no. 2 Sonata (*Moonlight*) on an 1805 Brodmann. We went backward in time, through Khachaturian, Fauré, Schumann, Mendelssohn, Liszt, Chopin, and Bach, their music filling the large space, once a library, on instruments made between the early twentieth century and the late 1700s: Bösendorfer, Chickering, Steinway, Bechstein, Graf, Broadwood, Tröndlin, Pleyel, Érard—a United Nations of musical sound covering more than two centuries. Many hours later we ended on a beautiful c. 1795 unsigned Viennese-style piano with geometric marquetry and a reverse-color keyboard (the accidentals are white, the regular keys black). Absent a foot pedal, Mike used his knee to control the dampers and played Mozart's haunting A-minor sonata, K. 310, composed just a dozen years before this piano had been made. In Ashburnham the great composers are vibrantly present, not only through their music but sometimes their fingerprints as well: the Fredericks have an Érard that once belonged to Ignacy Paderewski. As you walk through the crowded Study Center, you can touch the pianos, examine their innards, play their keyboards, and most of all learn from the Fredericks *how to listen* so you can experience what composers, pianists, and audiences heard when these instruments were the new, new thing. "We don't call ourselves a museum, because we are hands-on," Pat says. The Fredericks want you to see, feel, but mostly *hear* the world from which these instruments hail.

I came to Ashburnham expecting to hear a mechanical story, and instead what I got was a musical one. Yes, over the centuries the piano evolved through engineering innovations: beginning in Italy, then leaping from one country to another as technicians made improvements and contributions like members in an orchestra passing a melody back and forth; onward to Germany, then Austria, England, France, America. But the message the Fredericks work hardest to convey is that the instrument developed not so much through technology but through music. "I have a dim view of people who write books about the piano," Michael says to me somewhat ominously, almost before I have hung my coat in the entryway. This is because most books tend to present the story of the piano as a neat, linear narrative, an inexorable march of technology and innovation that ultimately, as pianos got bigger and more powerful, leads to the Steinway concert grand we hear today under the fingers of such diverse artists as Maurizio Pollini, Keith Jarrett, Yuja Wang, and Harry Connick, Jr. "The problem with the piano literature," he says, "is it's always about science and 'progress.' It's all about patents. Most people who write about pianos have never heard the old instruments, and so they focus on the machinery." It's not that Michael Frederick isn't fascinated by the inner workings of his instrument; a former harpsichord builder, he has an almost encyclopedic command of the mechanical engineering and materials science behind keyboard instruments. Sure enough, while I was there he made head-spinning discursions on everything from "the law of levers" and the coefficient of expansion to the mathematics of temperament.

But the story they tell here is that the piano developed as musical styles and tastes changed over the decades since Cristofori's first experiments with *soft* and *loud*. What Baroque audiences favored—mathematical clarity in complex structures like fugues, and polyphony, simple harmonies, thin textures, a consistent mood throughout, a steady rhythmic flow that was often compared to a sewing machine—was very different from the wide ranges of tone color, unbridled chromaticism, chordal effusions, contrasting dynamics, and unexpected polyrhythms that bewitched Romantic salon-goers. It's true that at some level in the conversation about piano development there lurks a chicken-and-egg question: Did the mechanical developments influence the music or did the composers pull the technology forward? But whatever the answer (if one even exists), the revelation that greets you in Ashburnham is a musical soundscape from the nineteenth century that simply doesn't exist anymore, one that's characterized by a surprising variety and multiplicity of voices.

During the golden age of pianos, this era in the early nineteenth century when Chopin began writing music, countries had their own distinct sounds. Makers in Vienna cared about the preferences of Viennese audiences, not those in London, Paris, or New York. While each atelier had its own signature sound, it catered to local taste. German-style pianos evolved from a culture of clavichord playing, whereas the English tended toward harpsichords, and each heritage was reflected in the instruments. Pianos made in Vienna favored a sweet, singing tone in the treble and a warm, precisely audible bass. The English, by contrast, favored a dry treble—Pat Frederick likens it to a xylophone—and a full, robust bass. The design of the French pianos Chopin loved was originally inspired by the English, but by the 1830s they had acquired their own characteristics, chief among them an uncanny ability to project a multitude of tone colors over a changing dynamic range, from very loud to incredibly soft. What this means is that a melody played in the right hand can be louder and even carry a slightly different timbre than the accompaniment played in the left. The high and low registers act almost like different instruments in an orchestra, accompanying each other in a choreography of tones that can sound beautiful together while each simultaneously maintains its own clear, individual character.

Until I went to Ashburnham, I hadn't understood how richly different the nineteenth century sounded from our own. Today our concert stages (and recording studios) are dominated by a handful of brands—Steinway, Yamaha, Bösendorfer, Fazioli —whose high- and low-pitched notes, both soft and loud, have been made to blend into a smooth continuum and are built for power and volume. Manufacturers today want their sound to reach a listener in the farthest seat of the highest balcony in the biggest concert hall. A few weeks after my first visit to Ashburnham, I took a subway across town to the Steinway factory in Queens to see how the modern grand piano has been made since the time of the American Civil War. The recurring theme of my tour, echoed in every section of the factory, is sound production: both quality and quantity. It starts outdoors, with huge piles of Sitka spruce, specially selected for soundboards because they grow on the shady side of the hill and therefore contain more tree rings, which can produce a bigger sound. The most dramatic moment of a Steinway tour is the room where the immense cases of concert grands are created in layers bent on huge metal presses. The multiple rims make the case stronger, and allow vibrations of the strings and soundboard to focus inward, thereby maximizing the volume of sound. The large, cast-iron frames—so massive they're fabricated in a foundry in a different location—also enable a key innovation that separates the modern Steinway from Chopin's Pleyel: cross-stringing. This is a design scheme in which the bass and treble strings cross over each other and yield a lusher, bigger volume of sound. But because the two layers of strings cause sympathetic vibrations, the richer sound comes at a cost: it's muddier; it's harder to hear the distinct character of each pitch because so much vibrating is going on. This trade-off, Pat Frederick observes, was consistent with goals of the Industrial Revolution for standardization and uniformity in manufactured products. "They wanted to smooth everything out, make it even, then mass-produce it." No matter how you listen to music these days, whether in Carnegie Hall, a piano bar, or streaming over the internet, you are hearing in the piano an even—and to critics like the Fredericks, a "homogenized"—tone that is the distant legacy of the Industrial Revolution. "What we are doing here," Mike says by way of contrast, "is preserving ecological diversity in classical music." The composer and author Jan Swafford paid a visit to Ashburnham and found, in exploring the Fredericks' collection, insights into the artistic intentions of early composers. "They wrote for those sounds, that touch, those bells and whistles," he observed in an article titled "In Search of Lost Sounds." When, for example, Beethoven composed his *Moonlight Sonata* in 1801, he directed the performer to hold down the pedal throughout the entire first movement, so the strings would never be damped and the sound would create the subtle effect of "one harmony melting into another." On a modern piano you have to pedal constantly after each measure, otherwise the effect you get is what Swafford called "a tonal traffic jam." This doesn't make the music any less beautiful, but as I heard for myself, it changes it quite dramatically, creating a different soundscape from the one Beethoven knew.

By the time Chopin arrived in Paris, there were ninety-one different piano makers, up from twenty-four in 1805. It had taken Cristofori twenty-five years to build twenty pianofortes; in 1831 alone the ateliers of Paris cranked out eight thousand. The city would soon be christened "Pianopolis," not only for the number of instruments streaming out of its factories but also for the diversity between brands. The passion for piano music grew so feverish that the two leading French manufacturers, Pleyel and Érard, built their own concert halls that could accommodate hundreds of people. Duels between pianistic superstars—*Liszt vs. Thalberg!*—were advertised in newspapers. Orchestras also grew, both in the number of players—from around thirty-five in Mozart's day to eighty in Chopin's—and diversity of voices, which in the Romantic era came to include large-bellied brass instruments like the newly invented ophicleide (a giant keyed bugle similar to a modern tuba) and trombones fitted out with multiple valves. This new fascination with massive sounds found a perfect champion in Hector Berlioz, whose *Symphonie Fantastique* premiered in Paris at the dawn of the new decade, in May 1830. Berlioz was famous for deploying huge orchestras, and this new symphony called for more than ninety instruments, including "at least" four harps, fifteen violins, nine double basses, and four timpanists who each play a different note on their drums. He was also inventive about the way he manipulated sounds. For example, he instructs horn players to change notes by stopping the bell with their hand instead of using a valve, which created a muffled, semi-muted effect. Most revolutionary, though, was the written program Berlioz created for *Symphonie Fantastique*, an actual storyline that was printed and distributed to the audience before each performance. Subtitled "Episodes in the life of an artist," it begins with the protagonist's opium-fueled obsession for a beautiful woman and ends with a march to the scaffold and a witches' sabbath. Even the program's *idée fixe*, a phrase Berlioz coined for the musical theme that's repeated in various moods in all five movements, has an insistent quality that, for all its resonant power, is far removed from anything Chopin—the artist who "proposes, supposes, insinuates, seduces, persuades [but] almost never asserts"—would have written.

The *Symphonie Fantastique* in 1830, *Robert le Diable* in 1831: this was the musical climate in Paris when Chopin arrived. And yet, as the universe of sound and Gothic imagination was expanding, Chopin retreated. He became an outlier: as everyone else was trying to get louder and bigger, he perfected a tone that was often so subtle audiences complained he was weak. Some critics used a form of code to avoid harsh criticism: "How light his touch is!" they would say. In letters home Chopin told his parents "it is being said everywhere that I play too softly, too delicately, for people used to the piano-pounding artists here." Even reviewers who once "praised me to the sky" complained that he lacked "energy." His first Paris concerts earned plenty of praise, from Robert Schumann's visionary 1832 review ("Hats off, gentlemen, a genius!") to a more thoughtful analysis by the critic Fétis, who marveled at the way Chopin "abandoned" himself to his own instincts, rejecting previous models and creating "a complete renewal of pianoforte music" and an "entirely new way of expressing himself on the instrument, using an abundance of original ideas of which the type is to be found nowhere." As a young man in Warsaw he had responded to this same kind of criticism about his sound by changing pianos, putting aside his favorite Polish instrument, a Buchholtz with a very sweet and extremely soft tone he used for his debut concert, in favor of a more refined, singing Viennese Streicher piano for the follow-up recital a few weeks later. Reviewers who had found the first concert lacking in "energy" now praised his "pearly" tone and great "clarity" of sound. But by 1835 Chopin had had enough of the public's opinion; he simply removed himself from the arena. "I am not at all fit for giving concerts," he said to Liszt. "The crowd intimidates me, its breath suffocates me, I feel paralyzed by its curious look, and the unknown faces make me dumb." Throughout his entire career he would give some thirty public recitals (Liszt, by contrast, is estimated to have given more than a thousand public concerts in a single eight-year period); he dreaded them so much George Sand once joked about an upcoming recital that "our little Chip-Chip," as she lovingly called him, "should play without candles or audience and on a dumb keyboard." Instead of concertizing he focused on writing and teaching by day, and improvising and playing new compositions in small salons at night. "Concerts are never real music," he confided to a promising student. "You have to give up the idea of hearing in them the most beautiful things of art."

There was another pressure he was compelled to resist, which also grew out of society's craze for large, narrative-fueled orchestral forms. From his early days at the Warsaw conservatory there was an expectation in musical circles that Chopin would write the century's great national opera. Once in Paris, where he became famous practically overnight, he was pressed by everyone—his teacher, family, friends—to compose what was then considered the pinnacle of musical form. *Write it for Poland*, they begged. His sister Ludwika insisted in a letter that Chopin's prodigious talent was underserved by just the piano and a handful of concerts; "*operas* must make you immortal," she insisted. In a newspaper review Robert Schumann predicted Chopin "will not rise any higher" or assert a major influence on the art of music because of his fixation on "the narrow sphere of piano music." Józef Elsner, who taught Chopin harmony, theory, counterpoint, and composition, was the voice that resonated most, for he understood his pupil's "inborn genius" better than anyone. Elsner, who was also Poland's greatest living opera composer, believed "Nature intended" that Chopin take his place alongside Rossini and Mozart. Year after year, in touching, fatherly letters, the professor tried to move his student away from his all-too-evident devotion "simply to piano-playing [and] the same species of composition." Only the opera can "show your talent in a true light and win for it eternal life," he said in an 1834 letter. It was his greatest hope that Chopin would comply. "As I journey through this 'vale of tears,' " Elsner wrote, "I would like to live to see an opera of your composition." Chopin's replies to his teacher are filled with respect and consideration for this revered man. He uses humor and Polish-language puns to soften the blow; asks for the old man's blessing and points out the scores of "gifted young men, pupils of the Paris Conservatoire" who are "sitting waiting with folded hands for someone to produce their operas, symphonies or cantatas." He felt pressure and competition all around him but was determined "to stand more firmly on my own feet." No one could extinguish what he confessed to Elsner was "my perhaps too audacious but noble wish and intention to create for myself a new world." The center of that world would not be the orchestra or the opera, it would be the piano. And here too he was an outlier.

The grand piano was prized not just for its power, versatility, and range, but also, before Chopin came along, its unique ability to imitate all the instruments in an orchestra. Performers were praised for making it sound like a violin, harp, flute, or horn. Mendelssohn referred to one of his scherzos for piano as "my little trumpet piece." With its wide range of seven octaves, Liszt enthused that the piano "embraces the range of an orchestra; the ten fingers of a single man suffice to render the harmonies produced by the combined forces of more than one hundred concerted instruments." He and other composers incorporated techniques in their piano writing that mimicked instruments in the orchestra, like the "tremolando," which creates waves of sound on a string instrument like the violin, or the glissando, commonly used on the harp or trombone to produce a cascade of rapid-fire notes. But not Chopin; he never used these techniques in his writing. For him the piano was already everything; he was content to make it sound like *itself*. Beethoven, one contemporary critic observed, wrote music "for the piano"; Chopin's music was "for pianists." This is why, all deference to Cristofori, Chopin is universally credited with having created the modern piano.

In May of 2018, two weeks after hearing Maurizio Pollini play Opus 35 in Carnegie Hall on the special Steinway he tours with, which has been modified by an Italian super-technician named Fabbrini, I returned to Ashburnham to hear Russian pianist Olga Vinokur play the sonata on an 1859 Érard. The recital was part of the Frederick's summer concert series held in a classic New England Protestant church just up the road from the Study Center, a weekly event that attracts people from all over the region and, frequently, from overseas. It was Mother's Day, and Vinokur had made the unusual decision to play Chopin's funeral sonata as part of a Romantic program that included works by Debussy, Fanny Mendelssohn, Robert Schumann, and Giuseppe Verdi. The contrast between the two concerts could not have been starker: in the first, a mature, older man—Pollini was seventy-six—played a hyper-modern piano in an enormous hall filled with more than thirty-five hundred strangers; in the second, a young woman played a 159-year-old instrument in an intimate, brightly lit church with an audience of fewer than one hundred people, many of whom knew one another from the community. It was,

I thought, as close as you can get in the United States to the experience of a nineteenth-century Parisian salon. Most unexpected—and unfamiliar—was the sound. I had arrived early to watch Vinokur practice, and stood with Pat Frederick in the back of the church as she ran through her program, beginning with the Nocturne in D-flat major, op. 27, no. 2, a piece that enfolds you in the impossible beauty and poetry of Chopin's sound. At a summer festival I had attended a few years earlier I made a note of what scholar Jonathan Bellman said about this work, calling it "a pianistic reimagining of a tragic bel canto love duet that elevates every operatic cliché—the sigh, the affective turn to minor, an impassioned inversion of tenor and soprano parts, the last breaths, the liberated soul's final ascent—to the timeless and universal." The Érard, with its rich, carrying tone and the glorious balance of bass and treble—two voices that operate distinctly and in concert but never overshadow each other—made Bellman's final observation manifestly true. "If you don't hear it," he said, "you have a heart of stone." Pat, for whom the sound of this nineteenth-century instrument is as familiar as her husband's voice, said to me as we stood together in the back of the church: "It does bring tears to your eyes, doesn't it?" It was the sound that Chopin and his students, friends, fellow expats, and small salon audiences heard in Paris; it was "the world of my own" that he had created in his adopted home.

Back in the Study Center, as the sun was setting and the recital long over, Mike pulled a white cloth off the 1845 Pleyel, raised the music stand, and invited me to sit. This instrument (serial number 11,820) is similar to the last Pleyel Chopin owned and played, an 1846 grand on which he gave the final concert of his life in London (serial number 13,819). The Frederick's Pleyel has been retired from use because the original hammer felt is too fragile, but in 2010 Chinese pianist Yuan Sheng recorded all of Chopin's preludes, nocturnes, ballades, and impromptus on it. After I explored the keyboard of the Pleyel, playing a few pieces I had brought with me, Mike launched a track on Sheng's CD, the Prelude no. 15 from op. 28, popularly known as "Raindrop." On this mellow, delicate piano Sheng pulls you directly into Chopin's world, bringing out the mingled qualities that Chopin's student, Karol Mikuli, admired in his teacher: "He gave a noble, manly energy to appropriate passages with overpowering effect—energy without roughness—just as, on the other hand, he could captivate the listener through the delicacy of his soulful rendering—delicacy without affectation."

What I heard in Ashburnham, in Sheng's recordings on the 1845 Pleyel and Vinokur's live performance on the 1859 Érard, are the qualities of the piano Chopin loved, the ones that fueled all his musical innovations: its capacity for carrying the long line of a song, for imitating a multitude of voices, for now seizing the rhythm like the percussion instrument it essentially is, then gracefully defining the wind, like an Aeolian harp. These two pianos produce tones of perfect, bell-like clarity from the sepulchral bass all the way up through the octaves to the celestial treble, from *pianissimo* to *fortissimo* and every dynamic in-between. Most of all, though, what's going on here is a strikingly intimate communication between composer, machine, and listener. It's everything that a modern concert is not. Unless, of course, it is played in a modest hall on period instruments. . . .

In the fall of 2018 I spent the better part of two weeks in Poland—virtually, that is—watching on YouTube as a miraculous musical story unfolded in Warsaw. All year the country had been celebrating the one hundredth anniversary of regaining independence from the "Satanic Trinity," that coalition of Russia, Austria, and Prussia that, beginning in 1772, imposed a series of partitions that effectively erased Poland from the map of Europe. To commemorate the centenary the Fryderyk Chopin Institute, official keeper of the composer's legacy, decided to recreate the soundscape of Chopin's time by inaugurating a new international piano contest to complement its storied Chopin Competition, inaugurated in 1927 and considered one of the world's most important music competitions. The founders, two professors at the Warsaw Conservatory, designed the original competition to restore Chopin's reputation, which had lost some of its luster after World War I. He was not regarded as modern enough, his music was considered too subtle, his works were being played increasingly rarely and, most worrisome, with excessive embellishment—"hysterical" use of rubato, too much pedal, thunderous pounding on the keyboard, emotional histrionics. They wanted to restore historical accuracy to modern performance practice and, in the process, reignite the waning "cult of Chopin." The competition succeeded brilliantly and has grown in prestige with each edition; held every five years (except for a hiatus during World War II), it has launched the careers of some of the world's greatest concert artists, including Martha Argerich, Maurizio Pollini, Garrick Ohlsson, Krystian Zimerman, Stanislav Bunin, Fou Ts'ong, Kevin Kenner, and Daniil Trifonov. In the mid-1990s an American journalist visiting Warsaw was amazed at the country's almost universal fixation on a piano competition. "Poles Gaga over Chopin Competition," his headline read, in an article that called it "the World Series of music."

In September 2018, with Chopin's popularity around the world now soaring, the Institute inaugurated a new competition, this one to be held entirely on period pianos, the instruments on which and *for* which Chopin composed his music. They also took a different, and illuminating, musical approach: during the first round, performers were required to play a prelude and a fugue from Bach's *Well-Tempered Clavier*, which had a profound influence on the young Chopin, as well as works by other Polish composers who were active during his lifetime: Maria Szymanowska, Karol Kurpiński, Józef Elsner, and Michał Kleofas Ogiński. The purpose of the Competition on Period Instruments was to go even further than its august predecessor by actually restoring the authentic *sound* of Chopin's music as it was heard in nineteenth-century salons. To bring back, for the benefit of a twenty-first-century music lover accustomed to powerful Steinways, Bösendorfers, and Yamahas, "the original color and mechanics" of the instruments he used and loved, and to let them "grasp the unique, specific character of Chopin's music, with its one-of-a-kind articulation and harmonic language." This, the Institute conceded, "has been lost in interpretations on contemporary instruments." Echoing almost to the word what Pat Frederick had told me during my first visit to Ashburnham, a staffer commented in a television interview that "modern piano companies will be angry with me when I say this, but contemporary pianos sound alike." This makes them reliable, he observed, but limits their expressive capacity and removes them far beyond the world of nineteenth-century Europe, where scores of manufacturers worked so hard to achieve a unique, distinct, sound for their individual creations. "The aim of this competition," he said, "is to seek the beauty that is somewhere in these differences."

With its partners, Polish National Television and Radio 2, and aided by a worldwide live-streaming internet platform, the Institute invited people from around the globe to enter, and experience, the lost sonic world of Frédéric Chopin. Thirty young pianists from nine countries arrived in Warsaw to make a difficult choice. On offer was a wide variety of pianos from makers Chopin knew and loved: Érard, Pleyel, Broadwood, Graf, plus a newly commissioned facsimile of the

1825 Polish Buchholtz he used when he was just starting out. The sun had not yet risen in New York when the first performer, a young Pole named Ewa Tytman-Csiba, walked across the stage and sat before the keyboard of an 1837 Érard. Listening to her play Chopin's Étude in C minor, op. 10, no. 12, known as "Revolutionary," brought the significance of this event home to me. Supposed by historians to have been sketched out in Stuttgart when Chopin learned the November Uprising had been brutally crushed, this piece went on to become a musical evocation of Polish nationhood, and it's not by coincidence that Zbigniew Dębicki chose it as the final soundtrack of *Frederic: The Resurrection of Music*, where it's played during the last, epic battle between Frederic and the evil Mastermind X, over the soul of music. Here, in the intimate Kameralna Hall at the Warsaw Philharmonic, it was being recalled in celebration of a century of independence and freedom by a twenty-eight-year-old Pole on a piano Chopin himself would have known. The next performance, by a Russian named Dmitry Ablogin, on an 1842 Pleyel, began with a startling gesture: before each piece in his recital repertoire, Ablogin performed a brief improvisation of his own. It was an old-fashioned act of "preluding," the common practice of nineteenth-century salon artists who experimented in the key of the piece they were about to perform to accustom the ear of the audience to that tonality and settle them in the moment. In his next round he played a mazurka Chopin was composing at the same time the 1842 Pleyel on which Ablogin performed it was being built. This work (op. 50, no. 3 in C-sharp minor) astonished the notoriously verbose George Sand, who described it in a letter to Eugène Delacroix as being "worth more than forty novels and . . . more eloquent than the entire century's literature."

It was the beginning of an unforgettable two-week period that brought the old world in concert with the new; when the piano itself became as important as the composer and the music, and where we the audience were invited to listen in an entirely new way to the most familiar works. The fortnight in Warsaw recreated a signature quality of Chopin's world, something long lost to our age of perfect, smoothed-out, and (in the Fredericks' opinion) homogenous modern pianos: a wide range of different voices and timbres, tonal colors, and dynamic contrasts. It may have taken some time to adjust to the soundscape of these pianos, but the reward was an encounter with a universe of uncommon diversity, subtlety, and fresh, simply awesome beauty. The competition closed with Chopin's Concerto in F minor, op. 21, composed when he was nineteen years old. Each of the winners—Tomasz Ritter, Alexandra Swigut, and Naruhiko Kawaguchi—took turns on an 1842 Pleyel, and each played a movement of the concerto, accompanied by the excellent period Orchestra of the 18th Century. It was a poignant and unusual collaboration: three pianists born in the twentieth century, playing music written in the nineteenth, to celebrate, in the twenty-first, the liberation of one of Europe's most tormented countries.

After the competition I wondered what it was like for these young artists to re-engage with Chopin's music on period instruments. In interviews many spoke of the challenge of accommodating to the older machines: how they had to modify their touch in relation to the lighter actions, and work harder to bring out the more nuanced, singing tones. They learned that playing forcefully, as one might on a Steinway, produces only what Chopin called "barking" or "a pigeon-hunt" on the more delicate Pleyel. In an email after the competition one participant, Joanna Rózewska, told me she'd had to retool her technique, a process that took many weeks, but once she did, she realized she could "create a completely different world." Many of the pianists echoed this notion, and spoke with wonder about the wide range of "colors" they discovered in the old pianos. Mostly though, the competition brought them closer to Chopin, causing them to reexamine the way they hear and interpret his music. These instruments, Tomasz Ritter said, "help you read the composer's text."

There was only one American who competed in Warsaw, Eric Clark, and he trained and made his audition tape at the Frederick Collection. Eight months after the competition I met Eric in New York, and we sat in my loft talking about Chopin and the unusual event that had unfolded in Warsaw. What, I wondered, was the legacy of the competition in his practice and performance almost a year later? To answer, Eric spoke about the fundamental challenge that faces virtually everyone who chooses to participate in a competition: that inner battle between emulating successful, popular, or conventional styles, or "going your own way." Do you try to guess what the judges are looking for? Or do you do your own thing? It's a conundrum, and he was forthright about his own experience. Looking back on his two recitals in Warsaw, he gave himself a mixed review. In the first round he took some risks, allowed for spontaneity, resisted the convention to play everything as evenly and perfectly as possible. "I felt like this competition presented an opportunity to try some bold choices," he said: to move away from mainstream playing, take advantage of the different sense of touch and sound and interpret things—phrasing, certain accents, when to use rubato, whether or not to play the hands together—just a bit differently, perhaps more improvisationally, to capture the spirit in which the music was composed. But in the second round he played more "conventionally," almost as he would on a modern Steinway. In fact, for the longest, most important work he would play during that round, the Opus 35 Sonata, he chose an 1837 Érard, the brand Chopin chided for its "ready-made tone." Eric had experienced the veracity of Chopin's observation himself, having used the competition's 1842 Pleyel for some of the major works during his first-round recital. But as the stakes grew higher in the second round, he turned to the Érard. It was safer, he said, not so risky. And, perhaps, less effective, since he failed to advance to the third round. "But I noticed," he said, "the week after I got home from Poland I gave a recital on a modern Steinway, almost the same pieces I played in Warsaw. I felt myself reaching for more spontaneity and freshness, more license to do what occurs to me intuitively. And I think it was one of the best recitals I've ever given in my career. I had this freedom, and flow, and I felt like I was really singing at the piano, and things were just kind of occurring to me in the moment. And this friend of mine who was in the audience came up to me afterwards and said 'I've never heard it that way before, it was wonderful.' It was strange because it was just very easy for me physically. And I thought: *Now I see, it doesn't have to be that difficult.*"

It's a comment that surely would have made Chopin smile. What we know from the reports his students left behind is that his greatest goal as a teacher, beyond the development of technique, was their capacity to find, then express, their own voice in the interpretation of his music. He probably would have hated the idea of a piano competition, but I think he would have appreciated the results of this one.

THREE

Teach with Love

Back in Pianopolis in 1838, at around the same time she was drafting her epic "declaration of war" to Albert Grzymała over the heart of Chopin, George Sand was busy with another project: trying to comprehend the mechanics of her new lover's art. She did this in her typical way: by the pen, in a genre of her own invention. *The Seven Strings of the Lyre* is Sand's retelling of the Faust legend, which was newly, and wildly, popular at the time. The Faust story appealed to the Romantics for many reasons, from its blend of horror and dark humor to the intertwining of science with magic. But at its heart is a story about human duality, the notion that we contain multitudes and that a battle between good and evil lurks within our breasts and could break out in any one of us at any time. Eugène Delacroix contributed seventeen lithographs to an 1828 reissue of Goethe's *Doctor Faustus* (it was first published in 1808), and the tale inspired parts of both Berlioz's *Symphonie Fantastique* and Meyerbeer's *Robert le Diable*. In 1835 it was turned into an opera for the first time; the production lasted five hours and was, according to Chopin's report to his family back home, "a frightening but powerful fantasy."

Sand approached the Faust story from a female perspective, using the struggle between a tormented philosopher and his deal with the devil as a way of exploring how a woman, long controlled and underestimated by powerful men, could liberate herself through art, even if it would kill her in the end. Neither novel nor play, the "little fantastic drama" (her words) is cast in the form of a Socratic dialogue. This had been a popular genre in the eighteenth century but had fallen out of fashion; now Sand enthusiastically reclaimed it for *Lyre*. The unconventional format allowed plenty of leeway to tap into the web of Romantic juxtapositions that preoccupied her: faith versus science, art versus industry, male versus female. But this strange little book goes beyond the traditional Faustian counterpoints into a subject that had taken center stage in her life: music. Just a few months into the new romance with Chopin she assembles a cast of characters who, in a tortured love story that revolves around a bewitched stringed instrument, attempt to separate the science and logic of music from its mystery and emotional power.

At the center of the story is a revered philosophy professor, Albertus, who's wracked by doubt over the power of science to interpret the universe. What he now seeks is love, specifically that of Helen, the orphan who is his beautiful young ward. Helen is in possession of a magical lyre that resonates the "harmonies of the upper world," meaning it could speak to her in the language of God. To everyone else, however, the instrument is either mute or caterwauling. In Sand's version of the tale it is Helen, a powerless woman surrounded by men of science and philosophy, who has privileged access to knowledge, and it comes to her through the language of music. Mephistopheles in Sand's account yearns to possess Helen, destroy the lyre, and bring damnation—through despair of love—to Albertus. His business is with the philosopher's large but untutored heart, and he manages to convince the professor that if he takes apart the lyre by breaking each of its seven strings he can leave behind the restraints of science and learning, gain access to the mysteries of love, and beat out his younger students in the battle for Helen's hand in the bargain. The whole drama circles around an existential tension between the languages of poetry and reason: one that lets us feel, the other that lets us know. The message of *Lyre* is that music, written in a special code of its own that's based on science and mathematics but speaks directly to the Romantic soul, is the language that, if we can only learn to *hear*, will lead us to the fullest expression of humanity: the ability to love and be loved.

In her memoir Sand recounts that her father was playing the violin when her mother delivered her, and thus was "born in music." We know from her autobiography and thousands of letters that Sand, herself an accomplished musician, spent hours in conversation with friends unpacking the question *What is music made of?* This would became a central theme of *Lyre*. Never one to hide her intellectual light under a bushel, Sand finds plenty of opportunities to show off her knowledge, salting the text with references to "perfect ratios," "algebraic equations," and the ways in which an instrument's physical properties—wood, metal, animal gut—interact with the laws of harmony and melody to create music. In Act IV she even proves her up-to-the-minute scientific bona fides by having Mephistopheles refer to state-of-the-art acoustical experiments that had recently been conducted in the water pipes of Paris.

Lyre circles around an endeavor that preoccupied many musicians in piano-crazy Europe: how, exactly, to teach the growing corps of passionate amateurs to effectively use all those levers, pedals, escapements, dampers, and other technical innovations to actually *make music*. At the time Sand was writing *Lyre* there was an avalanche of method books put out by the many "schools" of pianism that emerged during the early years of the nineteenth century. Every famous (and not-so-famous) pianist wrote one—Clementi, Kalkbrenner, Hummel, Adam, Zimmerman, Kontski, Reicha, Fétis, Moscheles, the list goes on and on. Most of these names are long forgotten, but any poor soul who studied piano in our own century knows the misery inflicted by Carl Czerny, student of Beethoven, teacher of Liszt, whom Chopin described as "a good fellow . . . [who's] more sensitive than any of his compositions." Czerny's works (he wrote more than a thousand) may not appear on modern playlists, but he identified archetypes of technique still in use today, as my tattered copy of *The Preliminary School of Finger Dexterity*, op. 636—its cover long separated from the twenty-four tortures inside—can attest.

Independent as he was, Chopin was not immune to the lure of the *méthode*—that attempt to quantify in words the rules and principles of music for the serious piano student. At around the same time he dashed off the melody of the *Trio* in his funeral march, he was also making notes for his own treatise, a project he worked on, in fits and starts, between 1837 and 1844. Chopin never completed his method; it remained, in his words, a "sketch," but in its surviving fragments one can see signs of his unorthodox approach to the piano as well as hints about what kind of teacher he was. And brief though it was, the work was clearly important to him, because he carefully preserved the thin sheaf of pages and, on his deathbed, asked that they be given to two composer friends "to see whether any use can be made of it." After his death the manuscript became scattered, passing eventually to his sister Ludwika, who gave it to Princess Czartoryska, who in turn left it to her student, a Polish pianist named Natalia Janotha, who contributed a few extracts to an 1896 study of Chopin's works. Another forty years elapsed before Alfred Cortot, the celebrated

French conductor, teacher, and pianist (who had written his own treatise on piano technique), purchased the manuscript in London. In 1949 Cortot published the first, almost-complete transcription, but it was later discredited because of omissions and misreadings. Finally in 1970 Chopin's method saw the light of day. It was Swiss musicologist Jean-Jacques Eigeldinger who found, collected, and decrypted the notes and manuscript pages that had floated around Europe all those decades. More than a hundred years after it had been abandoned by its author, Eigeldinger published the most faithful transcription yet of the long-lost how-to book by one of history's greatest pianists.

To complete his project Eigeldinger went not to Paris, Warsaw, or London, but to New York. Here, at the Morgan Library and Museum on Madison Avenue—which sits, in a nice coincidence, directly across the street from the Polish Consulate—Chopin's manuscript found a final resting place after Cortot's death in 1962. It's where Eigeldinger spent many weeks painstakingly decoding what another scholar described as Chopin's "runic scrawl." In fact, the pages more closely resemble a highly redacted legal document than a musical how-to. This is what initially struck me when I went to the Morgan to examine the manuscript for myself. The first sentence, written in Frédéric Chopin's hand, is clear enough (though written in Polish); it instructs the student on proper positioning of the elbow in relation to the keyboard. But after carefully turning the page with a little wooden paddle the librarian gave me to avoid making physical contact with the paper, I was greeted by a riot of crossings-out, insertions, hastily drawn representations of musical notes on a staff, and the occasional doodle. A case in point is Chopin's depiction of demisemiquavers—notes with a value of 1/32nd—which looks like the rendering of a forest in an architect's landscape plan. Some of the pages are lined with music staves, some are just blank sheets. The crossings-out vary too: some are thick, as though Chopin dragged his pen deliberately over a word or phrase to erase it entirely and forever, while other strike-outs get just a simple line through a word, allowing history to record the edit. Several of the manuscript pages have been left blank, as have the reverse sides, so one assumes Chopin wasn't worried about conserving paper. It's as though he was writing at a feverish pace, his hand unable to keep up with his brain. "The pen burns my fingers," he once wrote, and here we can see it for ourselves. The pages comport with Sand's description of his composing process, which she recorded as "the most heartbreaking labor I have ever witnessed." In her memoir she described how Chopin would go promenading in the garden and ideas would flood his consciousness: "His creativity was spontaneous, miraculous; he found it without seeking it, without expecting it." But then, when he returned home and sat down at his desk, he was unable to recapture details of a musical theme that had been his walking companion. "He would shut himself up in his room for days at a time, weeping, pacing, breaking his pens, repeating or changing a single measure a hundred times, writing it and erasing it with equal frequency, and beginning again the next day with desperate perseverance." Traces of this indecision and impatience are on virtually every page of what Eigeldinger published as Chopin's *Projet de Méthode*, or "Sketch for a Method."

But what's also there are qualities that distinguished Chopin as an innovator, things that made his approach to composing *and* teaching uniquely his own. For example: right at the beginning, in just the sixth sentence of the *Méthode*, he establishes a connection between the keyboard and the human voice. He does this when introducing basic notation and the long "ladder of lines," today known as the *staff*, that composers use to render music in writing. It's the fundamental concept that launches every musical education and is a fixture of treatises going back to the first known example, written around 1600 in Venice. But what signals a real difference here is that tablature, for Chopin, represents much more than just musical notes and the intervals that separate them on a keyboard. They are "the sound which all voices . . . a man, a woman, a child . . . can sing." He reiterates this several times in the *Méthode*, as though to suggest that a piano, this complex machine that now occupied a place of honor in the parlor of so many homes, exists to conjure, or imitate, the voice of *every human being*. The "singing tone" was, by the 1830s, already a piano cliché, perpetuated by instrument manufacturers and devotees in a kind of promotional catchphrase, the way "hi-def" or "HD" became the sine qua non of film and television in our own time. But it was not a conventional metaphor that anyone applied to *technique*. What Chopin did was embed the idea of the singing tone into the study and practice of playing the instrument; for him the two were inseparable. This is why he endlessly badgered his pupils about going to the opera and taking voice lessons, which to him were as important as practicing scales and arpeggios. "You must sing if you wish to play," he would tell them.

He also thought about the human anatomy, and especially the fingers, in a new way, going against prevailing conventions that the establishment—represented by the plethora of methods and treatises they published—expected piano teachers to abide by. Chopin didn't accept their timeworn practices, based as they were on an unscientific notion of "symmetry" between fingers. In the *Méthode* he punches back: "For a long time we have been acting against nature by training our fingers to be all equally powerful." On the contrary, he believed each finger has its own power and personality, which is determined by its shape and position in the hand. This natural inequality of the individual fingers was a source of great variety of sound and colors;

rather than "destroy the particular charm of each one's touch," Chopin advocated, the student should *develop it*. So he came up with his own system, much to the horror of the prevailing "schools," which included a wholehearted embrace of the thumb on black keys (once considered so controversial as to be verboten); a technique of sliding the finger from one key to its neighbor; and marking his scores with suggestions based on the individual capability of each finger to create a beautiful sound. Again and again he told his students: "One must sing with the fingers." His sense of sound was intimately connected with the sense of touch. He admonished students over and over again: You must "caress the key, never bash it!" But his unorthodox approach went beyond just the digits: Chopin grounded his understanding of technique in a close study of the pianist's essential anatomy: that interconnected appendage consisting of shoulder, arm, elbow, wrist, fingers, and all the ligaments that connect them. "Just as we need to use the conformation of the fingers, we need no less to use the rest of *the hand*, the wrist, the forearm and the arm." He considered the entire mechanism one organic whole. This was a seismic shift. "For the first time in the history of piano pedagogy," musicologist Alan Walker observed, "precedence was being given to the physical comfort of the hand."

During the period when he was drafting his *Méthode*, Chopin was also composing parts of the funeral march from Opus 35, and I was taken aback during a piano lesson one day when I discovered that his teaching philosophy reveals itself right there, in the very first measure of the *Trio*. In a descending passage of quarter notes in the right hand, Chopin suggests you play the first two notes with one and the same finger: the fourth. In the score below, which was owned by one of his students, you can see the number "4" marked twice in the top line in Chopin's hand:

Score belonging to Chopin student Jane Stirling, with his finger notation "4-4."

When I first began studying the sonata my teacher, Rafael Cortés, crossed out Chopin's recommendation and replaced it with a more traditional sequence he thought would be more comfortable and straightforward for me: a stepwise progression beginning with the pinky that would launch a simple pattern of 5-4-3-2. But in our lesson the following week he took it back, erasing his suggestion and restoring Chopin's. "Actually," he said, "this is a very good fingering because he's asking you to raise your wrist in the middle of the phrase, which allows you to then drop your whole arm down on the pad of that fourth finger to articulate the second note. The weight of your arm falling like that will really let you sing those notes."

During this exchange Rafael was hitting on another of Chopin's more maverick ideas, which concerns the vitality of the wrist. Without being aware of it, he was practically quoting one of Chopin's favorite students, a young Latvian named Emilie von Gretsch, whose description of her lessons contributed greatly to the modern understanding of what he was like as a teacher. In her diary one day Gretsch described "another new, simple way of obtaining a marvelous result" that followed from Chopin's love of opera. "True to his principle of imitating great singers in one's playing," she wrote, "Chopin drew from the instrument the secret of how to express breathing. At every post where a singer would take a breath, the accomplished pianist . . . should take care to raise the wrist so as to let it fall again on the singing note with the greatest suppleness imaginable." If a student hesitated or was clumsy (which apparently happened quite often), he coached them with gentle admonishments: *facilement, facilement . . .* Go easy, he urged; play it without tension. He advised them to drop their hands—*laissez tomber les mains*—and in so doing put the force of gravity to their sonic advantage. What concerned Chopin most, his student and disciple Karol Mikuli wrote, was to free the pupil from "every stiffness and convulsive or cramped movement of the hand, in order to obtain the primary requisite of good playing, *souplesse* [suppleness], and with it independence of the fingers." All this was essential because Chopin believed a beautiful sound resulted from the performer's *touch*, a seemingly simple yet vexingly challenging physical labor that involves simultaneously understanding a physical mechanism *and* anticipating the beauty it will create. Rafael once described this as taking apart a rose, petal by petal. "We have to do this to see how the rose is built: that's technique." Gretsch confided to her diary that "attain[ing] this *souplesse* is the most difficult task I know, but once you succeed in doing it, then you laugh with joy at the beautiful sound, and Chopin exclaims, '*C'est cela, parfait! merci!*' ['That's it, perfect, thank you!']"

This physical technique also allows a performer to attain the glorious bel canto sound Chopin loved. Music critic Anthony Tommasini explains the mechanics of bel canto in his book *The Indispensable Composers*, describing how the singer strives for a perfectly even, smooth, vocal line throughout the entire range of her voice. "Ideally," he says, we don't want to "hear a singer shifting gears, in a sense, from low to middle to high registers, exposing what are deemed 'breaks' in the voice." (For those listening at home, Tommasini cites "*Casta diva*" from Bellini's *Norma* as "the epitome of a bel canto aria." This was, coincidentally, Chopin's favorite opera, and he wrote a beautiful piano transcription of it.) Using the technology of the pedal in synch with a carefully coordinated movement of the anatomy, a pianist can sustain that long line until it's time to take a breath. Students who had a hard time remembering to deploy the technique got a bold, diagonal slash through passages where Chopin wanted them to lift their hand and breathe, like a soprano in the middle of her aria. In his *Méthode* he simply wrote: "The wrist: respiration in the voice." Later he tied it all together: "A supple hand; the wrist, the forearm, the arm, everything will follow in the right order." It was an organic approach designed to get young pianists to regard the mechanics of their own anatomy as fundamental parts in a grand act of respiration. The trick, and the training, was to coordinate them in order to achieve a beautiful, singing tone. This is what trickled down from 1830s Paris to my loft in West Chelsea, where I struggled to lift my wrist and capture the voice, and sound, Chopin wanted in his sonata.

Every teacher carries within them the training, philosophy, and legacy of their own instructors. The day I began studying with Rafael, back in 1995, at a small community music school in midtown Manhattan, he recounted the story of his own pianistic journey; this was his way of framing his teaching method and preparing me for both the physical and mental task ahead. He had cycled through the traditional conservatory system, beginning at Peabody in Baltimore and continuing in Germany on a Fulbright Scholarship. He was trained in the classic twentieth-century style, with a fixed hand and curled fingers lifted high, by teachers whose own legacies extended backward to the early days of the piano's development: two years of master classes with Leon Fleisher, who studied with Arthur Schnabel, who studied with Theodor Leschetizky, who studied with my future nemesis Carl Czerny. In his twenties, after collecting bachelor's and master's degrees, Rafael began experiencing pain in his hands and realized something was wrong. "It turned out I had to leave Peabody to learn how to play the piano," he says, somewhat ironically. He had the good luck, after his return to New York and many years of searching, to find a new teacher, Edna Golandsky, whose training also went back to Czerny but via a different path that began with a Russian pianist. Later in her career Golandsky became the principal teaching assistant to Dorothy Taubman, who in the 1950s was instrumental in pioneering a new, ergonomic approach to physical movement based on coordinated motion. The goal was to enable pain-free playing that would also lead to greater artistic results. Her system, called the Taubman Technique, was not without controversy, but has since been the subject of peer-reviewed scientific inquiry and been used by many professional pianists—including Leon Fleisher—to retrain and salvage great careers. The biomechanical technique Rafael learned from Golandsky is rooted in an organic system that unifies the body's movements: rotation of the arm, proper alignment of the forearm, hands, and fingers, and, most important of all, a faithful release of tension in all the muscles immediately after a note or chord has been sounded.

Substitute the word *release* with *souplesse* and you're not all that far from the Rue de la Chaussée d'Antin in Paris, where, during the period when he began drafting both his *Méthode* and Opus 35, Chopin gave piano lessons, retraining not just the bodies of his students but also their minds.

And what of Chopin's teachers? Every book about him discusses two centrally important men: Adalbert Żywny, a Bohemian who lived in Warsaw and worked with Chopin between the ages of six and twelve, and Józef Elsner, who taught him harmony, theory, counterpoint, and composition at the Warsaw Conservatory. (He also studied the organ for a time with a composer/organist named Václav Würfel.) Żywny wasn't a pianist or even a piano teacher himself, he was a violinist; he schooled Chopin in the basic principles of music, but most important of all he bequeathed to his young prodigy a love of J. S. Bach. In those days this was not par for the course, as it is today. (Another thing Rafael did in my first lesson was promise that whatever kind of music we might be working on, I would *always* have a practice piece by Bach.) Bach's music had fallen out of favor by the end of the eighteenth century and was known only to a relatively small number of specialists. The turning point didn't come until the 1820s, some seventy years after Bach's death, when Felix Mendelssohn's grandmother gave him a copyist's manuscript of *The St. Matthew Passion* and, with that single gift, changed the world of music by bringing Bach back into it. Adalbert Żywny was one of that handful of specialists who knew and loved Bach, and when Chopin later lectured his pupils to *toujours travailler Bach* ("always work on Bach"), it was because this was how his own education began.

Elsner, as we saw in the last chapter, was a father figure to Chopin during his formative years, and mainly taught him counterpoint and composition. Like Żywny, he too was not a trained pianist; as a musician he's best known as an opera composer, though he also wrote symphonies, string quartets, a Latin Mass, and more than fifty cantatas. But in addition to teaching him the nuts and bolts of composition, Elsner bestowed on Chopin a unique—and liberating—gift: a teaching philosophy rooted in the Enlightenment values of individualism, independence, direct engagement with nature, and, I was surprised to learn, love. One of Elsner's chief influences was a progressive Swiss educator named Johann Heinrich Pestalozzi, whose theory of education was informed by a new and holistic idea: to educate the *whole* child, striving for an equilibrium of what he called "head, hands and heart." For Pestalozzi there existed an "inner dignity" in each individual, and he believed that "without love, neither the physical nor the intellectual powers will develop naturally." This was perhaps why, to the astonishment of his Germanic colleagues, Pestalozzi banned flogging from his school. He also favored direct experience with nature, practicing the art of observation, and using all the senses to process and evaluate information. He encouraged young people to pursue their own interests and draw their own conclusions. "Let the child be as free as possible," he wrote, and "do not teach by words anything which you can teach by actual experience of things as they are." Pestalozzi himself was a devotee of Rousseau (he named his only child Jean-Jacques) and the 1762 novel *Emile: or On Education*, which argues against rote learning and for direct engagement with nature and the outside world. Rousseau was writing during a golden age of scientific invention—new devices could calculate longitude, measure the acuteness of an angle, establish the distance between two points, identify what an object weighed—but he deplored the effect all this new technology was having on human perception. "The more ingenious our tools," he wrote in *Emile*, "the cruder and more awkward our senses become. By surrounding ourselves with instruments, we no longer find the instruments within us." Rousseau believed children should be taken outdoors to learn from nature. Teach your child to fly a kite, he urged in *Emile*, and from the shadow it casts over the high road, let her observe the angle of the sun and thus learn how to take a scientific measurement.

It's this spirit of inquiry and creative independence, passed down from his own teacher, that Chopin nurtured in his students. Beyond the usual keyboard exercises, he insisted they practice active *listening* as a part of their studies, which included practicing in a dark room so they'd be unable to see the keys and notes. "Only then does the hearing function with all its sensitivity," he told them; "then you can really hear yourself, noticing every fault, while the hand acquires an assurance and boldness that it cannot find when the player is constantly looking at the keys." *Head, hands, heart.* He saw his work as enabling young pianists to discover their own sound as well as develop a correct technique. "We each understand this [piece] differently," he once told a student during a lesson, "but go your own way, do as you feel, it can also be played like that." To another, who was nervously preparing to perform his brand-new Opus 35 sonata in public at a *soirée*, Chopin asked, "Why do you play less well today?" When the pupil, Friederike Streicher-Müller, explained she was afraid, he praised her performance of his work, then invited her "to play this evening as nobody has played before you, and nobody will play after you . . . !" These words "restored my composure," Friederike later reported, and she went on to have a successful recital with much applause from the audience. With his serious students Chopin customized his guidance to each individual, taking on board not only their physical abilities but also psychological barriers they may have placed between themselves and the art of creating music. For example, he urged Emilie von Gretsch to "Forget you're being listened to, and always listen to yourself." He gave her permission to *be herself*: "When you're at the piano, I give you full authority to do whatever you want; follow freely the ideal you've set for yourself and which you must feel within you; be bold and confident in your own powers and strength, and whatever you say will always be good." The message got through; later she confided in a letter: "I think he can read hearts." Halina Goldberg, the only scholar who has extensively written about the philosophical link between Pestalozzi and Elsner, used a kind of shorthand to describe what came down to Chopin from his mentors, and what he in turn appears to have practiced with his own pupils: "teach with love."

Most scholars believe that Chopin, an autodidact at the keyboard, actually benefited from not having had a formal piano teacher at any time during his life. Freed from constraints imposed by the traditional "schools" of pianism, he was left to explore and innovate on his own. As Goldberg describes in her book *Music in Chopin's Warsaw*, his teachers nourished his artistic genius and encouraged him to experiment in order to find his own voice. Żwyny and Elsner may not have been what we would call "great educators," but they helped shape Chopin's musical and aesthetic talents, and allowed him to go forward and create that world of his own. In teaching composition, Elsner believed "one should not dictate rules, especially to students whose talents are apparent; let them search alone, so they can surpass themselves; let them have the means of finding that which is still unknown." When people asked Elsner why he gave Chopin so much freedom with the rules of theory he replied: "Leave him in peace. His is an extraordinary path, for he has an extraordinary gift. He does not follow the old rules, because he seeks those of his own." The tools—melody, harmony, counterpoint, thoroughbass, tonal progression, sonata form—were, for Chopin, readily at hand, just like the inbuilt beauty of the Érard. It was the encouragement toward independence and individualism—like finding one's own, distinctive voice on the Pleyel—that enabled true artistry.

Also in the spirit of Pestalozzi and Rousseau (and later Maria Montessori, who was strongly influenced by their philosophy), Chopin urged his students to get out into the world: to visit museums and look at masterpieces of art, take invigorating walks, go to the opera, read a good book. Whereas the young Franz Liszt, to stimulate his students, would read aloud a page from Chateaubriand or a poem by Hugo, Chopin developed his own language of personal imagination at the keyboard: *Pretend there is a shepherd in a grotto,* he would say to them, or *an angel passing over the sky.* He made stories out of music and textured them with nuance and suggestion. Explaining the inner drama of one of his nocturnes, he told one student: in the first two chords "a tyrant commands"; several measures later, his victim "begs for mercy." This was a muscle he had developed in grade school: young Frédéric and his pals would gather together after dusk and tell scary stories to each other—about Polish kings, famous battles, robbers climbing through windows in the dead of night—which Chopin would illustrate with moody music at the piano. There's a legend, perhaps apocryphal, from his early Paris years that illustrates this inclination toward imaginative freedom and independence that must, in some way, owe a debt to Elsner via Pestalozzi via Rousseau, which concerns the haunting Nocturne op. 15, no. 3 in G minor. Chopin was apparently in the middle of drafting this piece when he attended a performance of *Hamlet.* According to the story, he returned home from the theater and inscribed at the top of his manuscript: "At the cemetery." But when the piece was ready to go to the printer, he had a change of heart and expunged the descriptive label. "Let them guess," he reportedly said. He hated exaggeration, histrionics, a heavy, didactic hand. It was subtlety and simplicity that he prized. To one student he said: "No noises, no 'effects,' just simplicity, as in all that is beautiful." To his friend Wilhelm von Lenz he expressed his style even more concisely. "I indicate," he said; "it's up to the listener to complete the picture." Perhaps you might think of a graveyard when you hear the G-minor Nocturne. But if you do, it's not because the composer suggested it.

I think it was this same dislike of the didactic approach that caused Chopin to stick his uncompleted *Méthode* in a drawer. Most of the piano manuals published around this time were filled with mechanistic, repetitive exercises he regarded as just "a new genre of *acrobatics* . . . like learning, for example, to walk on one's hands in order to go for a stroll. Eventually," he wrote, "one is no longer able to walk properly on one's feet, and not very well on one's hands either." Guidebooks, he concluded, don't "teach us how to play the *music* itself." In his manuscript he had tried to explain how to educate one's fingers, hands, forearms, shoulders; how to approach technique in an organic way, using physical touch and the natural force of gravity to produce a beautiful sound. But in the end words didn't do it for him, and he put the *Méthode* aside for good. To one student he had simply stated: "Put all your soul into it!" No amount of pages dedicated to correct fingerings, proper hand position, or mastering an economy of movement could ever teach a student how to do *that*.

FOUR

Interlude with a Vampire

By the fall of 1838 Chopin and Sand were in love and inseparable.

To arrive at a point where she could choose her lovers at will, Sand had accomplished something exceedingly rare in 1830s France: at a time when divorce was prohibited by law, she legally separated from her husband, was allowed by the court to retain her property, and was granted primary custody of her two children. For a woman born in 1804, the same year the Napoleonic Code codified in law the supremacy of men and required a married woman to "live with her husband . . . and follow him wherever he moves," this was an astonishing achievement, and it didn't come without a prolonged, public court battle waged by her husband, Casimir Dudevant. When the long "conjugal and maternal war" was over and she had finally won, Sand relished what she called her "superb and unabridged independence." What she seems to have valued most about being liberated from her marriage was the unencumbered freedom to write—to live by her pen and her wits. In the mid-1830s George Sand took a man's name (she was christened Amantine-Aurore-Lucile Dupin), began wearing trousers, smoking cigars, and wandering the streets and theaters of

Paris without burden of gender. Now she had won the heart of Frédéric Chopin and was free to pursue her ideal of true love, that "pure" state between equals in which she could give her exclusive attention to another without, as she had put it in the epic letter to Grzymała, "reflecting that I am a woman."

These joys, however, were tempered by the specter of illness. Sand's teenaged son Maurice had begun suffering from acute rheumatism and violent headaches, and doctors believed his heart was enlarged. Chopin too was sick, beginning to present symptoms of tuberculosis, the illness that had claimed his sister Emilia's life and would also cause his own death. Both Maurice and Chopin needed a change of climate, as did Sand—not for her physical health but as a means of escaping all the tongue-wagging in Paris about her recent affair with Maurice's tutor, Félicien Mallefille. Distraught over Sand's abandonment and humiliated because it happened right after he had published a glowing review of one of Chopin's ballades, Mallefille challenged his rival to a duel with pistols and even went after his faithless lover with a dagger. Luckily no one was hurt. On October 18 Sand embarked on the long journey with Maurice and his younger sister, Solange, that would take them via Barcelona to the Balearic island of Majorca. Chopin would catch up with them in a few weeks for the sea crossing. The evening before he departed, he paid a visit to Saint-Gratien, villa of the Marquis Astolphe de Custine, where he played a Pleyel piano in his favorite setting: a beautiful château, amid a small group of friends. It was in this salon on October 21, 1838, that Chopin shared, probably for the first time in public, the funeral march from Opus 35. Perhaps he improvised on the melody and perhaps he played it as we know the final version today. But this evening resulted in the first written account by a listener.

It's worth pausing here for a short detour to look at the life of

Custine. He plays a minor role in the story of Chopin, although his fixation with the composer was surely outsize (if not entirely reciprocated). But in many ways he embodies the spirit, and sense of possibility, of Paris in the 1830s, straddling both the old world and the new in ways that only one other figure in this chronicle—who happens to be George Sand—can truly match. That they both competed for the affection and respect of Chopin connects them in just one of several intriguing ways. The Marquis is also inextricably—if rather strangely—linked to the creation story of Opus 35. He is glancingly mentioned in most books about Chopin, but his own story has been largely ignored, which is surprising because Astolphe de Custine is one of the most fascinating figures in Chopin's orbit and, arguably, in all of nineteenth-century France.

Astolphe's grandfather was a hero of the American Revolutionary War, having fought in a French regiment on behalf of the colonies. Later, under the Reign of Terror, he was one of thousands of aristocrats brought up on charges of sedition by the government's Committee of Public Safety. During his trial Astolphe's mother, the Marquise Delphine de Sabran, left her infant son in Normandy with a nurse and traveled to Paris where she sat loyally—and regally—at her father-in-law's feet in the judiciary hall. To get there she had to first pass through a volatile, bloodthirsty mob that gathered on trial days. Her presence in the courtroom combined striking physical beauty with unyielding personal courage; it aroused such emotions that the ladies in the gallery, known as "furies of the guillotine," were reportedly brought to tears. Having such a woman in his courtroom so enraged the prosecutor that one day, before she departed, he alerted a group of assassins outside. To reach a hackney coach Delphine had to first walk down a long flight of steps outside the tribunal and pass through a dense, angry crowd. As she descended, she caught the eye of a woman

Astolphe later described as "the most hideous fishwife" cradling a baby in her arms. Amid cries of "traitor!" this perfect stranger handed her infant child to Delphine. "Take him," she said, "you can return him to me at the foot of the steps." The gumption of one impoverished woman and a vulnerable child opened a safe passage through the crowd to the coach and driver, and Delphine escaped unharmed.

After the trial, her father-in-law was guillotined. Five months later so was her husband, Astolphe's father, who had served the government as a diplomatic minister under Louis XVI. Delphine herself was imprisoned for six months in one of the many convents that were turned into prisons during this period, and she too was headed for the guillotine but, in the end, was saved by an unlikely hero: one of Robespierre's lackeys who had participated in a search of her apartment for evidence of betrayal against the state. As they searched, Delphine drew caricatures of the invaders, displaying a "courageous gaiety" that prompted one of them to fall in love with her on the spot. It was he, a mason named Jérôme, who saved Delphine from the scaffold—not with a spontaneous act of bravery like the fishwife's, but through a more enduring act of personal courage and ingenuity. There was during this period a "fatal box" of papers inscribed with the names of prisoners that went each morning to the chief prosecutor and from which he selected, starting at the top of the pile, those who would be executed that day. Every night Jérôme snuck into the office and placed Delphine's dossier at the bottom; he did this for six months. When she finally was released from prison, she was in ill health and broke, the government having plundered her husband's considerable estate. Still, she managed to put together enough cash to help Jérôme escape to America and spent the rest of her life rebuilding, for the benefit of Astolphe, the family fortune. Over the years she took many lovers, including François-René de Chateaubriand, the writer, diplomat, and politician who is considered the father of France's Romantic literary movement and later became, to Astolphe, a spiritual mentor. Germaine de Staël, the first female writer in France to achieve literary and commercial success, modeled the heroine of her debut novel, *Delphine*, on this remarkable woman. It was a groundbreaking book that explored the limits of a woman's freedom in post-Revolution aristocracy, and its blatantly feminist outlook caused Napoleon Bonaparte, no admirer of women's rights, to exile Mme de Staël from her homeland.

To such unlucky but extraordinary parents was the Astolphe de Custine born in 1790, the year after the storming of the Bastille. He grew up in a culture of violence and fear, and the stories of his family's misfortunes, told to him over and over again by servants, haunted him throughout his life. "My first sentiment," he later reflected, "was that of a fear of life," an "impression of terror" that had saturated his youth. What makes his story so unusual is the way he continually reacted with cool independence to the social, political, and artistic gyrations of his times. In her fascinating biography Anka Muhlstein observes that "the Revolution had robbed Custine, the aristocrat, of his property, shaken his confidence in the world with which he was familiar and destroyed the society from which he sprang. But it gave him, in exchange, the assurance that he had a right to freedom and the conviction that he was accountable neither to the old order nor to the new." He later declared "I am certainly anything but a revolutionary, still I am revolutionized." As Mulhstein shows, he went on to prove it "by developing an absolute independence of spirit . . . [and] living precisely as he intended." His greatest personal trial occurred in 1824 when he was caught having relations with a soldier. A group of men beat him senseless and left him for dead, yet this violent attack and the scandal that followed served not to oppress Custine but to liberate him. He went on to become an open homosexual who lived with the same man for thirty years, until his own death, in preparation for which he hired a team of lawyers to write an iron-clad will ensuring that Edward, his lover, would receive his estate. He did. And yet Astolphe had also married a woman he greatly admired, had a son with her, and run a modern a household in which Edward cared for his soon-to-be-ailing wife, Léontine, "like a brother." Léontine died at age twenty; their young son, Enguerrand, died three years later, followed shortly thereafter by Delphine. Custine was left alone with Edward, his entire family gone, to reinvent himself.

Like Sand, Custine was improvisatory when it came to relationships. He and his mother shared an unconventional notion of equality, addressing each other, for example, with the informal *tu* instead of the traditional *vous* that was used in aristocratic families. He developed, then lived by, his own philosophy, regarding the ideal state of marriage as two independent halves united in friendship. This is the spirit that informs a letter he wrote to Chopin in 1837, when the composer was waiting in vain for Maria Wodzińska's reply to his marriage proposal. In consolation the Marquis suggested: "If it is love that has failed you, let us see what friendship can do." Throughout his life Astolphe's mother, mentors, and friends came to accept his unorthodox lifestyle, which revolved around a group of friends he dubbed "the regulars," which included multiple lovers and at one point involved a five-year ménage à trois with a Polish count.

Also like Sand, Custine was liberated by becoming a professional writer. They were both born into a time, just following the Revolution, when being an artist was newly regarded as more than just a respectable profession—it was a calling, a kind of social ministry that could educate and improve society. By the time he started writing poetry and novels in the 1820s, Custine wryly observed that "the sound of Paris is the sound of a quill scratching on paper." A true Romantic, Custine was attracted to new genres, and just a decade after the first guide to France was published, he took up travel writing as an art form, experimenting with an epistolary style instead of traditional narrative. This was how he made his name as a writer, and in the process discovered that traveling the world was another form of liberation. "To change one's country is tantamount to changing one's century," he wrote; it was the perfect occupation for "one who cannot conform to the ideas that govern the world." A perennial outsider—"I felt from my infancy that my lot had been cast in a place of exile"— Custine spent much of his adult life wandering the nations of Europe: through Italy, Germany, Switzerland, England, Scotland, and Spain, bearing witness to social and political change everywhere he went. Like the rest of his generation he was gripped by wanderlust, yet unlike his friends and fellow aristocrats who gravitated to Swiss mountains and Italian lakes, he sought out the unexplored parts of these new worlds, seeking his own, unmediated perspective. In traveling to England in the 1820s, for example, Custine was the first to discern, writing nearly twenty years before Dickens, the social consequences of the Industrial Revolution. He visited factories, mills, and mines, and observed the awakening that was occurring "in men of all classes in every country." He correctly predicted the "spirit of hostility" that would soon come to define the relationship between workers and the rich industrialists they served.

This was the spirit in which he approached his most famous and consequential trip. Having lived through a second wave of turmoil in his own country, the July Revolution of 1830 that replaced one monarch with another, and inspired by Tocqueville's recently published *Democracy in America*, which looked at a totally new system of representative government, Custine embarked on a journey to Russia in 1839. He was in search of "new arguments against the despot that reigns at home," and in a series of long, intimately observed letters he wrote the first—and only surviving—contemporary account of life under the Czarist Empire. Custine had wanted "to do something bold and novel." Well aware that reports about Russia predictably skewed in one of two directions, exaggerated praise or hateful calumnies, he states in his preface: "I am not afraid of making shipwreck on the one rock or the other." He set off on the arduous journey by himself, determined to study a nation and a system that might illuminate a better political way forward back home. Indeed he returned to France with a new view of the world, acknowledging that the despotism he witnessed in Russia had "modified [his] monarchical ideas" in favor of representative government. "If ever your sons should be discontented with France," Custine concluded in the last lines of his long travel narrative, "try my recipe; tell them to go to Russia. It is a journey useful to every foreigner: whoever has well examined that country will be content to live anywhere else." Banned in Russia immediately after it was published and again during the Cold War, *La Russie en 1839* remains in print to this day and is acknowledged by some contemporary experts as an uncanny prediction of the upheaval that would destroy the czarist system and lead to the totalitarianism of Stalin's Russia.

What's intriguing about Astolphe de Custine, and why I've lingered on his story, is the way he was so much *of* his times but also, simultaneously, transcended them. His life was colored, from his earliest days, by fear, violence, and political and social persecution, yet again and again he responded to the world's tumult around him by cultivating independence, both in his personal relationships and his work. His life illustrates in almost equal measure the liberations and oppressions of the Romantic era, a time when cross-dressing female writers and aristocratic homosexuals could enjoy freedoms that were unimaginable even a decade or two earlier. It's not surprising that Custine was magnetically attracted to Chopin, that singular artist who went his own way, quitting the public stage at the moment when everything—pianos, orchestras, audiences—were getting bigger and louder, and enabling a new brand of celebrity that everyone else seemed to find irresistible. Custine felt a particular sort of kinship with this Polish exile, maybe because he saw in him a fellow outsider. "One is alone with you in the midst of a crowd," he once confided in a letter. "One may love and understand one's neighbor through Chopin." The intimacy of the music and the shared sense of difference—Chopin as political exile, Custine as perennial outsider—spoke powerfully to him. Custine was fiercely protective of his friend, constantly worrying over Chopin's health and love life, doing everything possible to lure the composer to his estate, where he promised to "save" him from all that threatened and provide a place where he could work in peace. Chopin was the only person who had an open invitation to Saint-Gratien, who could come "whenever he wants and without warning me." It's reasonable to surmise that Custine was infatuated with the composer, but what moved him most of all was what his friend did at the piano. Chopin played not on the instrument, Custine said, "but on the human soul." It was not the music alone that affected him, but the deep "sense of *gratitude*" it engendered in him for the presence of art and beauty in his life. This was a gift Chopin gave to everyone who had the privilege of hearing him play; for Custine it resonated with particular power.

Occasionally—reluctantly, it sometimes seems, just trying to be polite—Chopin accepted the Marquis's overeager solicitations, and it was in Saint-Gratien one October evening in 1838 that he chose to say his farewells at the keyboard before departing for Majorca. The next day Custine sent a colorful letter to his friend Sophie Gay, which captures the essence of everything the Marquis relished in a Chopin salon recital, beginning with the colliding worlds he conjured at the piano. The original source of the letter, a biography published in the 1950s, identifies the first piece as the rousing Polonaise popularly known as "Military" (op. 40, no. 1), which Custine describes as "a joyous riot . . . dazzling with force and verve." Then, in a striking contrast, Chopin played a "Polish prayer," a work scholars suppose was a short piece named after its tempo marking, the slow and stately "Largo in E-flat Major." To hear these works back-to-back is to experience two utterly different emotional soundscapes, one soaring and heroic, the other meditative and sentimental. But they have something powerful in common: Poland. Both works are, by tradition, connected with Chopin's attachment to his homeland and its historic suffering. The Largo is based on a popular church hymn called "God, Save Poland"—whose refrain is "Return our Homeland to us, Lord!"—and the Polonaise has long been regarded as a "coronation" piece, a work scholars think Chopin composed in anticipation of his country's perpetually imminent ("Poland has not yet perished!") rebirth. In fact, this stirring, foot-stamping work became so associated with the Polish spirit of resistance it was broadcast nationally by Polskie Radio every day after the 1939 Nazi invasion of Warsaw. Custine's musical portrait intriguingly suggests that, on the eve of his departure for faraway lands with his new, unorthodox family, Chopin was looking backward, longing for his homeland.

It's the next passage in Custine's report that resonates in the story of Opus 35: the work that followed the "Polish prayer." Now Chopin moved into yet another emotional terrain and played "funeral marches that, despite myself, made me dissolve in tears." Custine exclaims: "It was the cortège that led him to his final abode; and when I thought I perhaps would not see him again after this, my heart bled." This is the most vexing moment in the Opus 35 story, because of course Chopin didn't die for another ten years, at which point his funeral march would, indeed, be played at his own funeral. In his melodramatic account Custine makes the odd prediction that ends up being true, a quirk that has gone unquestioned, even while it has been cited in various biographies and scholarly articles, for decades. The rest of his letter is equally flamboyant, for he goes on to accuse George Sand of being a vampire who has succeeded in sucking Chopin's soul from his body in just the first few months of their romance. "You have no idea what she has found a way to do in one summer," he complains to Sophie Gay. And then, weirdly, he proceeds to write a brief review of Sand's latest novel, *Spiridion*, first calling it "incomprehensible" and then grudgingly admitting she's a powerful talent (even a "genius"), capable of creating as much color on the page as the painter Rubens did on his canvasses. And yet, he concludes at the end of all this, she is "an evil individual." With this letter he was expressing what was on the minds of many of Chopin's friends, who believed from the beginning that Sand was dangerous. Tytus Woyciechowski, one of his closest schoolmates, who had accompanied him on the fateful trip to Vienna just before the November Uprising, wryly observed in hindsight: "I needn't have bothered keeping Frédéric from getting himself killed in the Warsaw uprising since he only wound up falling into the claws of Sand!"

Ultimately, the value of Custine's strange contribution to the Opus 35 story is the testimony he makes to the Romantic spirit. At a time when the most popular works of opera, symphony, theater, and literature were filled with magical prophecies and dark omens, his vivid imagining of the pale, bloodless composer being carried off to his final abode while accompanying himself at the piano was perhaps—at least in the hands of a writer who by all accounts lived in a world of his own making—business as usual. That he ties it all up with a bit of literary criticism only completes the gesture.

Did George Sand ever find out she had been compared to a vampire? The historical record is mute, but the name Astolphe comes up later, and I'm left to suspect that she did.

FIVE

Toujours Travailler *Bach*

It was an unorthodox travel party that boarded the steamship *El Mallorquin* in Barcelona on November 7, 1838, bound for Palma. Generations of Majorcans would remember its members as, to quote English novelist Robert Graves, "a domineering, cigarette-smoking, ill-dressed, irascible woman, living in open sin with a foppish piano-player, six years her junior, and teaching her children to be as bad Catholics as herself." The locals were terrified of consumption and therefore feared Chopin, quite literally, like the plague. They disapproved of fifteen-year-old Maurice's endless drawing (in place of studying), particularly his sketch of a "Monastic Orgy," which he pinned up on a wall; and they regarded his sister Solange (age ten)—a trouser-wearing tomboy like her mother—as rebellious, arrogant, and temperamental. But the intensely conservative and religious Majorcans were most derisive about Sand. News of the scandal over an earlier affair with a French playwright had reached Majorca after being minutely documented in Paris newspapers, and the locals were, it seems, as offended by the extramarital romance as they were by rumors she had "seduced, betrayed, and abandoned" him. Together the couple from France was seen, Graves writes, "not only as moral, but as physical, lepers."

Majorca in the 1830s was no Venice. Devoid of tourists, hard to reach, with a native language few Europeans could speak, it was virtually unknown as a travel destination. Sand's original idea had been to visit Italy, but a Spanish acquaintance recommended Majorca for its climate and exotic setting, and the idea of a faraway island in a foreign country powerfully appealed to her sense of adventure. One travels, she later explained, in "search of mystery and solitude, or to escape from the long shadow which our fellow beings cast over us, sometimes sweet, sometimes painful." She wanted to leave everything behind, from "the tedious duties of etiquette" and the simmering *scandales* over her latest love affairs, to the receipts, newspapers, and endless visitors that kept her from her work. She planned to stay at least a year, perhaps two. She would write; Chopin would compose; Maurice, fresh from his studies in Paris with Eugène Delacroix, would paint; Solange would study the classics. In fact the sojourn lasted just ninety-eight days, and while it wasn't the Romantic fantasy she'd envisioned, it did turn out to be one of the most notorious—and artistically productive—journeys ever undertaken by two artists.

There's a rich trove of primary sources about this trip, beginning with Sand's travel memoir *Winter in Majorca*. Published in 1841, it wasn't translated into English until much later, after Robert Graves discovered the island in the late 1920s during his own escape from a romantic scandal. It was Gertrude Stein who recommended the island. "Try Majorca," she told him. "Paradise—if you can stand it!" With the exception of a ten-year interlude during the Spanish Civil War and World War II, Graves lived there for the rest of his life, and his love of the island, its people, history, and landscape, embellish his translation of Sand's text in masterly footnotes that range from respectful corrections on matters of history, geography, agriculture, wildlife, religion, cartography, and weather to acid asides about her "fancy tales" and memory lapses. The brief but searing *Winter in Majorca* would top anyone's list of the most hostile travel books ever written in any language, but it has never lost its allure and has never gone out of print. Just a few weeks after it was serialized in the French magazine *La Revue des Deux Mondes*, a Majorcan writer with his own literary journal, José Maria Quadrado, published a "Vindication" that ran a Sandian five thousand words and set out to dissipate, point by point, "the black vapors with which so seductive a mouth has begrimed our reputation." This colorful argument between "the Lioness of Berry" and an aspiring young historian in Palma ensured that the sojourn on Majorca would never be forgotten—not by literary scholars, musicologists, or generations of travel writers. But even without the literary pyrotechnics that framed the trip for European readers, the Majorca visit had, by itself, enough elements of a nineteenth-century Gothic drama to make it enduringly appealing: a deserted medieval monastery on a windswept hill with a cemetery just outside its high, stone walls; a small party of foreign travelers rendered homeless by bad weather and illness, who find refuge in its cells; social and political unrest in the wake of a recent civil war; unexpected, relentless cold weather; reports of phantoms and imaginary drownings; a storm-tossed piano en route from Paris. And all this in a place that existed in Sand's imagination as paradise—an "El Dorado of Art"—but turned, quite rapidly, into "a living hell."

There was a single sentence in Sand's book that convinced me to make Majorca the first stop on my travels, and to go without delay. Writing about the landscape, she describes a combination of "severity and grace, melancholy and magnificence." If you were looking for a description in ten words or less of Chopin's work in general, and

Opus 35 in particular, this would do the trick. I was also mightily impressed by the fact that, in her Mount Everest of published writings, the only time George Sand ever seems to find herself at a loss for words is on this island. "As for me," she says at one point (a clause that could, one knows, begin virtually every paragraph in her oeuvre), "I have never so keenly felt the futility of words as in those hours of meditation" in the old monastery where they spent the bulk of their stay. "Religious impulses came to me frequently," she wrote, "but the only form of words found to express my enthusiasm was: 'Thanks be to God for the gift of sight!'" This woman of so many words—during the course of her long life Sand wrote some seventy novels, fifty volumes of other works, including novellas, short stories, plays, poetry, and memoirs, and twenty-six volumes of correspondence—now comes face-to-face with their inadequacy. Nevertheless she soldiers on, grasping for words to portray a place that, before her eyes, was "everywhere shifting its character with an abruptness I have never seen paralleled elsewhere." Her descriptions of the landscape both anticipate and provide a context for the exquisite juxtaposition of tenderness and violence, hope and despair, darkness and light that characterize many of the pieces Chopin worked on, revised, composed, corrected, or completed in Majorca, which include the collection of Preludes, op. 28; a gorgeous pair of Nocturnes, op. 37; the two Polonaises of op. 40; a Scherzo in C-sharp minor (op. 39); the Ballade op. 38, no. 2 in F major; and the Mazurka op. 41, no. 1 in E minor. With the major key, Poland-inspired *Trio* already drafted, and the heavy lament of the funeral march that had so recently haunted Astolphe de Custine now clearly in his mind, one can imagine no better place than this conflict-saturated landscape, with its exotic beauty and inherent danger, for stitching them together into the sonata movement we know today.

The Majorca trip began auspiciously. Chopin found himself in a magical place of rolling hills and myriad trees—cactus, orange, lemon, fig, pomegranate, olive, aloe, cedar—in fresh air that was "heavenly," under a warm sun that shone all day. "The sky is like turquoise, the sea like lapis lazuli, the mountains like emerald and the air as in Heaven," he wrote to his friend Julian Fontana. "Ah, life; I'm alive again, I am close to the most beautiful things on earth." But the weather soon turned. Within two weeks, Sand wrote, "all the flowers fell off the trees" and Chopin was spitting up blood. Writing again to Fontana and describing his meetings with doctors on the island, Chopin remarked: "The first said I was going to die, the second that I was dying, the third that I am already dead." Then the rains began, and over the course of the coming weeks the weather turned colder and darker. At first the party stayed in Palma, the capital city, but the streets were full of noise: blacksmiths hammering anvils, coopers banging mallets, sailmakers singing all day as they sewed. The party rented a house on a hill in the suburb of Establiments, which in later years acquired the ominous nickname Son Vent, or "house of wind." Intended for summer use, the home had no windowpanes or fireplace, only a complicated charcoal brazier no one could figure out how to use. "The damp settled like a cloak of ice over our shoulders," Sand wrote. Four weeks later the owner of the house evicted them, fearing it would be contaminated by Chopin's now well-publicized illness. This is when they moved to an abandoned monastery in the mountainous region of Valldemossa, about twenty kilometers northwest of Palma. The medieval charterhouse, or *cartuja*, was originally a palace for the short-lived dynasty of Majorca's kings, and in the early fourteenth century it became home to the contemplative Carthusian order. In 1836 Spain's president, Juan Álvarez Mendizábal, began confiscating ecclesiastical properties as part of a program to pay off official debt and enrich and reinforce his army amid an ongoing civil war. Any monastery or convent with fewer than twelve inhabitants was closed, and some were subsequently demolished. The Valldemossa *cartuja* was by now partly in ruins but had thirteen monks, so the building was saved, though its residents were banished. The state took over the complex and decided to rent the cells to anyone who wished to live there. Loyalty to the old monks and superstition about the government inspired few locals, so when the Sand-Chopin party arrived on December 15, the abandoned monastery had just three other occupants: a lone remaining monk, who was also a pharmacist; an eccentric housekeeper; and a sacristan with a scandalous backstory.

Valldemossa is, for people who love Chopin, a place of pilgrimage and reflection. The cell, or *celda*, where he spent the winter of 1838–39 is today a museum that has been owned and managed by a single family since 1932. The walls are adorned with reproductions of paintings (including a large one of the steamship *El Mallorquin*, which brought the first foreign tourists to the island), sketches (many by Maurice Sand), and photographs. Display cases include letters, receipts, memorabilia, and books. Also displayed are facsimiles of the manuscript pages for each of Chopin's preludes, offering visitors a chance to witness in situ the progress of his pen across the page, the often agonizing, "heartbreaking labor" Sand described in her memoir. In a glass case are copies of Chopin's death mask made by Solange's future husband, Auguste Clésinger, and a plaster cast of his exceedingly delicate left hand. Nearby is a wooden tuning key that belongs to the small upright *pianino* sitting near a window, cottage piano no. 6668, which Chopin had ordered himself, for the sum of 1,200 francs, from the Pleyel House in Paris. Before departing for Spain, he made arrangements for the instrument to be shipped by boat to Majorca, anticipating it would be available upon his arrival. But on November 15, a week into the trip, the piano had still not arrived. He asked Fontana to investigate, and to Camille Pleyel lamented: "I dream of music but I can't write any because there are no pianos to be had here—in that respect it is a barbarous country." Over time his desperation mounted. In a stream of letters from their various lodgings both he and Sand recount their distress over the wayward instrument. On December 14 they learned it had been loaded onto a merchant vessel in Marseilles, and were told to expect further delays. "Meanwhile," Chopin wrote, "my manuscripts sleep while I get no sleep at all. I can only cough and, covered with poultices, await the spring." Two weeks later the piano had reached Majorca but was sitting, useless, in the customs house in Palma, where bureaucrats were insisting on "a huge sum for the damned thing." Finally a prominent banker named Canut, whose family had helped Sand with the financial and logistical details of her journey to Majorca, joined with the French consul to intervene with local authorities. The Pleyel was released from customs and dispatched on the last leg of its perilous journey up the mountain to the monastery.

In *Winter* Sand executes some of her most vitriolic sentences in descriptions of Majorcan roads. Thanks to her we can imagine the piano's progress, perched in a strange local hackney carriage called a *birlocho*, its driver sitting on a plank with his legs outstretched and straddling a mule or donkey. In this setup, Sand observed, the operator experienced every movement of the creature as well as "every bump of his barrow: thus he drives a coach and rides a horse at the same time." Through it all the driver sang, interrupting himself only when the animal came to the brink of a precipice. Thus "dreadfully jolted," he would pause to utter a few "terrifying oaths," then continue again on his way. This, Sand writes, "is how one goes driving [in Majorca]: ravines, torrents, swamps, quickset hedges, ditches, all bar the path in vain; one does not stop for such trifles because, of course, they are all part of the road. At the outset, you may believe that this steeplechase is a wager in bad taste, and ask your guide what fly has bitten him. 'We are on the road,' he answers. 'But that river?' 'It is part of the road.' 'And that deep hole?' 'Part of the road.' 'And that thicket?' 'All parts of the road.' 'Fine!'"

The long-suffering Pleyel arrived in the monastery on or around the 10th of January, 1839. Over the course of the next thirty days, until he became too ill to remain on the island, Chopin completed his Preludes on it, then dedicated the entire opus to Camille Pleyel. He would have taken the piano home with him to Paris, but for the fact that the same customs officials who had held it hostage at the port now wanted to exact a steep fee in export taxes to allow it *out* of the country. It would be many months before the matter of the Pleyel was finally settled, but in the end it was purchased by the Canut family of Palma. No one else on Majorca would purchase a piece of furniture owned by a consumptive, no matter that it was Frédéric Chopin's hand-picked piano from the prestigious Pleyel House in Paris. Hélène Choussat, wife of Bazile Canut and an acquaintance of Sand's, reimbursed Pleyel the same 1,200 francs Chopin had promised, and sold off her own instrument (a French Pape, which Choussat believed to be "the best of Palma") to cover the cost. This is how Pleyel no. 6668, the oldest of the surviving pianos played by Chopin, and the only upright, came to be sitting on a little raised platform, covered with a magenta carpet, in *Celda* No. 4, where it continues to inspire awe, humility, and wonder in the thousands of visitors who make their way to Valldemossa each year.

I spent a week in Majorca in 2017 and was lucky to catch a full moon while I was there. Rising above the craggy, juniper-dotted peaks known in Catalan as *puigs*, it was so bright and big I could read by the light it cast, and in its magnificent presence was reminded that Robert Graves was obsessed with the moon on this island. In his book *Majorca Observed* he wrote: "I am prepared to swear that nowhere in Europe is moonlight so strong as it is" in the little mountain village where he lived for almost fifty years. On the first morning of my visit I stepped out on the little portico near my hotel room and was greeted by a chorus of bells coming from the terraced hills across the valley. With the zoom lens on my camera I found the source: wandering goats, each of whom wore a collar with a bell tuned to its own particular pitch. Chopin and Sand heard this same animal music, only it came from the necks of mules and asses. "It is well known that each country has a different tune," Sand observed in *Winter*, and the soundscape here is unforgettable. Each evening during my visit I ate dinner in an outdoor café on a quiet, cobblestoned plaza just outside the monastery wall, above what was once a cemetery. This is where Sand went late at night to wander and meditate in the darkness, sometimes in the company of her children, and they would have heard many of the same night creatures, especially owls, that I did. Come morning, the place is filled with birdsong, especially in late fall and early winter, when a great influx of starlings, thrushes, finches, waders, and wildfowl migrates from farther north in Europe. My morning walk from the hotel into the village would also have been familiar to a traveling party in the nineteenth century: up a narrow road encased on either side by ancient stone walls that appears in a lithograph made by artist Jean-Joseph Bonaventure Laurens in 1839. If you use Google Street View to locate this road, the Carrer del Camí Antic, as it makes its approach into Valldemossa, and compare the view to Laurens's drawing, you'll observe that not much has changed; the monastery's handsome Gothic bell tower still dominates the landscape, and even the presence of cedar and palm trees abides. The only sound missing today is the clacking of castanets, a ubiquitous background noise that delighted some visitors but drove Sand crazy. "This piercing clatter of wood [is] fit to rupture the eardrum," she complained.

The director of the *Celda de Frédéric Chopin y George Sand*, Gabriel Quetglas, is a descendant of Hélène Choussat and the family Canut, which had purchased Chopin's piano. He is also a publisher, and to celebrate the bicentennial of her birth brought out Mme Choussat's memoir, titled *Souvenirs*, which she wrote in 1875. The book contains valuable—and colorful—descriptions of the party that so scandalized the Majorcans, from Solange's boyish velvet blouse to the silver dagger in Sand's hair and the large, shiny cross she always wore around her neck. It was Mme Choussat whom Sand trusted with the installments of her latest novel, the Gothic ghost story *Spiridion*; she mailed the manuscripts, written in small notebooks, to Paris so they could be serialized in the magazine *Revue des deux mondes*. Gabriel's grandfather bought the *celda* in 1928, and ever since it has been managed by his family. Now in his early fifties, Gabriel is a bighearted, generous man who cleared an entire week of his schedule to show me around the island. We walked through the streets of old Palma, past the home of one of Chopin's doctors, which sits just a few blocks away from the old Jewish quarter. He took me to the preserved ruin of the Arab Baths, Majorca's only remaining Muslim monument, believed to have been constructed in the tenth century. Another afternoon we climbed a steep, rocky path through the mountains of Valldemossa to the ancient Hermitage de la Trinitat, established in 1648 as a refuge for hermits seeking a secluded and contemplative religious life. Chopin, Sand, Solange, and Maurice made this same journey through "somber green forests" and up a stony footpath that "cut our feet in pieces." It was at the beginning of the Majorca sojourn, when Chopin still had enough strength for rough walking, and this was one of the only long hikes he took on the island. Following in their footsteps, Gabriel and I finally emerged from the densely wooded path to the edge of a high cliff that looks out onto the Balearic Sea, and when I took in the view I instantly understood what Sand had meant when she described her own first impression here: "In Majorca alone I finally saw the sea of my dreams." The color blue that hangs over this landscape, from the sky above to the sea below, is so preposterous I thought the digital card in my camera had been manipulated by gremlins or otherwise corrupted before I downloaded photographs in New York. But I had simply beheld the very same sight that greeted Sand and Chopin, virtually unchanged and still bewitching: a lapis lazuli carpet of water stretching for as far as the eye can see, "limpid and blue as the sky, gently undulating like a sapphire plain," a sea that is simply unlike any other in the world.

Sand, who reveled in the landscape of Majorca but seemed to hate *all* the humans she encountered, was typically acid about the five or six hermits who still lived in the ancient cells that were built into the cliff at La Trinitat, calling them "the most stupid men in the world," apparently because they wore no religious apparel, had dirty beards, and didn't know the word *in any language* for ice. But they had seen ships from the French navy in 1830, passing below on the way to conquer Algeria. Cut off from the news of the world, they had no idea what the outcome was. *Did they succeed?* one hermit asked, and when Sand confirmed that they had, "his eyes opened wide" and he exclaimed that France was a great nation indeed. George Sand was the first woman who had ever visited the Hermitage, but it's sadly impossible to know what these men made of her because they left no record of the encounter. When I visited in late fall 2017, the same season that Chopin made the trek, the once thriving religious community had dwindled to just a single hermit, a man in his seventies whom we met in the gift shop. My high school Spanish was good enough to make out bits of his conversation with Gabriel about a recent book they had both read, and the fellow smiled warmly as he wrapped in brown paper a small religious icon and a history of the Hermitage I purchased. A few months later Gabriel emailed me to say that, while walking in the woods in search of moss with which to decorate his nativity scene, the man we had met, who was known as Benet, had disappeared. Teams from emergency services searched the rugged, inhospitable landscape for six days until finally, the day before Christmas, they found his body. He was the last hermit in Valldemossa, part of an eight-hundred-year tradition that included an unlikely visit by a frail pianist from Poland via France and his robust, iconoclastic female companion.

Back in the monastery Gabriel took me through each room in the *Celda*, completing a detailed picture of Chopin's stay here with stories, documents, and images. One morning we were speaking near the Pleyel, and I became, apparently, rather animated. A middle-aged woman took me by the elbow and said in a stern, librarian's voice: "Please be quiet. This is a sacred place." It was then that Gabriel told me about a recent visit by Nobuyuki Tsujii, a young Japanese pianist whose story perfectly illustrates the truth of that woman's statement.

In 2010, then in his late twenties, Tsujii set out to immerse himself in Chopin's Majorcan world. Nobu, as he's known to his legion of fans, wanted to experience for himself the sounds, smells, and sensations that Chopin knew in this place where he composed some of his most complex, beautiful works. A documentary crew followed him, first into the courtyard of Son Vent, where the wind was indeed so blustery you can hear air currents eddying around a videographer's microphone, buffering the sound of Nobu's voice as he stands with his mother, Itsuko, near a pomegranate tree. Nobu didn't make the typical tourist's journey; he brought a piano with him, and once it had been installed in the room where Chopin wrote—and shivered— he played a prelude from the op. 28 series. He then paused and, in tribute to a composer best known in the salons of Paris as a brilliant improviser, played around with his own melodies on the keyboard, improvising a piece he would later publish as "House of Wind."

The documentary continues with Nobu's arrival shortly thereafter at the *Celda*. Gabriel removes the velvet rope around the Pleyel and invites him to touch and even play Chopin's piano, which he does gently and with great tenderness. The instrument is badly out of tune, but the notes still have a beautiful, otherworldly tone, like church bells ringing in the distance. It's impossible to say what this *pianino* sounded like when Chopin himself played it in this room, but we do have an expert, contemporary description that captures what he loved about the Pleyel brand. It comes from Claude Montal's 1836 *The Art of Tuning Your Own Piano*, one of the first how-to books for instrument owners. Montal, sightless since childhood, taught himself how to tune pianos and became a prominent technician, lecturer, and manufacturer. He was also, incidentally, the man who kickstarted the tradition of piano tuning as a profession for blind people. Two years before Chopin purchased the storm-tossed no. 6668, Montal described with some amazement Pleyel's achievement. By modifying the English mechanism, reinventing the shape and materials used in the hammers, and innovating the use of veneer on his soundboards, Pleyel had created an instrument with a range never heard or even imagined by artists and piano makers before. Now the performer "could bring out in *piano* playing a soft and velvety tone, gaining in brightness and volume with stronger pressure on the keyboard." The upper register could become "bright and silvery, the middle one accentuated and penetrating, and the lower clear and vigorous." This piano was capable of creating an altogether new universe of sound.

When Nobu has finished sounding a few notes on the old Pleyel, Itsuko takes his arm and walks him to the wall nearby where a facsimile of Chopin's original manuscript for Prelude no. 15, popularly known as "Raindrop," is hanging in a frame. She takes his hand—Nobu is blind, so he can't see the music—and draws it over the score measure by measure. "How is his handwriting?" Nobu asks. "It is detailed and delicate," Itsuko replies. "There's parts where he rewrote it and covered all his mistakes in black as if to say, 'I don't need this part.'" Her son, an accomplished pianist who played Beethoven's monumental op. 106 Sonata, the *Hammerklavier*, in the Van Cliburn International Piano Competition, has never seen a musical score in his life; all the music he plays he learns by ear, listening to recordings that have been split into small sections by assistants, practicing over and over again until "the piece is perfectly in my body."

When he was a toddler, Nobu formed a special attachment to Chopin, and his young ear developed an uncanny sensitivity to his music. Itsuko wore out a CD of Chopin's works performed by Russian pianist (and 1985 Chopin Competition winner) Stanislav Bunin, music to which eight-month-old Nobu enthusiastically waved his little arms and legs while lying in his crib. When it eventually began to skip, she bought another Bunin recording, this one made when the pianist was quite a bit older. Performing artists often radically change their interpretation of beloved works as they mature with their instrument; Glenn Gould's recording of Bach's *Goldberg Variations* in 1955 and then, in a drastically slower version, in 1981, is no doubt the most storied example. Late in his career Bunin reflected on his early years as a pianist, describing himself as "a bird freely flying." As he grew older, though, he acknowledged that his playing had become more cautious. Bunin's later recording of the Chopin works was so different that Nobu failed to react at all. Finally Itsuko replaced the original CD, and the child's joy returned.

Even before he could walk, Tsujii's senses were keenly focused in the act and practice of listening, which is what made it possible for him to learn, as a young man, large, complex works by Bach, Mozart, and Debussy, as well as war horses of Classical and Romantic repertoire by Rachmaninoff, Liszt, and Beethoven. From his earliest days his sense of the world was connected to a keyboard, beginning with a little toy piano on which he repeated, to his mother's astonishment, melodies of songs she would sing in another room. Growing up, Itsuko read stories aloud to him and Nobu would improvise an accompaniment on the piano, creating, as young Chopin had done with his pals in Warsaw, a musical narrative to enrich her literary one. Early on Itsuko determined that her role would be to help Nobu experience the world: to translate colors, sensations, smells, and features of the landscape into a language he could access and share. She soon realized that Nobu wasn't missing out on the sights and features of the natural world she so dearly loved; he was simply seeing things in his own way. What was always clear to her—and what comes across in the several documentaries that have been made about his travels—is the joy, wonder, and awe he experiences in each new place he visits. Wherever he goes, a companion describes the scene before them, whether it's a work of art hanging in a museum, the ocean, a lobster, a lemon tree, a white swan in a lake, a New York Yankees game, or the exploding lights in a fireworks display. To one interviewer he explained that while he may not be able to see the faces of his parents, the stars in the sky, or the ocean, "still, I can see everything in my heart." When he plays with an orchestra, Nobu listens under the music for changes in the breathing of the conductor, using those respirations as his cue to rejoin the other players. His naturalness and utter lack of theatricality at the keyboard have a powerful effect on audiences. Richard Dyer, chief music critic for the *Boston Globe* and a juror at the Van Cliburn Competition, wrote of Nobu's performance, for which he shared the gold medal in 2009: "Very seldom do I close my notebook and just give myself over to it, and he made that necessary." Van Cliburn himself told a reporter: "He was absolutely miraculous. His performance had the power of a healing service. It was truly divine."

Having closed the museum for the day, Gabriel has given Nobu permission to spend time alone in the cell—"to face Chopin," as the pianist says he came here to do. After everyone has left and night has fallen, the camera records Nobu getting up from a cot that has been placed in the tiny room where the composer slept. In a letter to his friend Fontana, Chopin described this chamber as bearing "the shape of a tall coffin, with an enormous dusty vaulting." In this room, he wrote, there is a silence so heavy that "you could scream—[and] there would still be silence. Indeed, I write to you from a strange place." Slowly, Nobu feels his way through the darkened room to the Pleyel, where he plays the opening bars of the "Raindrop" Prelude, a work that, like the funeral march from Opus 35, is divided in three sections that portray a soul-stirring contrast between major and minor; "the squall and the lullaby," as one writer put it. Then he stands at the window and whispers into the night air. He begins to weep. "I am here, Chopin. I've come to the monastery. Yes, here, inside." It's a poignant scene in part because of the heavy silence, which is broken only by the bell-like, out-of-tune sounds of the Pleyel and Nobu's sobs. He pauses and speaks again, this time to himself, meditating on the meaning of his visit. "I thought about different things about myself, things I cannot express in words," he whispers. He feels Chopin's presence in the room, even hears his voice speaking to him, sharing the story of how, when he was ill in this place and fighting his disease, he composed music and this gave him hope. "He tells me to keep composing," Nobu says, "to keep having experiences like this one, to be with different people in many environments. To *hear* different things wherever I go." He bows three times to Chopin's Pleyel, and the movie fades out. The next, and final, scene takes place the following day. Nobu is in the adjacent room, sitting before a Steinway grand piano that has been brought here from Palma. Behind him hangs a reproduction of Eugène Delacroix's famous portrait of Chopin. Nobu now plays the entire "Raindrop" Prelude, the clarion richness of the Steinway's sound echoing through the stone walls of the monastery, bringing its modern voice to notes that may have been written down in this very room 170 years ago.

To bring a Steinway concert grand up a mountain to a monastery is, these days, both easy and commonplace. There have been Chopin festivals in Valldemossa since the 1930s, featuring renowned artists, from Alfred Cortot to Garrick Ohlsson. But the sight of this modern piano in Chopin's tiny room is both jarring and wondrous, as is its sound. Throughout *Celda* No. 4 Gabriel has installed speakers, so visitors hear a constant, soft soundtrack of Chopin's music as they move through the three rooms. Hearing the work played live, though, has a special resonance in this "sacred place."

Like all the Preludes—pieces that, by tradition, served as a kind of musical throat-clearing for a pianist before she commenced an announced program—the fifteenth is brief, lasting no more than five minutes. Robert Schumann described the twenty-four pieces that make up op. 28 as "beginnings of studies or, if you like ruins, a mad jumble of eagles' plumes." Each has an idea that Chopin plays with, and in the "Raindrop"—I'll get to the somewhat annoying name in a moment—he juxtaposes a beautiful major-key melody against an ominous minor-key rumble of chords, inserting violence, gloom, and agitation into a little narrative that circles back, in the end, to a peaceful reverie. It's almost the mirror image of the *marche funèbre*, which he also worked on here: optimism at the edges, despair in the middle. The piece also has that quality of emotional precision that's so powerful in Chopin's music. You can see this for yourself, in Chopin's own hand, in the last few bars of the manuscript page that the museum has framed and hung on the wall. Amid the familiar little forest of cross-hatchings and erasures, Chopin writes, in measure 79, *smorzando*: dying away. A measure later he writes *slentando*: slow down, but gradually. And then, in the final bar, *ritenuto*: slow down immediately. Precise, disciplined, exact—and achingly beautiful. All this emotion has been so carefully planned out, yet it sounds like an improvisation.

What Nobu's performance of no. 15 brought to mind when I watched the documentary was a conversation that took place long ago in this room that's often associated with the "Raindrop" Prelude. It's a story Sand recounts in her memoir which illuminates at least one aspect of her complex relationship with Chopin and it begins with (what else?) a disastrous road trip. She and Maurice are returning home from a shopping expedition in Palma one evening when torrents of rain render the road virtually unpassable. When they finally arrive in the monastery, shoeless and well past nightfall, she hears Chopin at the piano playing "a marvelous prelude." Entering the room, she sees he is weeping. Sand recalls: "On seeing us come in, he rose, uttered a loud cry, then said with a wild expression and in a strange tone of voice, 'Ah, just as I imagined, you have died!'" After finally settling down, he describes a dream in which he saw himself drowned in a lake, "heavy, icy drops falling rhythmically on his chest." Awaking alone in the cell, he calmed himself at the piano, playing the piece that greeted Sand and Maurice as they entered. And so, in this mood, drenched from her travels and facing the haggard composer by candlelight, she makes an observation. *Listen*, she says, "to the drops of water falling rhythmically on the roof." She suggests he has experienced a kind of "imitative harmony" created by the strange duet of rain and piano. Chopin angrily, vehemently rejects Sand's interpretation, protesting her "naïveté" in believing his notes were aural imitations. As is clear in the manuscript, they are anything but; they are hard-won, carefully planned, finely crafted elements in a work of art. Chopin hated programmatic music that dictated an emotional trajectory for the listener. (This didn't stop his publishers, who went ahead and added their own titles to his works without his permission. *The Zephyrs*, *Murmurs of the Seine*, *Adieu Warsaw*, *The Infernal Banquet* are just a few.) Sand, to her credit, immediately stood down. "He was right," she says. "His genius, full of the mysterious harmonies of nature, translated them into sublime equivalents in his music, and not by a servile imitation of sounds." But she couldn't quite leave it there, and in the next sentence reaffirms that the composition he was playing that evening was "certainly full of raindrops resonating on the tiles of the monastery." Actually, it certainly *wasn't*. The weather in Majorca was sunny and dry the week I was there, but I asked Gabriel if he ever heard raindrops inside the *celda*, and he was equally adamant. No, he said, you can only hear rain falling in the garden outside the window, never from inside the cell itself. The sound of the famous raindrops came from Sand's rich imagination.

For me, the value of this oft-told story about the beloved fifteenth Prelude is that it permits us to eavesdrop on a conversation between two remarkable artists. They were as different as night and day, a study in contrasts; they came to this faraway place for the same purpose—to work and to heal—and the landscape, which loomed large for each of them, was both enabler and inhibiter. The variety of the beauty was so inspiring that everyday concerns, like, for example, the expense of a trouser button, were for Chopin "just a grain of sand, when one has this sky, this poetry that everything breathes here, this coloring of the most exquisite places, colour not yet faded by men's eyes." He truly inhabited the monastery and its landscape, the brightness of its flora and fauna and the dark, mysterious charms of its architecture. The monastery, by contrast, truly inhabited Sand. She eagerly embraced the Gothic elements of her setting: the cemetery through which she wandered late at night and the "weird spectres" she encountered in and around the abandoned monastery; the impassable roads and bone-chilling cold; the strange native people with their ancient, inscrutable ways; the phantom raindrops on the roof. "Undoubtedly," she admits in *Winter*, "the romantic elements so evident before my eyes inspired in me certain reflections on romanticism in general." She couldn't, it seems, resist imposing all this on her partner's work, hearing in his preludes the "visions of dead monks and echoes of the funeral chants which besieged him." But it seems to me quite possible that these were tropes that besieged *her* on Majorca, not him. And that, perhaps, the caricature of this trip that has come down to us through the ages is in large part another example—and a magnificent one at that—of Romantic storytelling and embellishment; in the spirit, one might say, of the Marquis de Custine, whose imagination also ran wild when he heard Chopin play the piano. Of course none of this matters because in the end we have the work they produced there: music and literature of singular vision and inventiveness that continue to engage people of all ages in unexpected ways.

* * *

For Chopin there was yet another artist in the room besides his lover: Johann Sebastian Bach. He brought with him to Majorca just a single book, the score of *The Well-Tempered Clavier*, Bach's collection of preludes and fugues composed between 1722 and 1742. In later years this work would come to be regarded as a kind of sacred text, music's "Old Testament," as the late nineteenth-century conductor Hans von Bülow put it, but "The 48" had fallen out of favor since Bach completed it and was not, when Chopin carried it from Paris to Majorca, part of the standard repertoire. I asked Yuan Sheng, who recorded all of Chopin's Preludes on the Frederick's 1845 Pleyel and is also a Bach expert, why he thought Chopin chose to bring that particular music with him. "Well, for Chopin Bach is God, and that book is like a Bible," he replied without hesitating. "It has everything, all the resources he would need: harmonic, contrapuntal, melodic, and structural. It has many different styles: French, Italian, German; sacred, secular, you name it, it's all there. But most of all," he added, "it's a real piano book, a book for *piano writing*." Sheng smiled and added: "Think about it: Chopin is traveling to an island, and he can't take much luggage. This one book will sustain him for however long—maybe even the rest of his life, because he was ill when they departed for Majorca and had no way of knowing how much time he had left." *The Well-Tempered Clavier*, Sheng was suggesting, is the perfect "desert island book" for a pianist/composer.

In a letter to Fontana Chopin sets the scene: "Between the cliffs and the sea a huge deserted Carthusian monastery . . . you may imagine me with my hair unkempt, without white gloves and pale as ever. . . . In front of the window are orange-trees, palms, cypresses; opposite the window is my camp-bed under a Moorish filigree rose-window. Close to the bed is an old square grubby box which I can scarcely use for writing on, with a leaden candlestick (a great luxury here) and a little candle. Bach, my scrawls . . ."

Chopin venerated Bach and particularly "The 48"; he could play them entirely from memory, and once, after performing many of them for a pupil, remarked: "It's not something you forget." By the time he arrived in Majorca, he was deep into a project to pay homage to the composer he admired most, his Preludes, op. 28: twenty-four exceedingly short pieces that form a complete cycle, inspired by *The Well-Tempered Clavier*. The two collections are different in format: Chopin made his way through the twenty-four keys that make up the harmonic universe of Western music, known as the Circle of Fifths, by taking large leaps, whereas Bach proceeded in small, incremental steps. Bach followed each prelude with a fugue; Chopin didn't. But they both used this highly structured format—a cycling through of all the available tonalities a keyboard instrument could muster—as a way of exploring the musical landscape of their instrument, which for Bach was an organ, harpsichord, or clavichord and for Chopin was a more modern pianoforte. These were, in effect, experiments in *color*, a word that turns up in writing about music as frequently as it does in photography or painting, although musicologists use a more fancy word: *chromatic*. (One of the delights of twenty-first-century life is computer technology that enabled an American composer, Stephen Malinowski, to build a "Music Animation Machine" that uses multi-colored animations to display a musical score online, thereby opening an entirely new vista for listening to—and visualizing—the harmonic landscape of classical works.) There were other composers before Bach who cycled through the twenty-four tonalities, but it's Bach who is universally considered to be the one who changed music forever with *The Well-Tempered Clavier*, a collection he created mainly as a teaching tool, not as a formal opus for publication. Nevertheless, it had a revolutionary effect, bestowing on later generations a range of color that was virtually limitless. The keyboard composer, like an Impressionist painter, now had a new palette with dozens of colors to work with, instead of just a few. For Chopin, the Preludes, op. 28 was an opportunity to riff on his idol Bach's game-changing work by creating a complete cycle that embraces the widest possible range of moods in the briefest of pieces. Some are as short as thirty seconds; others last for six minutes or longer. The preludes are emotional vignettes, tiny works that contain a universe of emotion. Citing their "sheer brevity" and compositional genius, scholar Jim Samson calls the Preludes "among Chopin's most radical conceptions." The external patterns are, he says, straightforward enough, "but lengthy tomes could be written about the subtle and varied means" by which Chopin executes his art. In fact there is indeed an ever-growing mountain of scholarship about these works, as research accrues and new tools of analysis become available. One constant, though, is the spirit of innovation in which Chopin approached this project, building on Bach's teaching exercises, pushing at the edges of the keyboard's tonal horizon, and creating a group of pieces that could be used either as a spark for improvisation in a salon performance or as a more formal part of a concert program. The landscape of Majorca, for all its asperities and conflicts, together with the companionship of Bach and Sand, his two artistic muses, allowed Chopin to create what Samson calls "a remarkably innovatory conception quite unlike anything he had written before."

This is the other conversation that took place in the old Carthusian monastery: a musical one between Johann Sebastian Bach and Frédéric Chopin. Out of sentimentality, I had carried my copy of *The Well-Tempered Clavier* on the plane from New York to Majorca. It was in my knapsack, nestled alongside Chopin's Preludes, when I visited the *Celda*, but I needn't have bothered; the museum has its own copy in one of the glass cases: a water-stained, slightly rumpled mid-nineteenth-century French edition engraved with the name of a woman from Marseilles who might have—but scholars haven't been able to confirm—been a student of Chopin's. Behind it, hanging on the wall near the Pleyel, are the framed facsimiles of Chopin's handwritten manuscript for each prelude. Standing there in that old, stone sanctuary, you can't miss the connection between the Bach "48" and Chopin's op 28. And there's another intriguing detail, beyond the music, that links these two composers: each worked on his project to explore the universe of tonal narrative under challenging conditions and without an adequate instrument. Bach worked on Book I of *The Well-Tempered Clavier* in a Weimar prison, where he spent four miserable weeks after being arrested for what seems to have been a trifling affair—perhaps, biographer Christophe Wolff conjectures, having lost his temper with a duke over an employment contract after he had accepted a new position as music director at another court in a different town. In any case, it appears likely he composed some portion of "The 48" during his incarceration in this cold, unhappy place, without any keyboard instrument and during a period that marked "the absolute low point" of his professional life. Chopin was by no means miserable in Majorca; in fact, he would look back on this sojourn as a time of such happiness that could be "sufficient for a lifetime . . . suffused with such female tenderness and musical inspiration." In his letters home he calls Sand "my angel," and describes how she tirelessly nursed him and watched over her children's education, despite being continually harassed by "those Spaniards." He was awed by Sand's dedication to her work, how she would sit in bed for an entire day and do nothing but write. He was at times gravely ill, peripatetic; the weather was awful, the people were strange, the food nearly inedible.

But his biggest challenge was the lack of a proper piano. For some number of weeks, before the Pleyel finally arrived, he worked on a rented keyboard, but it was mediocre at best, an instrument George Sand described as "a poor Majorcan piano" that was probably—but no one knows for sure—a square instrument with a tiny sound. And yet he was able—as was Bach in Weimar—to produce some of the most innovative music of his career in this place, even without benefit of the instrument for which it was composed.

The museum in the *Celda* still resonates with all those musical and artistic conversations begun in the late 1830s between Chopin and Sand and continued, over time, by pilgrims like Nobuyuki Tsujii and countless others: musicians, writers, soldiers on leave, former American presidents, piano technicians, astronauts, philosophers, painters, and tourists from every country in the world—people who feel some connection to Chopin and come to this mingled landscape to gain access to what was among the most important creative episodes of his life.

SIX

Pulling out the Pickaxe

The dream of an artist's paradise on Majorca ended suddenly and badly. Chopin's illness grew acutely worse, and it became clear he wouldn't survive the damp, unexpected coldness of the Balearic winter. The party made a final, wretched road trip, with Chopin riding down the mountain in a two-wheeled cart pulled by a donkey because no one would provide a proper carriage to a man coughing up blood. The sea voyage was even worse: *El Mallorquin*, whose main purpose was to transport pigs from island to mainland, was now filled with a hundred hogs. Not only did they suffuse the ship with an awful stench, they cried pitifully as they were beaten by crew members under orders to keep them awake and standing on all four legs, lest they succumb to seasickness or other ills that would erode the owner's profit margin once they reached shore. Sand, an ardent animal lover, reserves some of her choicest vitriol for this final insult, describing the pigs as "gentlemen" and their masters as ignorant, greedy, dishonest brutes. In the end she all but consigns the captain to the jaws of her porcine shipmates. When the coastline finally heaved into view, she flagged down a French steamship moored in Barcelona's harbor and arranged transport for the whole party. As the weary travelers set foot on the handsome brig they cried out as one: *Vive la France!*

Sand, like Chopin, had embarked on the Majorca journey in a spirit of innovation. On the heels of *Seven Strings of the Lyre*, her retelling of the Faust legend from a woman's point of view, she now commenced work on another "novel in dialogue," using this hybrid form to delve into a subject that had long preoccupied her: gender identity in the modern world. The social politics that frame *Gabriel*, which she dashed off in just a few weeks after the party reached Marseilles, are rooted in the ancient feudal law of primogeniture, the institution that prevented women from owning property. The story is set in seventeenth-century Italy, where Jules, prince of Bramante, confronts a thorny problem of inheritance after his son and rightful heir dies along with his wife, leaving behind only a baby daughter. Rather than face the end of the familial line, Jules instructs his granddaughter's nanny and tutor to raise the child as a boy; thus is Gabriel born. "He" learns science, horsemanship, fencing, Latin and Greek, but most of all is steeped in a belief system that favors male power and superiority. In art classes Gabriel is shown heroic paintings of the abduction of the Sabine women and the sale of female slaves in the Orient. Literature consisted of stories about "repudiated queens, spurned or betrayed mistresses, Hindu widows scarified on their husband's funeral pyres." Early in the drama Gabriel's tutor proudly assures Jules that the job has been well done: he has imbued the youth "with the grandeur of man's role" in nature and society, and the concomitant "lowliness" of woman's. In every area of study the female is a creature depicted as "trying to free herself from her fetters only to undergo worse punishment." She is capable of success "only through lies, betrayal, and futile, cowardly crimes." When Gabriel learns the truth of "his" real gender at age seventeen, this is what rankles most. "An admirable ruse, indeed!" s/he replies. "To inspire in me the horror of women, only to throw it in my face and say, But this is what you are."

The first thing Gabriel does with this new self-knowledge is set out in search of Jules's rightful heir, a cousin named Astolphe (I mentioned earlier that the name would return . . .), so everything can be put to rights. The two share an instant, magnetic bond reinforced by riding, drinking, and getting into bar fights. Astolphe is initially discomfited by the strange attraction he feels toward Gabriel, but pays it little mind. Soon it's Carnival time and he convinces his cousin to dress up as a woman. The scene of Gabriel's transformation into *Gabrielle* reads like Sand's recollection of her own early days in Paris when flimsy, ladies' shoes caused her to sway on the cobblestones "like a boat on ice." Now she places her hero/ine before a mirror in a fashionable dress and gives voice to her own feelings about the claustrophobia of women's clothing. "How I suffer in the garment!" Gabriel complains. "Everything binds and stifles me . . . I feel so awkward. Can a woman not be pleasing without these simpering affectations?" Later, after the Carnival celebrations when Gabrielle is changing back into pantaloons and boots, Astolphe catches a glimpse of "him" and learns the truth. Sand being a true Romantic can't help but complicate—and corrupt—her plot with love, and so the cousins fall for each other. Gabriel becomes, in Astolphe's world, his "wife" Gabrielle, but they now share a dangerous secret that could be the ruin of them both. Gabriel must continue to stay in the frame as Jules's heir until "he" has succeeded in winning a special dispensation from the Pope to legally redirect the inheritance to Astolphe. But as the months drag on, Astolphe is consumed by jealousy, worrying that other men will experience the same intuitive attraction he felt and challenge his claim. More than anything, he fears the loss of control. Thus Astolphe follows the standard playbook on which Gabriel had been reared: he strives to conquer and dominate his "woman." Astolphe repays his cousin's honor by locking Gabrielle in a room, then visiting with a prostitute. In the final scene, in a tragic case of mistaken identity, Gabriel—once again in doublet and boots and returning from the Pope with dispensation in hand—is stabbed by a man whose life he had saved during the bar fight earlier in the story. Gabriel/Gabrielle is, in the end, betrayed by everyone, and dies alone.

What's striking about Sand's story is how modern it remains, almost two centuries after it was written. Plenty of other writers before her had grappled with the question of gender identity, from Shakespeare's *Twelfth Night* to Mozart's *Marriage of Figaro*, but it was usually to advance some lewd or comedic plot. Sand by contrast uses the question, the *problem*, of gender as a device to test the boundaries of personal freedom and explore the possibilities of friendship. She gives an answer of sorts early on when Astolphe asks his new friend Gabriel what he likes to do. "Greek, rhetoric, geometry, what?" Gabriel replies, now sounding a lot like George Sand herself: "None of that. I like my horse, the open air, music, poetry, solitude, and above all my freedom." These were the things George Sand prized, and in *Gabriel* she makes a heartfelt argument for their preservation in a woman's married life. Toward the end, in a scene with Gabriel's tutor, the enraged and jealous Astolphe threatens to reveal his cousin's secret so he can take command of the relationship. In a poignant reply the tutor begs Astolphe to "respect and revere" the two sides of his lover. "Let her live and die in disguise, happy and free by your side. As the heir to a great fortune, *he* will share it with you equally. As a chaste and loyal lover, *she* will be bound from within by your love for each other, though she be free."

Look, Sand seems to be saying, there's an ideal friendship that can exist between the sexes: it's possible, it's right here, all it requires is mutual respect for an individual's freedom, and a promise by each party in the relationship to enable the other. This is what the drama is really all about: how one can be truly independent and yet still love purely, deeply, and completely, another person. This work was a continuation of the theme Sand had struck in her long, "frightful letter" to Albert Grzymała—to whom she dedicated *Gabriel*—about partnering with Chopin. As it turned out, the ideal friendship ended up being a fantasy that Sand never managed to realize in her own life, but modern audiences continue to engage with her over this question of personal, and gender, identity in affairs of the heart. In 2017 a progressive theater group in Providence, Rhode Island, staged *Gabriel* with an all-female cast that included several actors who identify as gender neutral. In a "talk-back" with the audience afterward the director, Rebecca Maxfield, describes the work as "a parable for what women could be if they were raised the way men are." Sand's heroine doesn't just wear a man's clothing; she grows up in the zeitgeist of the male world, with all its assumptions, privileges, and prejudices. Into this reality Sand introduces the more subtle ambiguities of gender. The trans actor who played Gabriel/Gabrielle in the Head Trick Theater production points out that their character never picks a sex from the two options that are available in society. They (the modern pronoun used in this YouTube conversation) want access to *both*: to a fuller range of human experience and the privilege of improvising a *new* gender role in their relationship with both society and the beloved. The overarching theme of the piece is that the sex you're born with shouldn't dictate the role you play in life. In the end, Maxfield observes, Gabriel/Gabrielle has to die "because Sand can't see a way forward." But her work is still being used to explore the boundaries of a very different, twenty-first-century world, one that inherited many of the same problems and questions George Sand was doing battle with back in the 1830s——most especially in her relationship with Chopin.

The publication of *Gabriel*—the first installment appeared in *La revue des deux mondes* on July 1, 1839—serves as a cadence of sorts to the "thousand troubles" of Majorca, preparing a way forward for this odd couple. Generations of scholars and biographers have observed that upon their return to Nohant in early June Sand imposed a condition of chastity on the still-young relationship. It's unclear how Chopin felt about the new arrangement, but his health—he was ninety-seven pounds when they arrived home in early June—was so fragile he could engage in very little exertion without unleashing fits of coughing. Curtis Cate, Sand's biographer, surmises that she "found the physical act of lovemaking with Chopin considerably less exalting than his music." In any case it was clearly a momentous transition for Sand, because she took a knife into her bedroom and carved a date in the embrasure of her window: June 19, which scholars assume marked the first anniversary of the day they consummated their affair. Now, a year and many kilometers later, the date took on a fresh symbolic meaning, establishing the moment in time when Sand decided to craft a new, and certainly more modern, relationship with her fellow artist. After all those months of wrestling on the page with the *notion* of ideal friendship—first to Grzymała, then in *Gabriel*—Sand now put it to the test, casting herself in a multifaceted role: mother, caretaker, nurse, artistic enabler. She would write about this improvised state of relations often in her letters and memoir, sometimes in a loving way and at other times with bitterness and resentment. Her goal had been, perhaps, the same as that of her hero Gabriel, who announces to Astolphe early in the story: "I want to heal you, strengthen your better nature, raise you up, and lift you to the height of my ideas." Astolphe, not comprehending, jokes that his cousin is simply dreaming of "an ideal love the way I dreamed of an ideal woman." In other words, such *spiritual* equality between the sexes is a phantom; it doesn't exist. It's

Gabrielle's reply that echoes poignantly down through the ages: "You should have warned me from the first day you loved me that the time would come when I would have to change who I am to keep your love."

The traveling party finally arrived in Nohant on June 1, 1839, and it was here that Chopin would complete what he soon announced to his publisher as "a Grand Sonata." Still recovering from illness and travel, he was grateful for the birdsong and fresh air, though he confided to friends that he felt himself in "a strange outer space" and was not "made for the country." Throughout that summer Sand worried he was bored; to a friend she confided: "Chopin is still up and down, never exactly good or bad. He is gay as soon as he feels a little strength, then, when he is melancholy, he falls back onto his piano and composes beautiful pages." But to a friend Chopin wrote: "We are as happy as children." He was particularly delighted with the Pleyel he had ordered from Paris, which had arrived without incident, and began feverishly working to complete the works he had undertaken in Majorca and get them ready for his publisher. As they settled into their new routine in July 1839, Sand told a friend "he is enchanting us from morning until night." He may have missed the bustle of Paris, but in this country paradise he was cared for with love and devotion, starting each day with his favorite beverage, a mug of hot chocolate, and continuing through the day with music, society, and nature. That summer they established a daily pattern based on a combination of independence and proximity that would abide through the next eight years of their lives together. They had rooms of their own, which accommodated their different creative rhythms: Chopin composed at his piano during the daylight hours; Sand wrote through the night at her little desk in the room next door and arose in late morning or early afternoon. (She described her writing ritual as "pull[ing] out the pickax.") In the afternoons they took long walks or carriage rides through the Black Valley, visited ruins, read out loud to each other. In the evening they joined their house guests—Eugène Delacroix, Franz Liszt, his lover Marie d'Agoult, opera star Pauline Viardot—and the children, Maurice and Solange, at the dinner table, then gathered afterward in the salon to discuss their current work, the gossip of Paris, and the politics of the day. Then came the entertainment. This began simply, with games of charades, but eventually evolved into more elaborate skits and improvised dramas based on intrigue and adventure. Chopin assumed his old role at the keyboard, unspooling musical narratives that plunged his listeners into a deep state of meditation or sadness. Sand describes what would happen next: "Suddenly, as if to cancel this effect and the memory of its pain, he would turn and steal a look in the mirror, arrange his hair and his tie, and all at once mimic a phlegmatic Englishman, an impertinent oldster, a sentimental English lady, or a mercenary Jew," all the while accompanying himself on the piano, adjusting the rhythms and melodies to the evolving story. After the evening's entertainment the household went to sleep—everyone except Sand, who pulled out her pickax and worked until daybreak.

Nohant is the estate that George Sand—improbably—won in her own fight against France's ancient law of inheritance, prevailing in the courts to overturn her husband's legal right to a property left to her by her grandmother. It originally consisted of almost six hundred acres of woodland and farms, and was so large it wrapped itself around the hamlet of Nohant-Vic, including a twelfth-century church that still stands just outside the walls of the manor house. It was purchased during the height of the Reign of Terror in 1793 by Mme Marie-Aurore de Sax Dupin de Franceuil, Sand's aristocratic maternal grandmother, and is where this formidable woman took refuge after being jailed for hiding her wealth and valuables—a criminal offense under the Revolution's rules—in one of the many convents that had been converted into prisons by Robespierre. (In an eerie coincidence of place, Mme Dupin de Francueil was imprisoned in the same convent where Sand herself would later be educated as a young girl.) These were forbidding places: massive, cold, and dark, their windows barred and covered with a heavy fabric that screened out sunlight and any trace of the outside world. After being released from prison, Mme Dupin repaired to the sun-drenched, open farmland in this valley around the Indre River, using what was left of her fortune to purchase the estate. Soon she began laying out formal gardens amid acres of hemp fields surrounded by tall elm and walnut trees. Little Aurore, the future George Sand, was reared here by Mme Dupin de Francueil after her father died at the age of thirty in a riding accident. The imperious old lady, herself descended from a Polish king, then banished Aurore's mother, a commoner whose father eked out a living selling bullfinches and canaries on the banks of the Seine. She did this by buying off her daughter-in-law, paying her a hefty fee to remain in Paris and stay out of their lives. Aurore pleaded not to be "given away for money"; her mother, in assenting, caused her daughter's first heartbreak. Looking back on this event in her journal when she was twenty-six and in a direct address to Sophie-Victoire Delaborde, Sand wrote: "You betrayed me, you lied to me, mother. . . . You broke my heart. You opened a wound which will bleed all my life. You embittered my character and warped my judgment. You introduced into my soul a dryness, a bitterness I find in everything." For the wounded, parentless young girl the landscape around Nohant became a refuge, what she later described as "my frame, the garment of my own existence . . . the sanctuary of my first, my long, and my perpetual daydreams." Within three days of arriving home from the Spanish adventure, she confided to a friend: "I now fancy myself living in an Eden."

My first introduction to Nohant occurred in an unexpected way: via the brush of Eugène Delacroix. I was at an exhibit about public parks and private gardens at the Metropolitan Museum in New York when I entered a large gallery and was ineluctably drawn to one painting that stood out from all the others. It was displayed at the end of a long wall filled with glorious Impressionist masters: works by Bonnard, Monet, Vuillard, Cézanne, Corot, Morisot, each depicting some colorful, irenic scene: a lush garden with brilliant flowers; two young lovers at the seaside; a man reading a newspaper on a shady park bench; a handsome bridge arcing over a lily pond; a woman strolling under a blue sky. Then, at the very end, was *George Sand's Garden at Nohant*, a dark oil painting by Delacroix that more closely resembles a dense, overgrown forest than either a public park or a private garden. The work pulls you into its mystery, as though you've stumbled into a secret chamber in a woodland. At the center is a stone table; perhaps someone's work space? But where have they gone? At the left is a path that curves and wends its way to some unknown place, past a stand of hollyhocks whose bright pink blooms stand out against the green leaves and brown tree trunks and provide the only pinpoints of color in an otherwise crepuscular scene.

Delacroix was a frequent visitor to Nohant and he, like Sand and Chopin, was pushing at the boundaries of his craft, seeking to break from Neoclassical conventions and set himself apart. In 2018 the Met launched a huge exhibition devoted to his work; not tied to any anniversary, it was, the curator Asher Miller stated in the press preview,

"a once in a lifetime show to introduce the Delacroix you don't know."
The Eugène Delacroix visitors met in New York was an inventive artist preoccupied with working against the Academy, a painter who set
in motion a cascade of radical innovations that, Miller said, "resulted
in what we think of today as modern." "That bastard," Picasso said
of his predecessor; "he's really good." In gallery after gallery the Met
presented examples of how Delacroix forged his own path. In history
paintings, for example, he might place the hero at the very edge of the
canvas, as he did in *The Battle of Nancy and the Death of Charles the
Bold*. Here the composition prioritizes the spear of some anonymous
knight over the imminent death of the work's purported subject, the
"bold" Duke who is now pushed toward the edge of the frame and,
therefore, *out* of history. Delacroix frequently scandalized the establishment by eschewing the noble past altogether, painting people and
subjects of his own time. His breakout work depicted a gruesome
1822 military attack by Ottoman forces on inhabitants of a Greek
island. "Monsieur Delacroix rushes headlong without rules, without
moderation," a contemporary reviewer complained. Critics also seized
on his chromatic overexuberance: "Everything here is harsh, coarse,
rocky, rough, scruffy . . . he piles on the color . . . [and] paints with
a housepainter's brush." In portraits Delacroix was more interested
in the iridescence and texture of a subject's flesh than some classical
Michelangelesque ideal of human anatomy. He had studied and copied all the Old Masters at the Louvre, but invariably returned to his
studio to create unorthodox compositions, like the intimate *Women of
Algiers in Their Apartment*, an Oriental scene in which we, the viewer,
find ourselves peering into a room where colorfully dressed women
in pantaloons are at liberty to relax, smoke, and make conversation.

In flower paintings Delacroix abandoned the convention of fussy
vases and fantastic draperies; instead, as he wrote in his *Journal*, he

wanted to conjure "pieces of nature, such as they present themselves to us in gardens." Delacroix was fascinated with botany and frequently imported exotic species of flowers from China, Mexico, and Africa so he could deepen his understanding and accuracy in depicting the widest possible variety of flowers. His goal with his landscapes was to reinvent a genre by creating such stunning realism that his brush would lure viewers into a true contemplation of nature rather than just an appreciation of his decorative skills and mastery of classical settings and conventions. He cherished veracity but also wanted to create an emotional connection for his viewer. So when Delacroix painted George Sand's garden at Nohant, he captured not just a place but an *idea*: a tamed wilderness where the imagination could flourish, where artists work (the table) and wander (the path) in a state of solitude and natural beauty. It was a new concept of what a "garden" could mean, a little man-made world filled with "pieces of nature" that weren't necessarily orderly, as the French garden typically was, but were perfectly real. He was, like Chopin, an artist who had a deep sense of tradition but was, at the same time, indifferent to stereotyped models. This is what made his seductive, inscrutable painting of the garden at Nohant such a useful portal into the world where Chopin stitched together the four parts of what would later come to be known as his *sonata funèbre*. Made by a young painter who was upending classical traditions of form and content, and depicting the mysterious garden of a genre-busting, socially unconventional writer, it conjures the perfect setting for a work of music that so confounded early critics it would take almost a hundred years before its inventiveness could be fully appreciated.

I visited Nohant on a cold, sunny day in late November and discovered a landscape with its own rich story to tell. Walking through the grounds, I was struck by the juxtaposition of clean, straight lines, the classical *allées* of a nineteenth-century French garden, neatly aligned against the wild abandon of the forest that abuts it. If George Sand was truly at home anywhere, it was in this collision of worlds that she nurtured in her own backyard. Fascinated, like Delacroix, by botany, she planted a multitude of species in her flower garden: Bengal roses, violets, petunias, red azaleas, asters, goldenrod, anemones, verbena, hollyhocks, snapdragons. She created a kitchen garden big enough to sustain an entire household throughout the year, built a greenhouse for her exotic plants, and cultivated an orderly fruit orchard, its trees organized on a grid and yielding a diverse crop of apples, peaches, pears, quince, and apricots. But she also treasured the moody, dappled forest Delacroix captured in *George Sand's Garden at Nohant*, with its labyrinthine byways and mossy alleys protected by a heavy canopy of hornbeam, ash, maple, and lilac trees. These lead eventually to a small island lined with stones and surrounded by a moat. One feels the Romantic spirit in this place of mystery, contrast, and juxtaposition: Mme Dupin de Franceuil's formal, geometric garden beds that lead, as naturally as you like, to an unscripted wandering in the wood, a place for lonely daydreamers and those looking quietly inward. "Symmetry and strict order overwhelm me with gloom," Sand wrote in 1841. She found respite and joy in the riotous mix of colors she created in open, sunny spaces, which then prepared the way to an enchanted, lonely forest nearby.

But the real meaning of the place, as Edith Wharton remarked thirty years after Sand's death, in 1907, lurks "behind the row of tall windows opening on the tangled mossy garden." It was here, on the second floor, in a large, sun-soaked room, that Chopin completed his sonata. To get there a visitor passes through an elegant vestibule with black-and-white stone floor tiles and up a long, winding staircase. It's when you reach the top that you begin to understand how seriously Sand took her role as enabler to her fellow artist, because she took it down to the very bones of her house. As soon as you reach the second floor, you arrive at the door of Chopin's room, which sits in the center of a long hallway. Actually it's two large French doors that are covered in a complex weave of embroidered fabric. The house was noisy, filled with young children, kitchen staff, servants, and always a parade of guests. To help shield her sensitive friend and create an environment where he could work, Sand concocted an acoustic scheme to buffer the sound in his room: a thick web of horsehair, covered with a layer of heavy fabric on the outside. Then she installed a second set of doors to act as a further cushion against household noise. The entire corridor is laid with terra-cotta tiles; they are beautiful, but also a recipe for refracted sound, so Sand removed the section between Chopin's double doors and installed wood flooring instead. The result was a room that, for all intents and purposes, was soundproofed.

As I walked through the old château, Sylvie Jehl, my guide, pointed out aspects of the house that were modern for their time: a central heating system Sand installed; a toilet, which was one of the first of its kind; and the acoustic innovations she brought to Chopin's room. The phrase Sylvie kept coming back to, as we walked from the capacious kitchen through the many rooms of the house, was (roughly translated from French): "always maintain the best conditions to create." It's the informal motto of Nohant, a home Sand designed around the idea of unhampered creativity and good work. Most of the people in Sand's world were, in one way or another, creatives, and she increasingly saw her role as their enabler. Sand had also engineered a productive environment for her son, Maurice, by creating a sun-soaked atelier in the attic where he could pursue, in different areas of the large space, his many interests: drawing, painting, geology, natural sciences, theater. When you walk into the room today, it feels like Maurice just popped out for a walk: an unfinished painting is on the easel and nearby is a pot of paint. One glass case is filled with dried botanical samples, another with butterflies.

Maurice's teacher Delacroix himself spent weeks at a time in this house, in the most spacious room on the ground floor, which opened out on the garden. (It was originally Mme Dupin de Franceuil's boudoir.) Nohant provides a "nonchalant harmony that soothes and delights me," he told a friend in an 1842 letter. ". . . The hosts could not be kinder or more considerate. When you're not all together for luncheon or dinner, playing billiards or going for walks, you're in your own room reading, or guzzling on your sofa. From time to time you hear through the window which opens on the gardens wafts of Chopin's music, as he works in his own room; this blends with the song of nightingales and the scent of roses." It was far from what he recalled as the "feverishness" of Paris, a place where one could do "a little brain work" in order to, later on, "appreciate the delight of doing nothing." When he was not resting or working, Delacroix was able to engage in another of his great passions: the craft and artistry of music. He reveled in "endless tête-à-têtes with Chopin" during which they discussed the mechanics of painting and music: the science of reflections, the meaning of harmony and counterpoint, how the fugue corresponds to "pure logic," the chemistry of color, the genius of Mozart. Chopin was, for Delacroix, "the truest artist I have ever met."

It was in this environment, stimulating yet serene, that Chopin completed work on his sonata, an august Classical genre he approached in a spirit of renovation. Although he was still thinking about Bach when he arrived in Nohant—in his spare time he made corrections to the Paris edition of *The Well-Tempered Clavier*—Chopin's model for Opus 35 seems to have been a work by Beethoven: the op. 26 Piano

Sonata in A-flat major. This was one of his favorite teaching pieces and reveals a relatively young Beethoven—at thirty, he was around the same age as Chopin when he arrived in Nohant—playing around with traditional sonata form. In fact, op. 26 is the first of Beethoven's thirty-two sonatas to completely *abandon* what was by then ingrained in the classical world as "sonata form," a precise architecture of musical narrative based on the presentation, embellishment, and restatement of a theme: *exposition*, *development*, and *recapitulation*, each of which is expected to take place in a certain order and style. With this, his twelfth piano sonata, Beethoven chose to write something entirely new: "a sonata without sonata form." Among the rules he broke was the one governing tempo and the order of movements: instead of putting his slow movement in second place, as was common practice, he put it in third. Then he composed for that slow movement a funeral march "on the death of a hero." It's a stately and triumphant tribute that has a grand, militaristic quality throughout. Trills on the keyboard evoke drumrolls; upper register chords sound like trumpets; and the slowly rising and falling crescendos and decrescendos give the march a sense of dignity and importance. No one knows what hero Beethoven had in mind; maybe it was a general in Napoleon's army or a Homeric figure like Hector, Odysseus, or Achilles. This seems more likely because Beethoven was widely read in Greek and Roman literature and had a deep sense of the archetype of the brave, noble, classical hero. Beethoven himself clearly heard in this work something grander than the piano could, by itself, convey, because he later expanded it into an orchestral piece for winds and brass, making it the only movement from any of his thirty-two sonatas that he reimagined for orchestra. It was played at his own funeral (in an arrangement for men's chorus and solo piano) in 1827. It was also the only work of Beethoven's that Chopin was known to have played in public.

The funeral march was, by the time Beethoven began working on his in 1801, a well-established genre. Its most iconic quality—which Beethoven invokes in the opening measures—is what musicologists call "a grief motif" and Louis Armstrong summed up as the "rum tum tum": that universally recognizable collection of tones that everyone knows from Chopin's march: *dum dum da dum*. In musical language it's written *quarter note / dotted eighth + sixteenth note / half note*. It's as common in the genre of the funeral march as iambic pentameter is in the plays and sonnets of Shakespeare, and it goes back to the earliest surviving example: "The Queens Funerall March Sounded Before her Chariot," written by Henry Purcell for the funeral of Queen Mary in March 1695. This is a brief—just fifteen measures—work in C minor composed for muffled drums and slide trumpets. Its considerable emotional power comes not from any melody but from a very simple, pared-down rhythmic pattern: two values, long and short, repeated again and again, first in a whisper, finally in a howl. *Long, short-short, long.* Or: *dum dum da dum.* What Purcell did was stake out the territory for musical grief, which derives first from rhythm, second from melody. This of course makes sense when a work is played while on the march, because it's written for the feet first. You can find recordings of Purcell's haunting, quite beautiful piece online, and it, like Chopin's, has had a long life in popular culture. Many know it as the theme music from the film *A Clockwork Orange*, where it appeared in a weird, disquieting version for Moog synthesizer made by Wendy Carlos. (Carlos is best known for her album *Switched-On Bach*, made in 1968 when she was known as Walter Carlos.)

The turning point with the funeral march came a hundred years after Purcell, with the "*Marche Lugubre*" of François-Joseph Gossec, a Frenchman who composed his work as a tribute to soldiers killed during an army rebellion in 1790. It also bears the rhythmic signature of the "grief motif," though it's inverted (his begins *short-short, long, long*). Music theorist Raymond Monelle describes Gossec's lugubrious march as "almost bereft of melody." Instead, it gains its power from percussion: the startling interruption of silence by the crashing sound of a metal gong known as a tam-tam. A contemporary witness described how "the lacerating harmonies, broken up by silences and marked by veiled beats . . . spread a religious terror in the soul." Another wrote that "the notes, detached from one another, crushed the heart, dragged out the guts." Monelle explains that "such naked sensationalism was new to music," and it set the standard for funeral works, deploying powerful explosions of bass drums juxtaposed against softer, timpani rolls, eventually enhanced by a full orchestra with wind and percussion instruments that could evoke, in the dress of "a gloomy tone poem [the] grandeur and terror of death." Born in rhythm, the funeral march soon evolved into complex harmonic works, such as Beethoven's exceedingly beautiful, graciously elegant *Marcia Funebre Sulla Morte d'un Eroe* from the op. 26 Piano Sonata. By that point the "grief motif" had become a fixed part of the musical language of mourning. Scouring the literature, I found a dozen or more funeral marches that open with some variation on the rhythmic pattern that goes back to Purcell: Mozart's *Kleiner Trauermarsch* ("Little Funeral March") in C Minor, K. 453a; Cherubini's *Hymne Funèbre Sur la mort du Général Hoche*; and the slow movement in Dussek's *Grande Sonata* in B Flat, op. 74, just to name a few.

Chopin, it turns out, had used the genre early in his career when, at the age of sixteen, he sought to pay tribute to a personal hero of the Polish Enlightenment, Stanisław Staszic. A naturalist, geologist, and poet, Staszic was an ardent supporter of the French Revolution and a follower of Jean-Jacques Rousseau. One way he expressed his Enlightenment ideals was by dividing his considerable estate among local peasants and creating for them a cooperative community that included a school, a bank, and a hospital. He exhorted his fellow Poles to put their education and energy—"your work, your wit, your initiative, your ability"—toward improving the Fatherland, not fighting its occupiers. It's almost a direct echo of the teaching philosophy of Johann Heinrich Pestalozzi, who so influenced Chopin's most cherished teacher, Józef Elsner: *Head, hands, heart.* Poland's overlords reviled Staszic; Prince Constantine, brother of the Russian czar against whom the cadets of the military academy had revolted in the 1830 November Uprising, amused himself by ripping out pages of the Polish philosopher's treatise *The Human Tribe*—a massive work written in blank verse—and burning them in his fireplace. But Staszic's optimism and faith in his country remained undimmed. "Even a great nation may fall," he said in a speech; "only a mean-spirited one can be destroyed."

Chopin revered this Polish patriot, and kept as a relic a piece of the pall that covered Staszic's coffin, which passed by him during the funeral procession. He opens his musical tribute with the standard rhetoric of the funeral march, the stately "rum tum tum," and then, having set the pace in a traditional walking beat, spins out a minor key melody that is plaintive, almost tender, even as it reaches down to the lowest notes of his keyboard, to convey the depth of loss. And then Chopin proceeds to make a stark departure from tradition, laying down a precedent he would return to many years later in Nohant: he follows the funeral dirge with a sweet interlude, a major-key meditation to contrast with the minor-key lament. This is a lovely, slightly meandering tune in A-flat major that effortlessly, and without even a tiny pause, elides into a new statement of the funeral march that set the stage for it. The dirge, now back in C minor, runs its course, and the piece comes to an end. Here it is in an early incarnation: the squall and the lullaby, a mingled chorus that speaks for the departed, first in sadness, then in hope. The momentous, and I think it's fair to say unprecedented, departure Chopin made from Beethoven—and all previous models—was to arrest his funeral march in the middle and speak, suddenly, in a new voice, changing the narrative through a modulation of harmonics and, in the process, challenging the way a listener has been trained to think about, and hear, a funeral march. This *marche funèbre*, published posthumously as op. 72, no. 2, is a prequel of sorts to Chopin's Opus 35 march. That he used his un-orthodox formula again some fifteen years later makes one wonder if the influential figures of his early life, like his teacher, Elsner, who passed down the Enlightenment ideals for which Stanisław Staszic stood—were on his mind in Nohant as he stitched together the four parts of his new sonata, creating in the process a funeral march that was like no other.

And then he did something truly astonishing.

It was George Sand's custom to spend the warm months in Nohant and the winters in Paris, and as the summer was winding down Chopin turned his attention from composing and began a series of letters to his friend and factotum Julian Fontana about lodgings in the city. It's here that he reveals his fastidious, dandy-ish side, directing Fontana about the style of wallpaper he would find acceptable (maybe "pearl-grey" or something varnished and shiny with a green stripe, but in any case "not commonplace vulgar and petty-bourgeois"); the need for a proper waistcoat ("combining great elegance with simplicity"); a hat of this year's fashion; and close-fitting trousers of a particular dark grey color (but *without* stripes). He also gave instructions about Sand's needs, specifying a large kitchen, light-filled study, parquet floors, and separate rooms for the children, also insisting it be "quiet, silent, with no blacksmiths in the neighborhood, no ladies of the streets, etc., etc." The noises of Majorca and Nohant were still, clearly, echoing in his mind, and just as Sand had taken care of his needs in the country, he was now dutifully attending to hers in the city. The partnership was thriving and deepening, and the letters of each reveal a desire to continue the arrangement of proximity with independence. The only nonnegotiable detail for both artists—each of whom was painfully sensitive to the cold—was that their bedrooms have a southern exposure.

On the 10th of October Chopin returned to Paris carrying with him, among a half dozen other works, the completed sonata. He spent the winter of 1840 wrangling with his publishers and then, about six months later, made a radical and still little-known decision about the work: a tiny edit that undercuts the entire idea of the sonata and would be willfully ignored by generations of publishers and printers, right up to (and indeed well beyond) the copy I purchased from Patelson's Music House in New York in 1998: he deleted the word "funeral" from his "funeral march."

Chopin's usual practice was to arrange the simultaneous release of his sheet music in France, Germany, and England, and the process was complex, involving negotiations over the size of the advance (haggling he detested) and the securing of copyright. The timing of the international "publication date" was made all the more challenging by Chopin's constant revisions and changes. The French impression of the score, published by the firm of Troupenas, went through four revisions, or "states," between May 1840 and sometime in 1841. It was somewhere between the second and third versions—the exact timing is unknown, but is assumed to have been after July 5—that Chopin ran his pen through the word *funèbre*, leaving just the single word *marche* at the top of the third movement. This left Jeffrey Kallberg, an

American scholar who wrote the most detailed account of the publication of Opus 35, to wonder: "Is the most famous funeral march in the world not really a funeral march at all?"

Chopin left behind no record of his reason for deleting the word, but there's an intriguing clue that suggests he was now rethinking the idea of what a "hero"—a figure worthy of a funeral march tribute—might be, and it has roots in the time and place where my story began: the July 1830 Revolution in France that overthrew the Bourbon monarchy and installed the "citizen king," Louis Philippe. This was the political movement that inspired young Polish cadets at the Warsaw officers' school to launch their November Uprising, which caused such turmoil that Chopin was unable to return to his homeland after his musical excursion in Europe. In 1840, for the tenth anniversary of this important political event, the French government commissioned the country's most famous living composer, Hector Berlioz, to write an orchestral piece for the ceremonial unveiling of a monumental Corinthian column in the center of the Place de la Bastille. Berlioz's *Grande symphonie funèbre et triomphale* debuted on July 28, 1840, not in a concert hall but in the streets of Paris, played by a gigantic marching orchestra that accompanied a procession containing the remains of "heroes" who had died during the three days of the July Revolution. Their bodies had been exhumed from a mass grave at Montmartre Cemetery, placed in coffins in an enormous "funeral car," and transported to the Place de la Bastille by twenty-four black horses and a battalion of National Guard, government ministers, and detachments from the cavalry, artillery, and infantry. Upon reaching their destination, the remains were re-interred in a columbarium below the newly christened July Column. The streets along the parade route, which began at the Louvre Palace with a salute by the king himself, were lined with Parisians, and Berlioz himself marched at the head of his musical corps, conducting his new, triumphant funeral symphony. Onlookers missed most of the music, hearing just snatches of the work as the procession passed, but the spectacle was unforgettable: some two hundred musicians playing dozens of different wind and percussion instruments, including some that were extremely loud and others that were extremely odd, such as the Turkish crescent, a percussion stick in the form of an ornamental standard with bells and jingles attached. Berlioz was known to be adventurous when it came to instruments, not only for the way he used traditional ones in novel ways (he created new roles for the harp, English horn, and trombone in his orchestra), but also for using brand-new ones that few had ever heard before, like the newly invented saxophone. So while they may have missed the melodic lines and some of the finer points of his symphonic orchestration, the crowds along the parade route heard what Berlioz designed for them: the grand, sonic boom of all those trombones, bassoons, clarinets, piccolos, flutes, oboes, cornets, trumpets, ophicleides, tam-tams, and bass drums. This was a new kind of spectacle in the streets of Paris, and it was such a public relations success Berlioz was invited to re-perform the symphony twice the following month.

Chopin was (briefly) a close friend of Berlioz, but he hated his music. We know this from several sources, including Delacroix, who wrote that he detested "music that is nothing without the assistance of trombones fighting against flutes and oboes"—exactly what Berlioz had conjured in his funeral symphony. Sand's daughter, Solange, described Chopin running away with his hands over his ears in the presence of such music. In a letter to a favorite pupil, Adolf Gutman, Chopin elaborated: "This is the way Berlioz composes: he sputters the ink over the pages of ruled paper, and the result is as chance wills it." That was what Chopin heard in the volcanic, "triumphant" funeral march for dead heroes that became all the rage in Paris during the summer when he was putting the final touches on his own march. The two works have something in common: each has roots in revolution, Berlioz's in the July Monarchy of France, Chopin's in the November Uprising in Poland. But how different were their evocations: one a "triumphal," public hand-wringing, the other an intimate conversation between friends that leaves them gossiping together in the end. Berlioz's multi-voice, flamboyant tribute to the revolutionary spirit was exactly the kind of programmatic music Chopin loathed. Berlioz may have been considered the quintessential French composer, but to Chopin he was an ink-splatterer. So it seems likely that when Chopin became aware of Berlioz's musical monolith and the extravagant public presentation of the *Symphonie funèbre et triomphale* he thought: *No, let them guess.* He deleted *funèbre*, left it at *marche*, and sent the revision off to the printer.

SEVEN

Death Comes to the Funeral March

Between the publication of Opus 35 in 1840 and his death nine years later, Chopin published dozens of works across a wide variety of genres, including those he had been composing in since his youth—mazurkas, polonaises, waltzes, ballades, scherzos, and nocturnes—and those that were new to him: a peerlessly beautiful Barcarolle (op. 60), the song a gondolier sings to passengers while gliding through a Venetian canal; the Berceuse op. 57, a lullaby into which Chopin infused echoes of a Polish song his mother sang to him as a child; and the poetic, impassioned Polonaise-Fantaisie op. 61, a work that combines so many different styles even Chopin himself didn't know quite what to call it. (Thousands of New Yorkers remember this dramatic work as the piece Vladimir Horowitz was playing at Carnegie Hall in November 1965 when a citywide blackout plunged the hall into darkness—and Horowitz continued without missing a note.) He wrote a third sonata for piano (published in 1845) and one for piano and cello, which would be his penultimate composition. His last was a Mazurka in F minor (op. posth. 68, no. 4), which a scholar described as just "one step removed from improvisation."

After skipping Nohant for the summer of 1841, the couple divided their time over the next seven years between city and country, living in the now customary state of independence, proximity, and constant work. "We are so busy we have almost no time to see each other," Sand wrote to a friend, even though "we share a common wall." He was busy giving lessons all day; she was "scribbling over paper the whole night." Chopin's health continued to fluctuate between attacks of rheumatism, coughing, and influenza, but when he was healthy in the country he joined the others for walks in nature (often aboard a donkey), folk dances with the local Berrichon people, and entertainments at the piano, where he acted out his celebrated musical dramas or performed parodies of Italian opera. He gave public recitals rarely, but since the return from Majorca reviews were, for the most part, ecstatic. In an 1841 article Liszt noted that "the voices that had criticized him have fallen utterly silent." He was crowned "the Ariel of pianists," and his printed works achieved huge popularity and commercial success around Europe. As for Opus 35, there are reports of Chopin teaching it to his pupils and performing it at musical soirées, despite Robert Schumann's outraged review in which he famously accused the composer of gathering together "his four maddest children" into a messy, rule-breaking travesty of sonata conventions.

Sand's impatience with Chopin begins to show up in her letters within just a few years of their return from Spain. She complains of his shifting moods; the sad state of his health, which put a damper on her own happiness and drained the household of laughter and joy; and, increasingly, his jealousy over her association with other men. By 1844 she didn't bother to conceal her frustrations: "I cannot hold it against him that he loves me so much he cannot get by without me" for more than a week, she wrote to a friend. In 1846, during their last summer together, Sand threw caution to the wind and went public with her dissatisfactions, recklessly publishing a novel about a catastrophically failing love affair that featured a thinly disguised caricature of Chopin whom all the world—except, it seems, the composer himself—recognized. What most outraged Chopin's friends was the fact that she wrote it literally under his nose. *Lucrezia Floriani* became notorious overnight and would dictate forevermore the way the world came to perceive the famous love affair between composer and novelist. The story is an anatomy of jealousy and a meditation on the disappointments of friendship and romantic love. The plot has enough similarities to the real affair—from the age difference separating the fictional lovers to the rule of chastity she imposes on him—that it was, to Chopin's friends and supporters, an unmistakable betrayal. This in turn enraged Sand. In her memoir, which was published five years after Chopin's death, she goes to great lengths to assure the reader that the portrait of Karol de Rosewald, the effeminate, sickly German prince in the novel, was not based on her lover. It's the last topic she covers in the enormous autobiography, and she introduces it in classic George Sand style: by first excusing, then victimizing, *herself*. "After the disappointments of my youth, too many illusions came to govern me," she begins. "My morbid skepticism was succeeded by too much ingenuousness and good will. I was duped a thousand times by a dream of an archangelical fusion of opposing forces in the great battle of ideas." And so on. In closing *Story of My Life*, the great Romantic warrior prefaces the *Lucrezia* debacle by highlighting her resoluteness, wisdom, fortitude, and compassion. By contrast, she portrays Chopin as a flighty genius who was jealous, intolerant, arrogant, imperious, and disloyal. The Prince Karol of her novel was not, she hastens to remind us, "an artist." He was just a character, "a dreamer and nothing more," and in any case, Chopin himself read her pages after she left the manuscript for him each morning, an act of transparency that, she implies, fully exonerates her. Sand concedes that he was kind, devoted, charming, and deferential—to *her*—but to everyone else he was capricious and jealous. Her sorrows grew, and Chopin—weak, moody, out of touch—was unable to bear his own misfortunes, let alone hers. It was Maurice, her son, who gave her real strength; this was the "natural bond" that would endure. Everything in Sand's formidable arsenal is here, including her practice of marshaling a battalion of words to make a case that her version of the truth is the supreme and final one. I take her decision to close the nearly 675,000-word memoir with this vigorous self-defense as evidence that she herself needed convincing, but I don't think she was entirely satisfied with it; only a few years after Chopin died, she allowed a new edition of *Lucrezia* to be published with illustrations of Prince Karol by the beloved Maurice which bear an uncanny resemblance to Chopin himself, not just his face and attire but also his posture. In one illustration Prince Karol sits in the same position, with arms crossed, that was captured in a famous 1836 watercolor by Chopin's erstwhile fiancée Maria Wodzińska, which had become a popular lithograph. None of it seems very ingenuous or, for that matter, archangelical.

The "rupture" between Chopin and Sand, as it has come to be known, was probably in the works for some time, but things came to a head over Solange's marriage to sculptor Auguste Clésinger in 1847, the year after *Lucrezia* was published. Sand initially believed this young artist was a talent on the order of Delacroix, and that his association with the family would bring honor and riches. In fact he was a scoundrel and a brute: boastful, arrogant, violent, a womanizer and serial debtor. Chopin suspected Clésinger was masquerading as a gentleman and had shared his concerns. Sand, who wanted to avoid her partner's disapproval, kept the news of the wedding from him. We know her feelings about what she now labeled their "fatal friendship" because she expressed them in another letter to Albert Grzymała, this one infantilizing instead of ennobling: "I think Chopin must have suffered in his little corner not to know anything and to be unable to give advice," but he "never understood human nature." Sand informs Grzymała she "accomplished prodigies of patience of which I would not have believed myself capable," and "I have reached a state of martyrdom." All the while her clueless lover was dying of his "insane attachment" to her.

After the wedding, things between Solange and her new husband deteriorated quickly, and it wasn't long before the sculptor racked up debts on Sand's account and, when confronted by his angry mother-in-law, punched her in the chest. Maurice showed up with pistols in her defense. What followed was a long war of silence between mother and daughter, as Sand again felt abused and taken advantage of. When Solange, now pregnant, fell ill in the aftermath, Chopin loaned her his carriage, a gesture Sand regarded as hostile and disloyal. The seed planted months earlier, with the publication of *Lucrezia Floriani*, was now a full-grown entity. Sand insisted that Chopin break with her daughter out of loyalty to her. His reply is beautifully generous and philosophical: "I cannot remain indifferent to her," he insisted. "You will remember that I used to intercede with you for both your children, without preference. I did this whenever I had the chance, being certain that it is your destiny to love them *always*—for those are the only affections which are not subject to change." In closing he wrote: "Time will do its work. I shall wait—still the same as ever." Sand's response was as defiant as ever. Whereas Chopin had tried to place himself in her world by imagining a love greater than anything he had ever felt, the bond between parent and child, she dug in. "I am entrenching myself in my role of outraged mother," she insisted. "Nothing henceforth will make me disregard its authority and dignity." She now calls her daughter "the enemy," envisions a new war, and invites Chopin to take Solange's side. "Adieu, my friend," she says in closing. The door was slammed shut on nine years of love and friendship, and this was their last exchange of letters. They met only once more, by accident, at the home of Charlotte Marliani, the friend who had suggested Majorca as an ideal destination for Europeans wishing to escape the ravages of a Paris winter. It was in March 1848 when they ran into each other in Mme Marliani's vestibule. Chopin asked if Sand had heard from Solange.

"A week ago," she replied.

"Then allow me to inform you that you are a grandmother. Solange has a little girl, and I am very glad to be the first to give you the news."

He tipped his hat and moved on, but then realized something important had gone unsaid. Sand had not inquired about the health of her own daughter, and in his weakened state Chopin sent his companion up the stairs after her to assure her Solange was well. Sand then returned to the vestibule to inquire if Clésinger was with her daughter—still, it seems, she was thinking of herself and the awkwardness of encountering the dreaded son-in-law. Finally she asked how he was. "I said I was well" he replied, tipped his hat again, and wandered back out into the streets of Paris. It was the last time they ever saw each other. Solange had more grief ahead; her infant died a few days later, and it would be several years before she reconciled with her mother. She, however, was at Chopin's bedside when he died a year and a half later, on the 17th of October, 1849.

Sand's part in the story is now over, but it's hard to leave her without a few more words—an attempt, at the very least, to articulate the contradictions that are embedded in the life and art of this extraordinary woman. For all the millions of pages she left behind, she remains, in the end, vexingly unknowable. She is at times tediously self-focused, and then, in an instant, generous to a fault. Her writing is often tendentious, except in those moments when she liberates herself from some moral lesson or political argument and opens a window onto a portrait of human nature or the natural world that stuns a reader for its acumen, vernal beauty, freshness, and originality. She has been treated harshly by fellow writers, historians, and especially Chopin biographers, even those writing in the twenty-first century, variously derided as overly voluble, self-serving, dishonest, intellectually immature. Balzac, one of her great friends, admired her strength and gracefulness but also decried her as "a curious animal." The poet Baudelaire didn't know Sand personally but called her a "stupid creature" and said if he ever met he would be tempted to throw a baptismal font at her head. One biographer called her work "an immense legal plea, advanced by an indefatigable lawyer"; another more cruelly remarked that she "lived her truths one at a time, each cancelling the last."

During the three years I spent reading Sand's works I veered—"like a boat on ice," to use her expression—from the ugly side her critics delighted in recounting to her deep, and often tender, humanism. For every instance where I wanted to throw her book against the wall, there were many long stretches where I found myself typing out her words so I would not, in the ocean she left behind, lose track of them. What's true about Sand is that she spent virtually all of her seventy-two years composing her own life. In the Preface to *Letters to a Traveler* she describes herself as "a wandering schoolboy," an apt metaphor because she was always moving from one place to another, always seeking to make discoveries about the world around her and then, with her pen, to analyze, pick apart, and explain them, first to herself, then to her millions of readers around the world. She was cruelly used by her mother and grandmother, and as a young girl was forced to make her own way in a world that did not—and never would—fully understand her. For me the most beautiful parts of Sand's memoir express the joy she took in uncovering the secrets of nature: in botany, minerology, geology, entomology, horticulture. She so delighted in human anatomy that for several weeks she hung the skeleton of a young girl in her bedroom. Her appetite for knowledge was simply voracious, and with every man she loved—whether her lover (Chopin), her friend (Delacroix), or her son (Maurice)—she was always on the hunt for innovative ways to enable them to satisfy their own creative appetites. "Always have the best conditions to create," Sylvie, my guide at Nohant, kept saying as we made our way around Sand's house and property. That was George Sand's religion, and she practiced it with a zeal that was in equal parts selfless and self-serving. That Chopin composed so many of his greatest works under her care is testament to the power of Sand's enabling influence. The poignant final encounter in Mme Marliani's foyer, which came eight months after the perplexing rupture over a carriage for Solange, reveals once and for all the tragic impossibility of her dream of the ideal friendship.

Edith Wharton may have found the "real meaning of the place" behind the windows where Sand reengineered spaces in order to create an ideal refuge for artists and friends, but for me the heart of George Sand's Nohant is elsewhere. The most affecting moment of my visit occurred in the woods, after Sylvie and I emerged from the dense overgrowth of Sand's little forest into a clearing. Here I was greeted by a bronze statue of a human figure in a quasi-balletic position, standing on a large gingko leaf with a little bird perched at its feet. It's a representation of Corambé, the imaginary friend young Aurore Dupin created when she was growing up in a household of conflict and tragedy. After the death of her father and banishment of her mother, Corambé came to Aurore's rescue in a dream, complete with its strange, untranslatable name. Sand writes about Corambé in various parts of her memoir, describing it as a "model character" who was pure and charitable like Jesus; shining and handsome as the archangel Gabriel. I've avoided a pronoun because Corambé manifested as both male and female; "it had no sex," she explains, "and put on many disguises." She assigned a special role to this figure, loving it "as a friend, as a sister, all the while giving it the reverence due to a god." It was an enlightened spirit in every way, from politics to religion. Corambé "would not have let a gasping Poland be devoured by bloodthirsty Russia," Sand wrote, nor would it have abandoned, back home in France, "the cause of the weak for that of the strong, or the moral and physical life of the poor to the caprices of the rich." The god she conjured would have been kindness embodied, "more Christian than the papacy."

In due course Aurore built an altar for Corambé, seeking out an untrodden, secret place in the densest part of the forest, an area beyond her grandmother's formal garden "where no one ever went and where even the eye could not penetrate during the leafy season." In the shade of three maples that rose from a common root this lonely little girl constructed an altar from pebbles, flowers, birds' nests, moss, and ivy. From the branches of the largest tree she suspended a string of pink and white shells she had collected on the property, forming a makeshift chandelier. She visited every day and brought her divinity an offering: not an animal, for to kill a bird or even an insect seemed to her "barbaric and unworthy of [Corambé's] perfect sweetness," but instead a frog, lizard, or butterfly she would trap and then, with delicacy and reverence, set free upon the natural altar. After her visits she carefully covered her tracks, lest anyone follow them to her sacred place. What appealed to her most of all was the way her tribute was hidden in plain sight, "in the depths of a virgin forest, while thirty or forty feet away were winding paths where people could go back and forth without suspecting a thing." Alas, her little brother did discover the sanctuary, and in a single moment it was forever defiled. Aurore destroyed her temple, dug a hole and buried the garlands, shells, and other "rustic ornaments" under the debris of the altar. From then on Corambé lived only in "the soul's sanctuary" of her heart and imagination, with no physical place of its own.

No one knows where the original site was, but in 1991 a visual artist named Françoise Vergier created a statue of Sand's deity as it revels in its natural state: nude, in the woods, with a bird as its only company. The people who run the Maison de George Sand, today a national historic monument, placed the sculpture in a circular opening in the center of the woods that can be reached via several different footpaths. Here, in a place where the future writer spent so many hours composing poems, daydreaming, wandering, observing, collecting and preserving bits of her natural world, a modern visitor can contemplate, to the sound of birdsong and rustling leaves, this singular woman and the existential contradictions that fueled both her personal and artistic imagination: her need for solitude and society, emotional connection and independence, maleness and femaleness. Vergier's Corambé reminds us of the battles she was always fighting and the value she placed on solitude and independence, not just for herself but for everyone in her orbit. Alone in the dappled forest, Corambé represents yet another sad theme that persisted in the life of both Aurore Dupin and George Sand: the inevitable loss of friendship and love.

For his part, Chopin wrote little after the relationship ended. He escaped Paris again for England after another political revolution inflamed the city in February 1848. By this time his teaching had become unsatisfying; young ladies sought him out simply in order to say they had taken lessons with the great Chopin, and his physical and emotional state was tragically declining. "I can feel neither grief nor joy—my emotions are completely exhausted—I am only vegetating and waiting for it all to end quickly," he wrote from London in July 1848. Chopin suffered a cruel blow while in Britain: his most trusted piano tuner "drowned himself," leaving the composer incapable of achieving the unique sound that had defined the outlines of his entire creative life. Scholar Jonathan Bellman wrote a poignant account of these days, which adds another gloss to the story of his decline. "If no one could tune to Chopin's satisfaction," Bellman observed, "then pianos were no longer responding to him the way they had previously, with their subtle tonal differences, their color, their vibrations, their *life*. It must have been natural, in such circumstances, for him to have seen music and especially the piano as more old, trusted friends that had abandoned him." He returned to Paris in November, once the political unrest had passed; his composing had all but ceased, and his teaching days were over.

On September 9, 1849, an ailing Chopin took up his final residence in Paris, moving into an apartment at 12 Place Vendôme, thanks to financial support from a circle of loyal friends. They also organized delivery of a splendid grand piano from Pleyel, but it's unlikely he ever played it. Upon arriving at the elegant building—it had formerly been the Russian Embassy—Chopin "took to his bed, and never left it." The scene of his final days has been much embellished and romanticized over the years, especially by people who were not present. In his novel *Smoke*, Ivan Turgenev notes that "In Europe there are nearly one thousand ladies in whose arms Chopin expired." There were other deathbed myths, including stories about stirring psalms and opera arias sung at his bedside. In reality the circle was much smaller; the people we know for sure who were present at Chopin's deathbed were his sister Ludwika; the ever-loyal Albert Grzymała; a Polish princess, Marcelina Czartoryska; and George Sand's daughter, Solange.

For me, the most affecting story about Chopin's last days comes from a friend, Charles Gavard, who sat beside the dying musician and read aloud to him. It has often been remarked, going back to the first biographies of the nineteenth century and continuing in the present time, that Chopin was not a great reader of literature. He left behind few books—mainly collections of Polish poetry—and the general impression of those who knew him was that he didn't much care for reading. But we know from Gavard that his personal library, which he brought with him to Place Vendôme, contained a pillar of Enlightenment thought: Voltaire's *Dictionnaire Philosophique*. It was a book Chopin valued for its "clear and concise language . . . and [Voltaire's] so sure judgments on the questions of taste." This is what he asked Gavard, an inventor and fellow artist, to read aloud in those final hours. In the end, it seems, Chopin circled back to the beginning: to words that expressed the Enlightenment ideals that had shaped his early education. Now isolated from society and so fatigued he could barely communicate in words, Chopin "begged me to take a book from his library and read to him." Gavard describes a touching scene, with Chopin doing "everything he could" to avoid making his friend sad, turning to literature in order "to shorten the hours," and choosing from a large tome the selection for Gavard to read aloud. Thus it was that some of the very last words Chopin heard during his lifetime were from Voltaire's essay on "Taste."

Voltaire began compiling his "Philosophical Dictionary" in the 1750s, organizing a series of essays on aesthetics, morality, civility, politics, and religion around the alphabet. The entry on "Taste" is a declaration of his views about art, music, painting, literature, and their importance to human society, and throughout his essay Voltaire accentuates the value of simplicity in all things that Chopin also espoused. "Without doubt," he states, "the best taste in every species of cultivation is to imitate nature with the highest fidelity, energy, and grace." Just as Chopin exhorted his students to go out in the world and experience its diversity—to visit museums and opera halls, read books, take walks in the park—Voltaire urged his readers to actively cultivate a broad range of interests. "Man molds and educates his taste in art much more than his sensual taste," he wrote. "A young man who is sensitive but untutored cannot at first distinguish the parts in a large chorus; in a painting, his eyes do not at first distinguish the shadings, the chiaroscuro, the perspective, the harmony of its colors, and the correctness of the draughtsmanship; yet little by little his ears learn to hear and his eyes to see." Study, observe, listen, Voltaire seems to be saying; then you can appreciate great works of learning and genius "with a portion of that spirit that appears in their composition." Voltaire could have been speaking of Chopin himself when he defined a connoisseur as one who recoils from "elaborate ornamentation . . . [and] the burlesque" in favor of "the simple and natural beauty" of *la belle nature*. It's an echo of what Chopin so often told his own pupils: "Simplicity is everything. . . . No noises, no 'effects,' just simplicity, as in all that is beautiful."

Before he died at two o'clock in the morning on October 17, 1849, he made one last request of Albert Grzymała. "In the name of the friendship you bear me," Chopin asked that his incomplete piano method be given to two composer friends, Charles-Valentine Alkan and Henri Reber, who "might derive something useful from it." Everything else, including all the unfinished musical sketches he left behind, should be burned. "I have always had a great respect for the public," he told his friend, "and whatever I have published has always been as perfect as I could make it." Even to the end, his desire for clarity and refinement were undimmed.

* * *

The first time Chopin's *marche* was ever played in an actual funeral was at his own, on October 30, 1849, at the Church of the Madeleine in the heart of Paris. It was most certainly this event that forever sealed the work as a *marche funèbre*, despite the author's best efforts to remove the programmatic note and allow "the listener to complete the picture."

The Madeleine is a massive structure, more temple than church, a fact that belies its strange history. First designed in the mid-1700s on parish land dating to the thirteenth century, the partially built church was demolished after its architect died, then reconceived in a new design. After the French Revolution the still-unfinished building and the land on which it stood became the subject of impassioned cultural debate: Should it be a library? A stock exchange? A bank? A railway station? In 1806 Napoleon supplied the answer: it would be a grand memorial to the French military forces, a "Temple to the Glory of the Great Army." After the fall of the empire and Napoleon's exile the building went through one more transformation before it was finally consecrated, in 1845, as a church dedicated to Mary Magdalene. Still, from the street it looks like an ancient Greek temple: fifty-two enormous fluted Corinthian columns encircle the building and support a pediment frieze filled with relief sculptures—not centaurs and lions, as you would expect in a classical edifice, but Christian figures in a tableau depicting *The Last Judgment*. Inside, the mixture of church and state is also vividly present: the interior of the dome is covered in a fresco portraying the history of Christianity, with Napoleon himself figuring largely. It's the only church in Paris to include a representation of the former emperor.

When I visited in the fall of 2018 France was celebrating the centennial of the Armistice that ended World War I, and as part of its regular series of Sunday concerts the Church of the Madeleine held a special recital in honor of the anniversary that included works by celebrated French composers. Members of a national police orchestra with roots going back to the French Revolution wore dress uniforms with the traditional braided cord laced through epaulettes; they were arranged in a circle under the cupola of this temple-church from which Napoleon, in ermine robes, looked down on them. I had come to the Madeleine to hear its grand organ, the same one that was played at Chopin's funeral, and a rarely performed work by Camille Saint-Saëns, *Cypress and Laurels*, made the perfect introduction. Composed in the early twentieth century in celebration of the Allied victory by a composer who was himself the Madeleine's organist for two decades, this is a sprawling, symphonic work that makes the organ its star soloist. Its massive sound reverberates off the marble columns and stone floors and wraps itself around you; you can feel it resonating in your bones as the heavy, sustained notes hang in the air for long, resonant seconds.

At Chopin's funeral it was Saint-Saëns's predecessor, Louis Lefébure-Wély, who performed on a newly installed forty-eight-stop instrument with four manuals (or keyboards), an event that likely would have pleased Chopin because Wély was considered the greatest organ improviser in Paris. The organ, like the piano, had recently gone through its own period of explosive growth and innovation: new technology in reed stops along with devices that allowed for greater wind pressure were giving organists and composers a vastly greater range of expressiveness. Like the piano, the organ was getting more powerful, more symphonic, capable of summoning multiple voices across a much wider dynamic range. With the addition of all those new stops, a single performer could mimic an entire orchestra: trombone, piccolo, bassoon, clarinet, English horn, viola da gamba. When a new, high-tech organ was exhibited at the 1826 Industrial Exposition in Paris, a prominent critic christened it the *grande orgue expressif*—the grand *expressive* organ—and announced: "Either I am very much mistaken or the moment of a revolution in organ music has arrived." Lefébure-Wély was the most celebrated organist of the day, a child prodigy who had been dazzling parishioners since he was eight years old. He assumed his first post as principal organist at an important Paris church at fourteen. Two weeks after inaugurating the Madeleine's new organ in 1846, he gave a haunting recital to benefit victims of a flood in the Loire, putting all those technical innovations to work in an improvisation that reproduced the sound of torrential rain, a river overflowing its banks, the moaning of victims, and the vibrations of thunder. Wély brought his audience to tears and was soon crowned "the monarch of the church organ." There was no one in all of Paris more suited to pay tribute to Frédéric Chopin at a keyboard of any sort than Lefébure-Wély, and he began the ceremony with two of Chopin's own works: Preludes no. 4 and 6, in E minor and B minor, from the collection of op. 28, completed in Nohant after the Majorca sojourn.

Sitting there in Madeleine so many years later, I thought about how stunning it must have been for the mourners at Chopin's funeral, people who had experienced the "soft and velvety tone" of his Pleyel, to suddenly experience the immense columns of air pushing through those long pipes and pronouncing in rich, booming tones—so loud they filled the entire church—these familiar works they had come to know in intimate salons. It was an unforgettable moment in Paris's long musical history; one observer described Wély's performance of the preludes as a wondrous interpretation that "produced a profound sensation [and] went straight to the heart."

It's possible to find organ recordings of Chopin's preludes on You-

Tube, but to get the full impact you need to be in a church. I wanted to experience that sensation of hearing this intimate, pianistic music played on "a grand expressive organ," so in early 2019 I made a visit to the Cathedral of St. John the Divine in New York, one the world's largest cathedrals. Its organ, originally built in 1910 by the Ernest M. Skinner Company, has 8,514 pipes that range in size from a pencil to a three-story building. As I sat in the organ loft high above the choir, the associate music director, Raymond Nagem, played the two preludes that Chopin's friends heard at his funeral, filling the vast cathedral space with melodies that were at the same time familiar yet startlingly new. A woman sitting below, near the altar, looked up from her book in wonder.

I arrived at St. John the Divine with a misconception that had influenced my imaginings of Chopin's funeral for almost the duration of my research for this book: the notion that hearing such non-liturgical music in a high church setting would have been jarring to parishioners. But when I mentioned this to Ray, he surprised me with another example of how nineteenth-century Paris was unlike any other place in Europe. During this time people went to the great churches every Sunday not just for religious reasons but for musical ones. Many people went to church for the same reason folks today go to jazz clubs, college auditoriums, and the local village green: to hear great, and often new, music. In 1830s Paris it was Alfred Lefébure-Wély who, more than any other organist in Paris, satisfied that hunger, going boldly against tradition to offer churchgoers a variety of music in every popular style. Even as a young man Wély had resisted the call of critics to stick to the classic liturgical repertoire of Bach and Handel. As one scholar observes, this "twenty-one year old already knew what *his* public wanted to hear and how to satisfy the popular taste in organ music more effectively than any other performer of his time." Visitors from Germany and England were particularly scandalized by what they heard in Paris churches: hunting songs, polkas, improvisations on popular opera arias, waltzes, even drinking songs. The French complained too; a historian wrote in 1839: "There is nothing more grotesque or irreligious at this time than the practices of the Parisian organists." This would change at the end of the century, when more conservative traditions returned, but at the time of Chopin's funeral the culture of improvisation and unorthodox musical style prevailed even in La Madeleine, one of the most prestigious churches in Paris. And so it was that my visit to a cathedral on New York's Upper West Side offered fresh and fascinating insight into Chopin's funeral, a moment when the greatest organ improviser of the day—a young musician who went his own way, despite what critics and the Establishment demanded—performed in tribute to a fellow independent spirit, the greatest piano improviser Paris had ever seen. It all seemed to me so wonderfully Chopinesque.

There was another dynamic at work in La Madeleine that day, which expressed itself in the music Chopin requested be sung at his funeral: the Mozart Requiem. It was the first time the work had been heard in Paris since 1840 when Napoleon's remains were returned from Saint Helena (Chopin and Sand had heard it sung in a dress rehearsal before the interment), but this time half the voices were disembodied: heard but not seen because they were hidden behind a heavy curtain of black cloth at the back of the church. This accommodation was a relic of French Catholic tradition that prohibited women from participating in any way in church services, let alone raising their solo voices in the house. After Chopin died, his funeral was delayed for almost two weeks, as his influential friends lobbied the archbishop of Paris for an exception to the ancient rule. Finally permission was granted, but it was a half measure: the women in the chorus and the two soloists, including renowned soprano Pauline Vi-ardot, were placed behind a large black curtain, where they sang, in-visibly, in tribute to their friend. It's impossible to know how many of the invited guests appreciated the irony of the moment: the final fare-well to a man who had spent most of the last decade of his life living out of wedlock with France's most famous feminist, sung by women whose voices were muffled behind a velvet cloth while those of the men filled the church. The performance was arresting nonetheless; a poet friend of Chopin later described how he felt the spirit of Mozart "hover and cry" over the "young soul" of his fellow artist.

Surely, though, the most stirring moment of all occurred when the Opus 35 funeral march was played in an orchestral arrangement as Chopin's coffin was carried into the church by his closest friends. The work had been hastily orchestrated by Henri Reber, one of the com-posers to whom Chopin had bequeathed, on his deathbed, the un-finished piano method. His transcription of Chopin's funeral march, which exists in a fragment at the Bibliothèque Nationale de France, is scored for a dozen wind and brass instruments, including flute, oboe, bassoon, trombone, violin, cello, and double bass. It's often the case after great artists die that they quickly enter the public domain and, having lost control of their own identity, become the property of the ages. It was Henri Reber who took Chopin's *marche* for pianoforte, re-stored the word *funèbre* to his orchestral score, and sent the work into the stratosphere, changing forever the way it would be perceived in the future. It was now and forevermore *Chopin's funeral march*. Having resisted, throughout his entire life, the pressure to write in the large, popular forms—operas, symphonies, cantatas, Masses—Chopin was, during the course of his own funeral and courtesy of his own music, expropriated from an intimate salon with a subtly nuanced pianoforte, and launched into the public sphere with a resounding, multi-instrument accompaniment. Some three thousand people had gathered outside the Madeleine temple/church, and as the massive bronze doors swung open at noon and pallbearers carried Chopin's coffin up the stone steps and along the nave toward the altar, they would have heard the now unmistakably heroic work, amplified by Reber's orchestra and broadcast into the streets of Paris for all to hear.

Chopin made another request about his final sendoff: during the burial he asked that there be no ceremony, no music, no graveside speeches. At the very end what he wanted was simplicity. It was a beautiful, clear October day when his coffin was lowered into the ground at the recently opened Père Lachaise Cemetery, five kilometers from the Madeleine Church. What the invited mourners did not know, as they quietly stood by and watched the coffin descend, was that part of the composer's corpse, his heart, was not to be interred in this place. There is a long tradition of "heart-burial," an ancient practice that connects a person's soul, represented by her heart, to a beloved place: a cathedral, church, or abbey; a personal estate; a homeland. Chopin had expressed to those closest to him that his heart be removed after his death and returned to Poland, but he could never have foreseen the long, strange journey the organ would take over the next hundred years. It's an oft-told story, worth recounting here because it manifests so many of the themes from Chopin's life, his music, and the afterlife of both.

During the autopsy the heart was placed in a crystal vessel filled with an amber liquid, probably cognac. With the Polish border still heavily guarded by a foreign army, Chopin's sister Ludwika secreted the jar in her voluminous skirts for the long carriage ride home. In her luminous novel *Flights*, Polish author Olga Tokarczuk imagines Ludwika's journey, conjuring first the image of Chopin's body in a chilly morgue, "overlain with flowers . . . [and lying] in semi-darkness, slight, gaunt, heartless," while his anguished friends petitioned the archbishop to allow his female friends to sing at his funeral. She lingers on the ingeniousness of his loyal sister's plan, using the "scaffolding" afforded by her crinolines and "the warm insides of her dress" to fool the Prussian gendarmerie at the border, maintaining her composure to the very end, until the precious "brown piece of muscle" had been safely handed over and she could finally collapse in tears. Thus was a part of Chopin returned to his homeland, but the heart would remain hidden for another four years, until Kalasanty Jędrzejewicz, Ludwika's husband, who resented her close alliance with her brother, had died. In 1855 the crystal jar, now interred in a small ebony box, was placed in the catacombs of the Church of the Holy Cross in Warsaw, where it was soon forgotten, until a journalist stumbled across it in 1878. Finally, in 1880, Chopin's heart was entombed in a stone pillar in the main part of the church, where it was consecrated and marked by a plaque carrying an inscription from the Book of Matthew: "Where your treasure is, there your heart will be also."

The heart rested there, untouched, for sixty years, until a new war broke out between ancient enemies. It was, ironically, a Nazi music-lover who engineered the removal of Chopin's heart from a church he knew would soon be destroyed by German bombs in the wake of the Warsaw Uprising of 1944. The urn containing the heart was transferred to the headquarters of a high-ranking SS officer, Erich von dem Bach-Zelewski, and eventually entrusted to a Polish priest for safekeeping until the war was over. In 1945 Chopin's heart made its final journey, first stopping at his childhood home in Żelazowa Wola, where a small piano had been installed for the occasion. Here a Polish pianist who had been a student of Paderewski, Henryk Sztompka, played the *Lento con gran espressione*, a work Chopin had composed in Vienna during the last happy days of his 1830 European sojourn, before he learned of the devastation caused by the November Uprising. This nocturne-like piece in C-sharp minor is often cited by scholars as an example of his innovative use of polymetrics: the melody is in one time signature (3/4) while the accompaniment is in another (4/4). It was discovered posthumously in 1875 and carried the dedication "To my sister, Ludwika." She knew the piece well, having inscribed it for her brother into Maria Wodzińska's autograph album some years earlier. Also in the home where the composer was born and in the presence of his own long-preserved heart, Sztompka played the famous Polonaise in A-flat major, op. 53, composed in Nohant in 1842 and universally known as "Heroic." This was the piece that was playing on a CD when Nobuyuki Tsujii's mother first noticed that her eight-month-old son was moving his little feet in time with the music.

Later that day the procession made its way from Żelazowa Wola to central Warsaw. The heart was returned to the Church of the Holy Cross and reinterred in its pillar in a ceremony broadcast by radio across Poland. It remained undisturbed for another five decades, until a team of forensic scientists, sworn to secrecy and working under cover of darkness in the presence of the Archbishop of Warsaw, exhumed the relic in April 2017 and, without opening the crystal jar, performed a series of observations. The issue of which chronically progressive, debilitating disease caused Chopin's death had been in dispute for some time—speculation included cystic fibrosis, alpha-1-antitrypsin deficiency, and mitral stenosis—and the original autopsy, conducted by a renowned French anatomist and physician, Jean Cruveilhier, had been lost in a fire of police archives in Paris in 1871. But in a paper published in the *American Journal of Medicine* the scientists, having observed signs of, among other things, a "frosted heart," confirmed his death from *pericarditis tuberculosa,* one of the most threatening complications of tuberculosis. After they finished their work, well past midnight, the scientists resealed the crystal jar, replaced it in the ebony cask, and reinterred it in the pillar at St. Mary's, where it will rest for another fifty years, until 2068, before being removed for further observation and, possibly, DNA testing.

In the meantime, the political wheel turns, new technologies come (and go), young pianists discover Chopin, and old ones rediscover him. The landscapes he knew and loved will change, but one thing seems certain: his music will keep showing up in surprising ways, as it did in early 2018 for an elderly pensioner in Nottinghamshire in central England. The ninety-three-year-old man's garden had been recently ransacked by hoodlums when two police officers stopped by to see how he was doing. Clearly disheartened, not just from the robbery but also the recent death of his wife, the gentleman was reminiscing about happier days when Craig Bull, one of the officers, noticed an upright piano in the corner with an open book on the music stand. The page was turned to Chopin's Nocturne in E-flat major, op. 9, no. 2, composed in 1830–31. "Well that's very strange," Bull said; "this piece was my grandma's favorite," one he played virtually nonstop when she was nearing the end of her life—"for hours and hours," he told the old man, "until my hands or back gave in." So without ceremony this cop sat down at the piano, still in his protective vest with a radio pinned to his epaulet, and played the entire piece, singing the notes, sitting still and upright, with a disciplined and, I must say, quite Chopinesque combination of restraint and feeling. His colleague filmed the whole thing, and in the foreground you can see the pensioner's hands fingering the air, conducting the much-loved work, then clapping in joy when it was over.

This piece, one of Chopin's most popular nocturnes, is an exceptional work because over the decades scholars have discovered as many as fifteen variants on the melodic line in scores belonging to Chopin's students. These *fioriture*, a word that comes from the Italian for "flowering," are remnants of his improvisation at the keyboard, written-out embellishments that reflect the wonderful, joyous playfulness that is among of the hallmarks of his music. I first heard all the variations at the Bard SummerScape festival dedicated to Chopin in 2017, when Australian pianist Piers Lane played them one after the other in a recital that was just mind-blowing. If I hadn't known otherwise, I would have believed Lane was making it all up, sending the melody soaring up and down the keyboard, jazzing up the rhythm, changing the dynamics, reimagining and reinventing composed phrases seemingly at will, like an improviser in a piano bar. Later, in a panel discussion at the Bard festival, the scholar Jonathan Bellman suggested that Chopin probably fashioned each *fioritura* for a different student, customizing the opportunity for playful improvisation to that pupil's unique ability. Here was a glorious example of Chopin's individualized, customized approach to teaching: the master giving students an opportunity to explore different pathways in his own music so they could hear, and also *feel*, in the process, the long, singing line as it's embellished, just as a soprano would decorate a bel canto aria. Bellman then played an extraordinary recording of a performance by Bart van Oort, a Dutch pianist who cycled through the ornaments, one after the other, on an 1842 Pleyel. At one point I closed my eyes and imagined I was in a jazz club. The music, so familiar yet now, suddenly, so new, sounded like it had been composed on the spot. When it was over, Bellman asked the stunned audience: "So where is the real Chopin version?" The question just hung in the air, unanswered but obvious. Chopin is everywhere.

If he were to magically return and burst through the gates of Père Lachaise like the superhero in *Frederic: The Resurrection of Music*,

Chopin would encounter a world that has much in common with his own: countries invade their neighbors; people flee their war-torn homelands, often unable to return; barricades go up in city streets; nationalism rages around the globe; new technology brings wave after wave of cultural and social change; dictators bloviate; individual voices are amplified. In this strange world he would also find himself, both his music and his life story, being reinvented and reclaimed in so many surprising ways and unusual places. If he had a voice in which to speak to us, I'm guessing his message would be unchanged: *Play it like no one else ever played it before. Play it from your heart. No matter what the others say, make it your own.*

Luckily, we don't need some magic technology to bring Chopin back, because he's already here. An artist who looks at once to the past and to the future, we can find him virtually anywhere, as fresh, inspiring, and inventive as ever.

A Note About the Dedication

Chopin was not quite twenty when he composed his piano concerto in F minor, op. 21, with its incomparably beautiful *Larghetto* in the second movement. He wrote very little for orchestra, yet this slow movement from his youthful concerto is, for me, among his most captivating works, one I listened to almost every day as I was research-ing and writing this book. It's nine minutes of music that never fails to fill the heart with joy. The movement opens with a call and response between the full orchestra—violins, cellos, violas, oboes, flutes, bas-soons, cornets, clarinets—everything but the piano, which emerges alone after a few measures, making an entrance that sounds, as Polish poet Jarosław Iwaszkiewicz described it, "like the opening of a gate to some haven of love and peace."

When Chopin wrote the *Larghetto* he was dreaming of mezzo-soprano Konstancja Gładkowska, his first Polish love and the woman he described as "my ideal." He was inexperienced in love, and to this day it's unclear if he ever declared himself, although he confided the infatuation to his closest friends. When, toward the end of her life and now blind, someone read aloud to her one of the first biographies of

Chopin, Konstancja claimed she had never known how he felt about her. But it's written right there, in a heart-stoppingly beautiful duet between bassoon and piano at the very end of the *Larghetto*. It's the notes from this brief musical conversation that appear on the dedication page, a moment when two voices rise up and over all the others in a tender love song, one that expresses what the heart wants to say much better than any constellation of words I could ever summon.

Acknowledgments

In recent years, say for the past couple of decades or so, our celebrity-enamored culture has been turning scientists into rock stars. Physicists, evolutionary biologists, software engineers, astrophysicists—most of us can name at least one bold-faced name in each category. After spending many years immersed in the world of music, I'd like to make a case for musicologists to join their ranks. What's remarkable about the great music scholars is how they can juggle so many wildly different disciplines at once, deploying with one hand the tools of science—mathematics, physics, acoustics, materials science—and with the other the more liberal arts of history, politics, biography, and literature. All in an effort to illuminate the inner workings of, and the source of beauty in, the profoundly complex art of music. I've been astonished again and again by the range of talent the great musicologists possess, and in my own journey of discovery to more fully understand the magic and scope of Chopin's genius, I wouldn't have gotten far without the work of these quite brilliant men and women.

First and foremost is Jean-Jacques Eigeldinger, whose *Chopin: Pianist and Teacher as Seen by His Pupils* is the irreplaceable work in my library. I think of it as the desert island book for Chopin lovers, one that can be read over and over as each page—and then every footnote—offers new insights into the artist and man: his aesthetic beliefs and teaching methods and philosophy, and even how he himself played the piano and interpreted his own music. Other Chopin scholars whose works were vital to my project and are, in my humble opinion, deserving of rock-star status include: Jonathan Bellman, Halina Goldberg, Jeffrey Kallberg, Lawrence Kramer, Anatole Leikin, Jim Parakilas, John Rink, the late Charles Rosen, Jim Samson, and Alan Walker.

A profound joy of this project was meeting two wonderful men whose personal and professional lives were touched by Chopin: David Aijón and Gabriel Quetglas. I'm deeply grateful for their unfailing kindness and generosity; for sharing research and resources, many of which I wouldn't have discovered on my own; and for reading portions of the book in manuscript and making corrections and suggestions. I feel that, through Chopin's introduction, we became lifelong friends. I'm similarly indebted to Patricia Frederick and Edmund Michael Frederick, proprietors of the extraordinary Frederick Collection of Historic Pianos in Massachusetts. Their vast knowledge about several centuries of instruments, composers, and music, as well as their artistry at the many different keyboards in their collection, is hard to capture in words; I urge you to go there and experience it for yourself. It's a unique place where the past comes to life in sound. Throughout the long process of research, writing, and fact checking, I was continually moved by the amount of time these generous people devoted to my efforts to, as Chopin once put it, "complete the picture."

I also wish to thank the following people who provided support in a myriad of ways, including with research, interviews, translation, and visits to historic monuments, or by introducing me to new music, helping me become a better listener to works I already knew and deepening my appreciation of Chopin's gifts as a composer, pianist, and improviser. They are, alphabetically: Nick Asano, Dagmara Binkowska, Gregory Brill, Samantha Caretti, Jennifer Croft, Zbigniew Dębicki, Moreno Donadel, Allan Evans, Adeline Fagel, José Garcia-León, Eugenia Santana Goitia, Lisa Greenwald, Tomoko Harada, Will Healy, Nina Hoffman, Andrew Horbachevsky, Marius Labaune, Maria Molestina-Kurlat, Marika Moosbrugger, Anka Muhlstein, Raymond Nagem, Elizabeth Olson, Peter Osnos, Gillian Pink, Dale Purves, Peter Rosen, Joanna Różewska, Ben Schott, Marisa Silver, Judith Tick, and Anna Zielinska-Elliott. I'm especially grateful to Eric Clark for speaking to me with such honesty and openness about his experience at the First Chopin Competition on Period Instruments, Sylvie Jehl for an unforgettable walk through George Sand's landscape in Nohant, Jeremy Kahn for allowing me to share here the story of his beloved wife, and Yuan Sheng for a richly fascinating and wide-ranging interview that, among other things, helped me truly understand the importance of Bach to Chopin.

I'm grateful to Polish artist Piotr Micherewicz for allowing me to use his portrait of Chopin on the cover and for his willingness to adapt some elements of the original illustration to suit an American marketplace. I thank the Bibliothèque nationale de France for granting permission to reproduce as endpapers pages from the score of op. 35 owned by Jane Stirling, one of Chopin's pupils. Thanks also to Oliver Kwapis for his patient and thoughtful work on the transcriptions that appear in the book and companion website. Special thanks to Silas Seandel for his love, friendship, and the precious gift of André Gide's *Notes on Chopin*; Jeanne Heifetz for our many long, engrossing conversations about art and music; and Claudia Kawczynska and David Black for their longtime support of my work as a writer. Gratitude also to Lissa Muscatine for her generous support.

Acknowledgments

I find myself somewhat lacking in words to express the depth of my gratitude to Rafael Cortés-Colon, my teacher and friend. Every week since 1996 we've spent at least an hour together at the keyboard, focused on a single work for piano. His multidisciplinary approach—looking at the art of the period, the political and social influences on the composer, his or her life story and national history—has been an incomparable joy and intellectual adventure. I'm a different, and better, person for this immersion in music, and remain humbled by his patience, wisdom, and artistry.

At Simon & Schuster I'm profoundly grateful to my editor, Emily Graff, who offered stalwart support throughout the entire process and astute feedback that made this a better book. Her assistant, Lashanda Anakwah, shepherded everything through the complex production process, offering patient and cheerful guidance at every stage. I also thank the copyeditor, Rick Willett, and the publicity and marketing team: Angela Ching, Elizabeth Gay, and Elise Ringo. I extend heartfelt thanks to S&S's publisher, Jon Karp, a man whose generosity, wit, and steadfast dedication to the unique voice and individual goals of each author I've admired for a great many years.

No doubt the finest gift of all to any writer is to be understood, believed in, and supported no matter what. I couldn't have written this book without being under the wing of Melanie Jackson, my peerless literary agent whose intelligence, unrelenting curiosity, deep reading into and around the edges of a subject, and intellectual generosity constitute a rare blessing. I also thank her masterful assistant, Matthew Dissen.

Finally, I end with a cadence on my partner, Ann Godoff. Of the many things she's taught me over the years, there's one essential truth that also informs the sonata of Chopin's that I spent so many years with. The power of this message inspires me every day: that love is as strong as death.

A Note About Sources

There are multiple versions in different languages of key primary sources in the literature about Chopin and Sand, and in the process of finalizing quotations in my own book I have consulted and cited multiple editions. Chopin's letters, which constitute the most important primary source for my research, have been collected and published in various editions since the beginning of the twentieth century. I have relied on two editions in English: Arthur Hedley's, an abridged collection based on Bronislaw E. Sydow's *Fryderyk Chopin's Correspondence* of 1955; and E. L. Voynich's, which is translated from the collection by Henryk Opieński and first published in 1931 as *Chopin's Letters*; and the original and definitive Sydow edition, published in three volumes by *La Revue musicale*, in collaboration with Suzanne and Denise Chainaye, Richard Masse, Éd., in French: *Correspondance de Frédéric Chopin*. Unless otherwise indicated, translated excerpts from that edition are my own. All of George Sand's letters have not yet been published in English. The bulk of quotations I've used from her letters are attributed in the notes to various books, collections, and articles, except in cases where I have translated the letters myself from the multivolume edition in French published by Éditions Garnier Frères, Georges Lubin, editor. I have relied on two English translations of Sand's travel memoir *Winter in Majorca*, one by Robert Graves and the other by Sara Wood.

The distance of time, nuances in language and translation, and corrections made after a work was published have all guided my decisions about which source to use. Each note specifies the edition cited.

Notes

Introduction: Bull's-eye

xvii *"he hits some kind of bull's-eye in my soul"*: Hofstadter, *Metamagical Themas*, p. 191.

xviii *"poised on the brink of atonality"*: Paul Badura-Skoda, "Chopin and Musical Structure," *The Chopin Companion*, p. 247.

xviii *"The left hand and the right hand"*: Chopin to Julian Fontana, August 8, 1839, *Selected Correspondence of Fryderyk Chopin*, Hedley p. 180.

xix *"what to do with a brick"*: Wesley Morris, "Her Rigorous Prose Inhabited Our Minds and Had Us Riveted," *New York Times*, August 7, 2019, https://www .nytimes.com/2019/08/07/books/toni-morrison-death-remembrance.html.

xix *an E natural*: For those with the score handy, this happens in measure 40–41 of the third movement of Opus 35. All citations are from the Jan Ekier Urtext PWM National Edition, published by the Foundation for the National Edition of the Works of Fryderyk Chopin. The Opus 35 volume is no. 10, "Sonaty Op. 35, 58," edited by Jan Ekier and Paweł Kamiński.

xix *her last breath*: Duke Ellington's "Black and Tan Fantasy" on YouTube: https:// youtu.be/uLJmgzMnOjQ. The quotation from Chopin's *Funeral March* begins around 14:50. Links to musical works in the text can be found on the companion website at WhyChopin.com.

xx *riffed on one of Chopin's Preludes*: Mieczysław Kosz, Prelude in C minor, from

Chopin's Preludes, Op. 28, no. 20, on YouTube: https://www.youtube.com/watch ?v=59khC-2TImo.

xx   *Polish jazz history*: Jacek Borowski, "Frédéric Chopin, Europe's first 'jazzman,'" "The First News," October 17, 2018, https://www.thefirstnews.com/article/frederic-chopin-europes-first-jazzman-2775.

xx   *"Chopin simply conquered our minds"*: Andrzej Jagodziński, liner notes to *Chopin Les Brillantes*," 2010. http://jagodzinski.art.pl/records/chopin-les-brillantes/#jp-carousel-770

xxiii   *"Chopin proposes, supposes"*: Gide, *Notes on Chopin*, p. 24.

xxv   *"Chopin seemed to be made of rubber"*: Niecks, *Frederick Chopin*, vol. II, p. 96. Niecks uses the word "caoutchouc" for rubber.

xxvii   *"or merely play the piano"*: Wilhelm von Lenz, "UÂàbersichtliche Beurtheilung der Pianoforte-Kompositionen von Chopin," *Neue Berliner Musikzeitung* 26 (1872), p. 289, quoted in Eigeldinger, *Chopin: Pianist and Teacher*, p. 86.

Chapter One: In a Word, Poland

1   *In a Word, Poland*: This phrase comes at the end of a letter by Chopin to Julian Fontana, a fellow Pole, composer, and pianist, who was Chopin's chief copyist and general factotum until he departed for the United States in the early 1840s. Dated April 4, 1848, it refers to the latest wave of political unrest spreading across Europe. The full quotation is: "You can see that all this breathes war, but no one knows where it will break out. If it does begin, the whole of Germany will be involved. The Italians have started already—Milan has kicked out the Austrians, but they still hold on to the provinces and will fight back. France will certainly help for she must take the opportunity to clear out a lot of scum from her territory. The Russians are sure to have trouble on their own hands if they make the slightest move towards Prussia. The Galician peasants have shown the way to those of Volhynia and Podolia, and the whole business will not be settled without frightful happenings. But at the end of it all is Poland, holy, great—in a word, Poland." Hedley, *Selected Correspondence of Fryderyk Chopin*, pp. 311–12

1   *"All the contemporary assaults upon society"*: Hugo, *Les Misérables*, p. 566.

6   *an army of Mongol warriors*: For the most trusted accounts of the legend of the Heynał Mariacki I've relied on two books by historian Norman Davies: *God's Playground*, vol. 1, pp. 71–72, and *Europe*, p. 365.

Notes

6 *the first mention of an hourly bugle call*: Marek Kępa, "Fact vs Fiction," Adam Mickiewicz Institute, Culture.pl, https://culture.pl/en/article/the-hejnal-trumpet-call-of-krakow-fact-vs-fiction?.

6 *"the longest running serial broadcast"*: Ibid.

6 *"the irruption of his horsemen"*: Davies, *Europe,* p. 365.

6 *"This country," Davies wrote*: Davies, *God's Playground,* vol. 1, p. vi.

7 *"annihilated . . . in cold blood"*: Ibid, p. 386.

7 *"With respect to us"*: Quoted in Mikołaj Gliński, "When Poland Was Nowhere: Foreigners Reflect on the Partitions and a Stateless Nation," Adam Mickiewicz Institute, Culture.pl, August 3, 2017, https://culture.pl/en/article/when-poland-was-nowhere-foreigners-reflect-on-the-partitions-a-stateless-nation.

8 *"We swear to each other"*: Davies, *God's Playground,* p. 126.

8 *"Satanic Trinity"* Adam Mickiewicz, quoted in Koropeckyj, *Books of the Polish Nation,* p. 197.

8 *"abnormal" history*: Miłosz, p. 200.

9 *"Poland was now an Idea"*: Davies, *God's Playground,* vol. II, p. 8.

9 *"people who have in them"*: Wikipedia, "Poland is Not Yet Lost" entry, footnote 2, Pałłasz, Edward. "The Polish National Anthem," Poland—Official Promotional Website of the Republic of Poland. Warsaw, PL: Ministry of Foreign Affairs. Archived from the original on 23 February 2013, retrieved March 7, 2013. https://en.wikipedia.org/wiki/Poland_Is_Not_Yet_Lost#cite_note-MFAoP-2.

9 *"through his music he imparted Poland"*: Goldberg, ed., *The Age of Chopin: Interdisciplinary Inquiries,* p. 84.

10 *according to one historian*: Orlando Figes, *The Crimean War: A History* (New York: Metropolitan Books, 2010), p. 79.

10 *"play the piano, have a good cry"*: Letter to Jan Matuszyński from Vienna, Christmas Day, 1830, in Hedley, *Selected Correspondence of Fryderyk Chopin,* p. 77.

11 *"Graves behind me"*: Ibid, p. 74.

11 *in the hands of the Muscovites*: Chopin's Album, entry dated Stuttgart, After 8 September 1831, quoted in Hedley, *Selected Correspondence of Fryderyk Chopin,* pp. 89–91.

11 *"beyond ten frontiers"*: Ibid, p. 89.

11 *"I pour out my grief on the piano"*: Chopin's "Stuttgart Diary," after September 8, 1831, Masse, ed., *Correspondance de Frédéric Chopin,* vol. I, p. 283.

Notes

12   *"a bliss of ambiguities"*: Bernstein, *The Unanswered Questions*, p. 211.

12   *For scholar Jim Samson*: Samson, *Chopin*, p. 75.

13   *"Important Autographs and Manuscripts"*: the source for details of the auction is the author's copy of the original catalog.

14   *acquired at the auction for $1,500*: this information was provided to me in an email by the Librarian at Grolier Club in New York City.

14   *low A flat that is intoned eleven times in a row*: Eigeldinger, *Chopin: Pianist and Teacher*, footnote no. 197, p. 157.

15   *"night winds sweeping over churchyard graves"*: Anton Rubinstein, *Music and its Masters: A Conversation*, 2nd ed., trans. Mrs. John P. Morgan, 2nd Edition, London: Augener and Co., p. 56.

16   *"Forgive me, dear Mr. Fryderyk"*: Chopin's *Letters,* Mme. Teresa Wodzińska to Chopin, February 28, 1835, Hedley, p. 125.

16   *"Goodbye, remember us"*: This quotation comes from Bernard Gavoty's *Chopin* (p. 189), a biography that has been challenged for accuracy on other points by some scholars, and the story may well be apocryphal. For her part, Maria ended up in an unhappy marriage that was soon annulled by the court of Rome.

17   *"passive nature"*: *Maria: une idylle d'amour en musique: Chopin à Maria Wodzińska,* première publication en facsimile du manuscrit de Chopin par Kornelia Parnas; version française de Gaston Knosp, Leipzig: Breitkopf & Härtel, 1910.

17   *"It is useless"*: Ganche, *Frédéric Chopin*, p. 186.

17   *"a lioness"*: William G. Atwood, *The Lioness and the Little One: The Liaison of George Sand and Frédéric Chopin* (New York: Columbia University Press, 1980), p. 44.

17   *"double chin, like a canon of the church"*: Gavoty, *Chopin*, p. 192.

17   *"Is she really a woman?"*: Samson, *Chopin*, p. 134.

18   *"her work is an immense legal plea"*: Gavoty, *Frederic Chopin*, p. 232.

18   *"as good as married"* George Sand's letter to Albert Grzymała, in Hedley, *Selected Correspondence of Fryderyk Chopin*, pp. 151–61.

19   *"When the heart, the mind, and the body"* Reid, *George Sand*, p. 62.

19   *"the chain beneath which my life"*: Quoted in Cate, *George Sand*, p. 195.

21   *We have suffered "thunderbolt"*: "Chopin: A Discourse, by Ignacy Jan Paderewski," trans. Laurence Alma Tadema, *Polish Music Journal*, vol. 4, no. 2, Winter 2001, https://polishmusic.usc.edu/research/publications/polish-music-journal/vol4no2/paderewski-on-chopin/.

22 *"He may lie there"*: FDR quoted in the U.S. Congressional Record, Senate Resolution 296, June 28, 2002.

23 *" 'We'll make Poland great again' "*: James Traub, "The Party That Wants to Make Poland Great Again," *New York Times*, November 2, 2016.

23 *"it was thanks to his music"*: Radio Poland, February 25, 2018, "Warsaw Concert Marks 200th Anniversary of Chopin's Debut," http://archiwum.thenews.pl/1/11/Artykul/351080.

24 *"Poles are born with Chopin"*: Malgorzata Bloch-Wisniewska, quoted in Tom Hundley, "Poles Gaga Over Chopin Competition," *Chicago Tribune*, October 18, 1995, https://www.chicagotribune.com/news/ct-xpm-1995-10-18-9510180258-story.html.

Chapter Two: Pianopolis

26 *"Poland for ever!"*: Hugo, *Les Misérables*, p. 933.

26 *"You find here the greatest splendor"*: Chopin to Alfons Kumelski, November 18, 1831, in Hedley, *Selected Correspondence of Fryderyk Chopin*, p. 93.

26 *"Paris is whatever you care"*: Chopin to Titus Woyciehowski, December 12, 1831, in Hedley, *Selected Correspondence of Fryderyk Chopin*, p. 97-98.

27 *"we will set the human spirit free"*: Tresch, *The Romantic Machine*, p. 224.

27 *"literally wired together"*: McCullough, *The Greater Journey*, p. 156.

28 *the ballerina's tutu*: Laurent Pelly in the DVD extra with cast interviews, *Giacomo Meyerbeer: The Legacy of* Robert le Diable, the Royal Opera, London (Opus Arte, 2013), https://www.youtube.com/watch?v=3m29rD1ZqVU.

28 *"practically drowns the whole orchestra"*: Chopin to Titus Woyciechowski, December 12, 1831, Hedley, *Selected Correspondence of Fryderyk Chopin*, p. 100.

28 "Robert *was to grand opera"*: John Tresch, "The Prophet and the Pendulum: Sensational Science and the Audiovisual Phantasmagoria around 1848," *Grey Room* 43 (Cambridge: Massachusetts Institute of Technology, spring 2011), p. 24.

29 *he was a sophisticated polymath*: Pollens, *Bartolomeo Cristofori and the Invention of the Piano*, pp. 2–4.

29 *But the harpsichord*: Harpsichords with multiple keyboards, or manuals, of course have a broader range of sound.

29 *In a pianoforte*: The original name was *gravecembalo di piano e forte*, later called *fortepiano* and eventually *pianoforte*.

30 *He added more tension*: Wendy Powers, "The Pianofortes of Bartolomeo Cristo-fori," Metropolitan Museum of Art, 2003, http://www.metmuseum.org/toah/hd/cris/hd_cris.htm.

32 *referred to a crucial part of the mechanism*: Arthur Loesser, *Men, Women and Pianos* (New York: 1990), p. 31.

33 *"a sound with a basically dark hue"*: Villa Medici Giuliani, *Chopin e il suono di Pleyel*, pp. 235–35, quoted in Walker, *Chopin*, p. 269.

33 *"silvery and slightly veiled sonority"*: Franz Liszt, quoted in Eigeldinger, *Chopin: Pianist and Teacher*, p. 25.

33 *"I need a Pleyel"*: Ibid., p. 26.

36 *compared to a sewing machine*: Kelly, *Early Music*, p. 51.

36 *each heritage was reflected in the instruments*: Edmund Michael Frederick, in Siek, *A Dictionary for the Modern Pianist*, Appendix C, "Historical Pianos and Their Relationship to the Standard Repertoire," pp. 259–63.

37 *maximizing the volume of sound*: Miles Chapin, *88 Keys*, pp. 76–77.

38 *"those bells and whistles"*: Jan Swafford, "In Search of Lost Sounds: Why You've Never Really Heard the 'Moonlight' Sonata," *Slate* magazine, March 2, 2010, http://www.slate.com/articles/arts/music_box/2010/03/in_search_of_lost_sounds.html.

39 *around thirty-five in Mozart's day*: Craig White, Yale University, Coursera on-line course: "Introduction to Classical Music," week 6, "The Classical Era," https://www.coursera.org/learn/introclassicalmusic/home/week/6.

39 *"at least" four harps*: Philip, *The Classical Music Lover's Companion to Orchestral Music*, p. 100.

40 *"proposes, supposes, insinuates, seduces"*: Gide, *Notes on Chopin*, p. 24.

40 *"it is being said everywhere"*: Chopin to his family, August 12, 1829, *Chopin's Letters*, Opienski, p. 54.

40 *"Hats off, gentlemen, a genius!"*: Robert Schumann, review of Chopin's Variations on Mozart's "Là ci darem la mano," *Allgemeine Musikalische Zeitung*, December 7, 1831, reproduced in Pianostreet.com, 2010, http://www.pianostreet.com/blog/files/schumann-article-on-chopin-opus-2.pdf.

40 *"entirely new way of expressing himself"*: François-Joseph Fétis, *Revue musicale*, March 3, 1832, quoted in Samson, p. 83.

41 *removed himself from the arena*: Eigeldinger, *Chopin: Pianist and Teacher*, p. 392.

41 *"I am not at all fit"*: Niecks, *Frederick Chopin*, vol. 1, p. 283.

41 *"without candles or audience"*: George Sand, quoted in Walker, *Chopin*, p. 438.

41 *"Concerts are never real music"*: Eigeldinger, *Chopin: Pianist and Teacher*, p. 110.

41 *"operas must make you immortal"*: Chopin's sister Ludwika to her brother, November 27, 1831, in Hedley, *Selected Correspondence of Fryderyk Chopin*, p. 96.

41 *Chopin "will not rise any higher"*: Robert Schuman, quoted in Kallberg, "Small 'Forms': In Defense of the Prelude," in Samson, ed., *The Cambridge Companion to Chopin*, p. 132.

41 *"inborn genius"*: Ludwika Chopin to Frédéric, November 27, 1831, quoting from a conversation she had with Elsner. *Selected Correspondence of Fryderyk Chopin*, Hedley, p. 96.

42 *"As I journey through this 'vale of tears'"*: Józef Elsner to Chopin in Paris, September 14, 1834, in Hedley, *Selected Correspondence of Fryderyk Chopin*, p. 124.

42 *"my perhaps too audacious"*: Chopin to Józef Elsner in Warsaw, December 14, 1831, in Hedley, *Selected Correspondence of Fryderyk Chopin*, p. 103–4.

42 *"my little trumpet piece"*: Edwin Hughes, "A Master Lesson: Mendelssohn's Scherzo in E Minor," *The Etude: Presser's Music Magazine*, October 1916, p. 711.

42 *"embraces the range"*: Franz Liszt, from *Revue et gazette musicale de Paris,* V/6, February 11, 1838, pp. 57–62, quoted in Eigeldinger, *Chopin as Pianist and Teacher*, p. 20.

43 *Beethoven, one contemporary critic observed*: Goldberg and Bellman, *Chopin and his World*, "Chopin Among the Pianists in Paris," by Sandra P. Rosenblum, p. 278. The critic was Fétis.

44 *"If you don't hear it"*: Jonathan Bellman, pre-concert talk, "Chopin and His World," at the Bard SummerScape festival, Annandale-on-Hudson, New York, August 18, 2017.

45 *"He gave a noble, manly energy:"* Eigeldinger, *Chopin: Pianist and Teacher*, pp. 275–76.

46 *the waning "cult of Chopin"*: The Fryderyk Chopin Institute and Medici.TV, "History of the Competition" (2015), http://chopin2015.medici.tv/en/page/the-competition.

46 *"Poles Gaga over Chopin Competition"*: Tom Hundley, "Poles Gaga over Chopin Competition," *Chicago Tribune*, October 18, 1995, https://www.chicagotribune.com/news/ct-xpm-1995-10-18-9510180258-story.html.

47 *"the original color and mechanics"*: "About the Competition," the Fryderyk Chopin Institute, http://www.iccpi.pl/en/competition.

47 *"modern piano companies will be angry with me"*: Aleksander Laskowski, spokesperson for the 1st International Chopin Competition on Period Instruments, "Rediscovering Music of Chopin Played on Period Instruments," Telewizja Polksa, August 9, 2018, https://polandin.com/38906486/video-rediscovering-music-of-chopin-played-on-period-instruments-full-interview.

48 *"worth more than forty novels"*: George Sand to Eugène Delacroix, quoted in Samson, *Chopin*, p. 198.

49 *"barking" or "a pigeon-hunt"*: Eigeldinger, *Chopin: Pianist and Teacher*, pp. 26, 32.

50 *"help you read the composer's text"*: Monika Scislowska, Associated Press interview with Tomasz Ritter, September 21, 2018, https://apnews.com/cfcfdd77d6e74b8da199e8b9fbefae5b.

Chapter Three: Teach with Love

53 *we contain multitudes*: Peter Pesic made this observation in an interview with Corinna da Fonseca-Wollheim, "Does Brahms's Obsession with Rhythmic Instability Explain His Music's Magic," *New York Times*, October 19, 2018, https://www.nytimes.com/2018/10/19/arts/music/brahms-92y-ohlsson-mark-morris.html.

53 *the tale inspired parts*: Letellier, *Meyerbeer's* Robert le Diable, pp. 46–52.

53 *"a frightening but powerful"*: Chopin to his family in Warsaw, August 26, 1829, in Hedley, *Selected Correspondence of Fryderyk Chopin*, p. 31.

54 *"little fantastic drama"*: Sand, *The Seven Strings of the Lyre,* letter to Christine Buloz, August 8, 1838, Introduction by George Kennedy, p. 16.

54 *"harmonies of the upper world"*: Sand, *Seven Strings of the Lyre*, p. 172.

54 *Helen, a powerless woman surrounded by men*: I am building here on an observation made by scholar Rachel Corkle in "Language and Music in Dialogue," *George Sand Studies* 31 (2012), p. 119.

55 *"born in music"*: Reid, *George Sand*, p. 16.

56 *"a good fellow"*: Chopin to his family in Warsaw, August 19, 1829, in Opieński, *Chopin's Letters*, p. 58

56 *"whether any use can be made of it"*: *Chopin's Letters*, Albert Grzymała to Auguste Léo, October 1849, Hedley, p. 375.

57 *It was Swiss musicologist Jean-Jacques Eigeldinger*: John Rink, in his review of Eigeldinger's *Esquisses pour une méthode de piano*, discusses the history of Chopin's *méthode* and notes that while he has great enthusiasm for Eigeldinger's achievement, "obviously the reconstruction is hypothetical and by no means definitive." *Music & Letters* vol. 75, no. 3 (August 1994), pp. 471–75, https://www.jstor.org/stable/737367.

57 *"runic scrawl"*: Kallberg, "Chopin and the Aesthetic of the Sketch: A New Prelude in E Flat Minor?," from "Early Music," August 2001, p. 414.

58 *"The pen burns my fingers"*: Chopin to Wojciech Grzymała, September 4, 1848, in *Correspondance de Frédéric Chopin*, p. 385.

58 *"the most heartbreaking labor"*: Sand, *Story of My Life*, Thelma Jurgrau, ed., p. 1108.

59 *first known example*: This refers to Girolamo Diruta, *Il Transilvano Dialogo*, written in Venice around 1600. The "ladder of lines" first appears on p. 6. In *Famous Pianists and Their Technique*, Reginald R. Gerig describes this work as "the earliest clavier method of any real importance" (p. 11).

59 *already a piano cliché*: Loesser, *Men, Women and Pianos*, p. 372.

59 *"You must sing"*: Eigeldinger, *Chopin: Pianist and Teacher*, p. 45.

59 *"For a long time"*: Ibid., p. 195.

59 *a source of great variety*: Ibid., p. 17.

60 *You must "caress the key"*: Ibid., p. 31.

60 *"For the first time in the history"*: Walker, *Chopin*, p. 249.

60 *During the period when he was drafting*: Chopin's pencil markings for fingering appear in the Jane Stirling edition of Chopin's autograph manuscript for Opus 35, p. 15, m5, held in the Bibliothèque Nationale de France, Rés. VMA.241 (IV, 35).

61 *"another new, simple way"*: Eigeldinger, *Chopin as Pianist and Teacher*, p. 45.

62 *What concerned Chopin most*: Eigeldinger, *Chopin: Pianist and Teacher*, p. 29.

62 *"We have to do this to see how the rose is built"*: Rafael Cortés, in an interview with the author. For a more detailed discussion of his philosophy about technique see *A Pianist: Wanderings of the Mind and Spirit, Essays on Music and Life* (New York: Cortes-Colon Impromptus, 2011).

62 *"attain[ing] this souplesse"*: Eigeldinger, *Chopin: Pianist and Teacher*, p. 45.

62 *"Ideally," he says, we don't want to "hear"*: Tommasini, *The Indispensable Composers*, pp. 214–15.

Notes

63   *a bold, diagonal slash*: One student who reported receiving these oblique strokes across the staff was Camille Dubois-O'Meara. Eigeldinger, *Chopin: Pianist and Teacher*, p. 112, footnote 79.

63   *"The wrist: respiration in the voice"*: Eigeldinger, *Chopin: Pianist and Teacher*, p. 40. In a footnote (number 80, p. 113) Eigeldinger clarifies that this statement does not appear in the Lehman manuscript and was written in isolation on a page presumably detached before Cortot acquired it in 1936.

63   *by teachers whose own legacies*: Cortés's other main teachers were: Lillian Freundlich, a student of Joseph and Rosina Levine, exponents of the Russian tradition; Roland Keller, a student of Ludwig Hoffman in Germany; and German Diez, a student of and assistant to Chilean pianist Claudio Arrau, who himself studied with Martin Kraus, a student of Liszt.

66   *"head, hands and heart"*: From the biography of Johann Heinrich Pestalozzi at http://www.jhpestalozzi.org and *The New World Encyclopedia*, https://www.newworldencyclopedia.org/entry/Johann_Heinrich_Pestalozzi.

66   *Pestalozzi banned flogging*: Mark K. Smith, "Johann Heinrich Pestalozzi: Pedagogy, Education and Social Justice," Infed.com, http://infed.org/mobi/johann-heinrich-pestalozzi-pedagogy-education-and-social-justice/.

66   *He encouraged young people*: Ibid.

66   *"Let the child be as free as possible"*: Postman, *Building a Bridge to the Eighteenth Century*, p. 156.

66   *"The more ingenious our tools"*: Jean-Jacques Rousseau, *Emile, or On Education*, un-paginated e-book version.

66   *let her observe*: Rousseau didn't, of course, use the pronoun *her* in *Emile*, but I surmise he would have come around to it eventually.

67   *"Only then does the hearing function"*: Eigeldinger, *Chopin: Pianist and Teacher*, p. 28.

67   *"We each understand this [piece] differently"*: Chopin to Carl Filtsch, Ibid., p. 13.

67   *"Why do you play less well today?"*: Chopin to Friederike Streicher-Müller, from her memoir referring to a *soirée* on December 20, 1840, in Eigeldinger, *Chopin: Pianist and Teacher*, p. 12.

67   *"Forget you're being listened to"*: Emilie von Gretsch in a letter dated April 30, 1844, in Eigeldinger, *Chopin: Pianist and Teacher*, p. 12.

67   *"I think he can read hearts"*: Emilie von Gretsch in a letter dated May 20, 1844, in Eigeldinger, *Chopin: Pianist and Teacher*, p. 13.

68 *"teach with love"*: Goldberg writes about Pestalozzi in her invaluable book *Music in Chopin's Warsaw* and used the phrase "teach with love" during a panel discussion I attended at the Bard SummerScape's "Chopin and His World" festival in August 2017.

68 *"Leave him in peace"*: Anatole Leikin, "The Sonatas," in Samson, *The Cambridge Companion to Chopin*, pp. 166–67.

68 *Whereas the young Franz Liszt*: Eigeldinger, *Chopin: Pianist and Teacher*, pp. 12–13

69 *"a tyrant commands"*: Chopin to Gutmann re: Nocturne op. 48, no.2 in F-sharp minor, in Eigeldinger, *Chopin: Pianist and Teacher*, p. 81, mm 57–100.

69 *"No noises, no 'effects'"*: Eigeldinger, *Chopin: Pianist and Teacher*, p. 54.

69 *"I indicate," he said; "it's up to the listener"*: Eigeldinger, *Chopin: Pianist and Teacher*, p. 128. The anecdote about the performance of *Hamlet* appears on p. 79.

70 *"a new genre of* acrobatics*"*: Ibid., p. 193.

70 *don't "teach us how to play the* music *itself"*: Ibid., p. 23.

70 *"Put all your soul into it!"*: Ibid., p. 15.

Chapter Four: Interlude with a Vampire

71 *"live with her husband"*: This quotation is from a petition filed by women against Article 214 of the Napoleonic Code, published in the *Gazette des femmes* in August 1836, and quoted by Moses in *French Feminism in the 19th Century*, p. 104.

71 *"superb and unabridged independence"*: Reid, *George Sand*, p. 70.

74 *"the most hideous fishwife"*: Muhlstein, *A Taste for Freedom*, p. 42.

74 *"courageous gaiety"*: Muhlstein, *A Taste for Freedom*, p. 67.

74 *"fatal box"*: Custine uses this term in recounting the story in Muhlstein, *Letters from Russia*, p. 36.

74 *Over the years she took many lovers*: Sand, *Story of My Life*, p. 1151.

75 *"My first sentiment"*: Custine, *Letters from Russia*, p. 25.

75 *"the Revolution had robbed Custine"*: Custine, *Letters from Russia*, p. x–xi.

76 *"the sound of Paris"*: Muhlstein, *A Taste for Freedom*, p. 220.

77 *"To change one's country"*: Custine, *Letters From Russia*, p. 68.

77 *In traveling to England . . . for example*: Ibid., p. 178.

77 *the "spirit of hostility"*: Ibid., p. 180.

78 *"If ever your sons"*: Custine, *Letters from Russia,* p. 654.

78 *Banned in Russia*: This case is made by Steven Erlanger in "Word for Word / The Marquis de Custine; A Long-Ago Look at Russia: (So What Else is New?), *New York Times,* June 16, 1996, https://www.nytimes.com/1996/06 /16/weekinreview/word-for-word-marquis-de-custine-long-ago-look-russia -so-what-else-new.html.

79 *"One is alone with you in the midst of a crowd"*: Astolphe de Custine to Chopin, dated after February 16, 1848, Paris, in Hedley, *Selected Correspondence of Fryderyk Chopin,* p. 307.

79 *"on the human soul"*: Astolphe de Custine to Chopin, April 27, 1841, in Hedley, *Selected Correspondence of Fryderyk Chopin,* pp. 193–94.

79 deep *"sense of* gratitude*"*: Astolphe de Custine to Chopin, June 28, 1849, in Hedley, *Selected Correspondence of Fryderyk Chopin,* pp. 189–90.

79 *Sophie Gay*: Gay is another colorful, entrepreneurial figure in Custine's orbit, treasured by him for offering what he most needed: "independence and friendship." Anka Muhlstein further credits her with having "invented an entirely new profession for herself: that of literary agent," *A Taste for Freedom,* p. 88.

80 *The original source of the letter*: Luppé, *Astolphe de Custine,* p. 202.

80 *The Largo is based*: Mieczysław Tomaszewski, Fryderyk Chopin Institute, Compositions, "Largo in E flat major," http://en.chopin.nifc.pl/chopin/composition /detail/name/largo/id/135.

80 *"God, Save Poland"*: Lyrics quoted from the Polish Music Center at the University of South California, https://polishmusic.usc.edu/research/national- anthems/boze-cos-polske/.

80 *the Polonaise has long been regarded*: Mieczysław Tomaszewski, Fryderyk Chopin Institute, Compositions, "Polonaise in A major, Op. 40, No. 1," http://en .chopin.nifc.pl/chopin/composition/detail/id/236.

80 *"funeral marches that, despite myself"*: In his fascinating article about the compositional roots of the funeral march, "Chopin's March, Chopin's Death," Jeffrey Kallberg suggests (on p. 14) that Custine's use of the plural, "marches," could signify that Chopin played his first funeral march, discussed in Chapter Six, during this evening too.

81 *even while it has been cited*: The letter was first cited in Luppé, *Astolphe de Custine,* p. 202.

81 *"incomprehensible"* . . . *powerful* . . . *"genius"*: Astolphe de Custine to Sophie

Gay, s. l. [October 15, 1838]. This letter is held in a private collection in the archive of Julien-Frédéric Tarn, Custine's primary biographer and author of *Le Marquis de Custine, ou Les malheurs de l'exactitude*, Paris: Fayard, 1985. A copy was made available to me in the original French; the translation is mine.

81 *"I needn't have bothered keeping Frédéric"*: Gavoty, *Frederic Chopin*, p. 288, footnote.

Chapter Five: *Toujours Travailler* Bach

83 *"a domineering, cigarette-smoking"*: Robert Graves, "Historical Summary," in Sand, *Winter in Majorca*, Graves edition, p. 177.

83 *News of the scandal*: Ibid.

84 *"not only as moral"*: Ibid., p. 180.

84 *"search of mystery and solitude"*: *A Winter in Mallorca,* Sara Wood, translator, referenced from chapter 4 of a not-yet-published manuscript.

84 *Maurice, fresh from his studies*: Walker, *Chopin*, p. 371.

84 *"Paradise – if you can stand it!"*: Paul Theroux, *The Pillars of Hercules: A Grand Tour of the Mediterranean* (New York: Fawcett / Random House, 1995), p. 56.

85 *"the black vapors with which so seductive a mouth"*: Graves, "Historical Summary," in Sand, *Winter in Majorca*, Graves edition, p. 199.

85 *an "El Dorado of Art"*: Sand, *Winter in Mallorca*, Quetglas edition, Chapter I, unpaginated manuscript.

85 *a combination of "severity and grace"*: Sand, *Winter in Majorca*, Graves edition, p. 120.

86 *" 'Thanks be to God' "* Sand, *Winter in Mallorca*, Quetglas edition, part 3, chapter 1, unpaginated manuscript .

86 *the pieces Chopin worked on*: The record is not 100 percent clear on which pieces Chopin worked on or completed during the Majorca sojourn, and some works are less certain than others. The list I've included is based on the research and speculation of the most respected Chopin scholars. At the time of this writing there is no way to know for certain.

87 *"The sky is like turquoise"*: Chopin to Julian Fontana in Paris, November 15, 1838, in Hedley, *Selected Correspondance of Fryderyk Chopin*, p. 162.

87 *"all the flowers fell off the trees"*: Sand, *Winter in Majorca*, Graves edition, p. 45.

87 *"The first said I was going to die"*: Chopin to Julian Fontana in Paris, December 3, 1838, Masse, ed., *Correspondence de Frédéric Chopin*, vol. II, p. 274.

87   *Son Vent, or "house of wind"*: The longtime tradition of referring to the Establiments house as "Son Vent," as many scholars do, was challenged by Gabriel Quetglas, who clarified in an email me that it's a mistake to translate "Son Vent" in this manner. In Catalán, he explained, "Son" refers to a surname, but there is no known owner of the house in question named "Vent." "Is it a mystery, an exception, a mistake?" he wondered. But the house is indeed elevated and therefore exposed to the wind. "It makes sense," he concluded, even though it's not entirely accurate.

87   *"The damp settled like a cloak"*: Sand, *Winter in Majorca*, Graves edition, p.46.

89   *"I dream of music"*: Chopin to Camille Pleyel, November 21, 1838, *Correspondance de Frédéric Chopin*, vol. II, p. 271.

89   *"Meanwhile . . . my manuscripts sleep"*: Chopin to Julian Fontana, December 14, 1838, Hedley, p. 165.

89   *"every bump of his barrow"*: Sand, *Winter in Majorca*, Graves edition, pp. 95–96.

90   *"the best of Palma"*: Choussat, *Souvenirs*, pp. 110–14.

91   *"I am prepared to swear"*: Graves, *Majorca Observed*, p. 13.

91   *"It is well known that each country has a different tune"*: Sand, *Winter in Mallorca*, Quetglas edition, chapter 7

91   *when a great* influx: Parker, *Walking in Mallorca*, pp. 40–41.

92   *"This piercing clatter of wood"*: Sand, *Winter in Majorca*, Quetglas edition, part 3, chapter 1.

92   *she mailed the manuscripts*: Choussat, *Souvenirs*, p. 111.

92   *"cut our feet in pieces"*: Sand, *Winter in Majorca*, Graves, p. 152. Note that the translation of "somber" comes from the Quetglas translation of the same scene.

93   *"In Majorca alone I finally saw the sea"*: Sand, *Winter in Majorca*, Graves edition, p. 152.

93   *"limpid and blue as the sky"*: Sand, *Winter in Mallorca*, Quetglas edition, part 3, chapter 4.

93   *"the most stupid men in the world"*: Sand, *Winter in Majorca*, Graves, p. 152.

93   *"his eyes opened wide"*: Ibid.

94   *part of an eight-hundred-year tradition*: Poet, logician, mystic, and philosopher Ramon Llull established the monastic life in Majorca in Miramar, where he founded a monastery and a school of oriental languages in 1276. Llull is a fascinating figure whose contribution to modern science extends from the study of language to mathematics. At the age of thirty he dedicated himself to

converting Jews and Muslims to Christianity, but his method was not purely faith-based: he relied on logic and science, using the vernacular language—he's credited with writing the first major work of Catalán literature—to achieve a broader influence. Llull created a system of information based on numbers that was later cited by Leibniz and is today regarded as the initial building block of computational theory.

94 *A documentary crew followed him*: The documentary, *Nobuyuki Tsukii Visits Chopin's Residence in Majorca*, was made by NHK in 2010. The translation from Japanese was commissioned by me. The film is available online at https://www.dailymotion.com/video/x3id9mz.

95 *the man who kickstarted the profession*: Fred Strum, "Claude Montal," Grove Dictionary Online, September 22, 2015, https://doi.org/10.1093/gmo/9781561592630.article.L2286091.

96 *"bright and silvery"*: Eigeldinger, *Chopin: Pianist and Teacher*, pp. 91–92, footnote 7.

96 *until "the piece is perfectly in my body"*: Chiho Iuchi interview with Nobuyuki Tsukii, *Japan Times,* October 17, 2019, https://www.japantimes.co.jp/culture/2019/10/17/music/pianist-nobuyuki-tsujii-sets-bar-high-new-concert-series/#.Xc1_Iy2ZOup.

96 *(Chopin Competition winner) Stanislav Bunin*: Bunin, it's worth noting, played a selection of compositions for another role-playing video game about Chopin, *Eternal Sonata*, released for Xbox 360 and PlayStation 3 by the Japanese developer tri-Crescendo.

97 *As he grew older, though*: Interview with Kumi Matsumaru, "Stanislav Bunin Loves Touring Japan, Even After 20 Years," *Daily Yomiuri*, indexed in Trans-News Annex, https://transnews.exblog.jp/3259378/.

97 *the child's joy returned*: The story of Nobu's reaction to Stanislav Bunin is recounted in the documentary *Touching the Sound: The Improbable Journey of Nobuyuki Tsujii*, directed by Peter Rosen, 2014.

98 *"Very seldom do I close my notebook"*: Quoted in Barbara Rose Schuler, "Japanese Pianist Nobuyuki 'Nobu' Tsujii Opens Carmel Music Society Season," *Monterey Herald*, October 6, 2011, https://www.montereyherald.com/2011/10/06/barbara-rose-shuler-japanese-pianist-nobuyuki-nobu-tsujii-opens-carmel-music-society-season/.

98 *"He was absolutely miraculous"*: Michael Granberry, "Cliburn's Passing Calls to

Mind Nobuyuki Tsujii Winning the Fort Worth Competition," *Dallas Morning News*, February 27, 2013.

98   *"the shape of a tall coffin"*: Chopin to Julian Fontana, December 28, 1838, Opieński, *Chopin's Letters*, p. 188.

98   *the squall and the lullaby*: Gavoty, *Frederic Chopin*, p. 93.

99   *"beginnings of studies"*: Robert Schumann, review in *Neue Zeitschrift für Musik*, quoted in Gavoty, p. 394.

100 *"On seeing us come in"*: Sand, *Story of My Life*, 1091–92.

102 *"just a grain of sand"*: Chopin to Julian Fontana, December 28, 1838, Opieński, *Chopin's Letters*, p. 189.

102 *"visions of dead monks"*: Sand, *Story of My Life*, p. 1091.

103 *"Between the cliffs and the sea"*: Chopin to Fontana, December 28, 1838, Hedley, *Selected Correspondence of Fryderyk Chopin*, p. 165.

104 *one of the delights of twenty-first-century life*: More about Stephen Malinowksi's work can be found at Musanim.com; his animated playlist of Bach's *Well-Tempered Clavier*, performed by pianist Kimiko Ishizaka, can be found on YouTube: https://www.youtube.com/playlist?list=PLtj_HurkS7ZyzWU6_fl H9RG2K2E1tWd1f.

105 *"among Chopin's most radical conceptions"*: Samson, *Chopin*, p. 157.

105 *either as a spark for improvisation*: This observation is made by Kallberg in "Small 'Forms': In Defence of the Prelude," in Samson, *The Cambridge Companion to Chopin*, p. 143

105 *"a remarkably innovatory"*: Samson, *Chopin*, p. 142.

106 *"absolute low point"*: Wolff, *Bach: The Learned Musician*, p. 184.

106 *of his professional life*: Keith Jarrett also produced one of the most influential works in the repertoire for solo piano on a lousy instrument in less-than-ideal conditions: *The Köln Concert*. Jarrett hadn't slept for two nights and was suffering from acute back pain when he arrived at the concert hall in Cologne, Germany, in January 1975 and found the wrong piano on stage. It was "tinny," didn't have the tonal range he wanted, and the pedals didn't work properly. Nevertheless he agreed to go ahead with the recital, sleep-deprived and wearing a back brace, in a performance that began at 11:30 p.m. at the Köln Opera House. The recording of his improvisations went on to become one of the bestselling albums in jazz history. In the documentary *The Art of Improvisation*, the head of ECM records, Manfred Eicher, reflects that Jarrett

played the way he did that night *because* the piano was so deficient: "Because he could not fall in love with the sound of it, he found another way to get the most out of it," adapting both his technique and artistry to the instrument at hand. Jarrett later reflected that, despite everything, he had a feeling of total trust in his own imagination, something I feel certain both Bach and Chopin shared.

106 *"sufficient for a lifetime"*: Franz Liszt, *Liszt's Chopin*, trans. Hughes, p. 126.

107 *a square instrument with a tiny sound*: In *Autour Des 24 Préludes de Frédéric Chopin* (page 27, footnote 23), Jean-Jacques Eigeldinger addresses the dispute over "the Mallorquin piano," clarifying the Valldemossa museum's position that the piano Chopin used before his Pleyel arrived was possibly a square instrument made by the Palma firm of Melchor Oliver y Suau, but it certainly was not a vertical piano, and was neither the Juan Bauza piano owned by Wanda Landowska nor the instrument made by Oliver Suau Hermanos of *Celda* No. 2. More about this can be found in the *"Saber Mas"* section of the museum's website, under *"Curiosidades,"* in *"Piano Fabricado Por Juan Bauza Propriedad de Wanda Landowska,"* http://www.celdadechopin.es/sabermas .php.

Chapter Six: Pulling out the Pickaxe

110 *Vive la France!*: Sand, *Winter in Majorca*, Graves edition, p. 165.

111 *"But this is what you are"*: Sand, *Gabriel*, p. 32.

111 *"Everything binds and stifles me"*: A century later, in a novel many believe was influenced by Sand's *Gabriel*, Virginia Woolf has her eponymous hero Orlando similarly complain: "Lord . . . these skirts are plaguey things to have about one's heels." (New York: Harcourt Brace Jovanovich, 1928), p. 154.

114 *"found the physical act of lovemaking"*: Cate, *George Sand*, p. 483.

115 *"a strange outer space"*: Chopin to his family, July 20, 1845, Opieński, *Chopin's Letters*, pp. 284–85.

115 *"Chopin is still up and down"*: Sand to Charlotte Marliani, August 24, 1839, *Correspondance de Frédéric Chopin*, vol. II, p. 351.

115 *"We are as happy as children"*: Chopin to Albert Grzmata, end of June 1839, *Correspondance de Frédéric Chopin*, vol. 2, p. 344.

115 *"he is enchanting us"*: Sand to Marliani, July 4, 1839, *Correspondance de Frédéric Chopin*, vol. 2, p. 344.

116   *"pul[ling] out the pickax"*: Reid, *George Sand*, p. 182.

117   *the same convent where Sand herself*: Walter D. Gray, "Historical Introduction," in Sand, *Story of My Life*, pp. 46–47; it was the Couvent des Anglaises.

117   *"You betrayed me, you lied to me"*: Cate, *George Sand*, p. 130.

117   *"my frame, the garment"*: Sand, author's "Notice," in *Valentine*, Paris, March 27, 1852, p. 2.

118   *"I now fancy myself"*: Sand to Charlotte Marliani, June 3, 1839, *Correspondance, 1812–1874*, p. 145.

119   *"a once in a lifetime show"*: Asher Miller, associate curator, Department of European Paintings, The Metropolitan Museum of Art, during the press preview for *Delacroix*, September 12, 2018.

119   *his breakout work*: The painting is the 1824 *Scenes from the Massacres at Chios*.

119   *"Monsieur Delacroix rushes headlong"*: Allard and Fabre, *Delacroix*, p. 19.

119   *"Everything here is harsh"*: Marie Mély-Janin, *La quotidienne*, September 12, 1824, quoted in Sébastien Allard and Côme Fabre, *Delacroix*, p. 19.

120   *"pieces of nature, such as they present"*: Delacroix, letter to Constant Dutilleux, February 6, 1849, p. 287.

120   *Delacroix was fascinated with botany*: This observation was made to me by Colta Ives, curator of the *Public Parks and Private Gardens* show in a private conversation during the Metropolitan Museim of Art's press preview, March 5, 2018.

121   *"behind the row of tall windows"*: Wharton, *A Motor-Flight Through France*, p. 80.

123   *"endless tête-à-têtes with Chopin"*: Letter to J.-B. Pierret, June 7, 1842, Delacroix, *Selected Letters*, p. 243.

124   *"a sonata without sonata form"* Andras Schiff, "Beethoven Lecture-Recitals," part 4, on the Piano Sonata in A-flat major, op. 26, https://wigmore-hall.org.uk/podcasts/andras-schiff-beethoven-lecture-recitals.

124   *an arrangement for men's chorus and solo piano*: "Beethoven's *Begräbniss*," arrangement of the third movement of Opus 26 by Ignaz von Seyfried, for men's chorus and piano, set to a text by Alois Jeitteles (published by Tobias Haslinger, 1827). Digital Collections, King Library Special Collections: http://digitalcollections.sjlibrary.org/cdm/ref/collection/sjsuLVBee/id/659.

124   *the only work of Beethoven's*: Andras Schiff, "Beethoven Lecture-Recitals," part 4

125   *theme music from the film* A Clockwork Orange: Wendy Carlos, https://vimeo
.com/179941656.

126   *"almost bereft of melody"*: Monelle, *The Musical Topic*, p. 127.

126   *I found a dozen or more funeral marches*: In the process of digging into the history of this somber (and almost exclusively) male-dominated genre, I accidentally stumbled upon what I believe to be the first funeral march ever written by a woman. Often confused with Chopin's march because both the melody and the rhythm are quite similar, "Flee as a Bird" was composed by Mary Dana Shindler at around the same time Chopin completed Opus 35. She was a young American wife and mother who began, as scholar Patricia Woodard wrote, "to pour out her grief in verse" after her husband and infant son died of malaria within two days of each other in 1839. Scored to the words of a Baptist hymn ("Flee as a bird to your mountain, thou who art weary of sin . . ."), Shindler's composition was published in 1841 and improbably went on to become an early standard of the New Orleans jazz funeral sometime later in the century. Jelly Roll Morton played a snippet of Shindler's dirge in his parody of the jazz funeral, "Dead Man Blues," in 1926. Louis Armstrong, who once told an interviewer he heard Shindler's tune at funerals when he was a child, made it famous in the 1950s with "New Orleans Function," the classic jazz funeral piece that begins with a heavy dirge (played on the way to the cemetery) and then, once the body is in the ground, kicks over into a joyous celebration called "Oh, Didn't He Ramble." Thus Schindler's piece, like Chopin's, embraces two contradictory moods. Mary Dana Shindler didn't write "Flee as a Bird" as a funeral march, but it was appropriated for that purpose pretty soon thereafter. When I was Googling "Chopin's funeral march" on the night train home from Chicago after visiting my dying friend, I made what is apparently a common mistake: I assumed that Morton and Armstrong's tunes came from the Polish composer who was born in 1810. Instead, as I later learned, they came from a woman born in the same year in America, who wrote a melody that bears an uncanny resemblance to the funeral march in Opus 35. She wrote it at the very same time, but on another continent. And like Chopin's march, "Flee as a Bird" was eventually appropriated for a jazzman's riff on a time-tested grief motif.

127   *burning them in his fireplace*: Miłosz, *The History of Polish Literature*, pp. 190–92.

Notes

127   *"Even a great nation may fall"*: Bobrowski, *A Memoir of My Life*, p. 40.

128   *"not commonplace vulgar and petty-bourgeois"*: Chopin to Julian Fontana, September 25, 1839, Hedley, *Chopin's Letters*, p. 184.

129   *This left Jeffrey Kallberg*: Kallberg, "Chopin's March, Chopin's Death," *Nineteenth Century Music*, p. 12. I am indebted to Kallberg's scholarship on the history of Chopin's funeral march for much of the material in this chapter, including Chopin's removal of the word *funèbre* and the speculation that he may have been reacting against Berlioz's *Symphonie Fantastique*. Kallberg's article is a fascinating investigation into the roots of Chopin's march, which includes some evidence I have not cited that speculates (but doesn't conclusively demonstrate) that those roots could stretch back even farther, to 1835. He also discusses at some length the possible influence of Rossini's opera *La Gazza Ladra* on the *Lento Cantabile* (or "Trio") section of the funeral march. The article can be found at: https://www.jstor.org/stable/10.1525/ncm.2001.25.1.3.

131   *"music that is nothing without the assistance"*: Ibid., p. 15.

131   *Sand's daughter, Solange, described*: Ibid.

131   *"This is the way Berlioz composes"*: Niecks, *Frederick Chopin,* vol. 1, p. 265.

Chapter Seven: Death Comes to the Funeral March

133   *his mother sang to him as a child*: According to the Fryderyk Chopin Institute in Warsaw, the song concerns the romance of Laura and Philo: "*Już miesiąć zeszedł, psy się uśpiły*" ("The moon now has risen, the dogs are asleep"), https://en.chopin.nifc.pl/chopin/composition/detail/name/berceuse/id/121.

133   *Chopin himself didn't know quite what to call it*: Mieczysław Tomaszewski for the Fryderyk Chopin Institute, on the Polonaise-Fantasy in A-flat Major, Opus 61, https://en.chopin.nifc.pl/chopin/composition/detail/name/polonaise-fan/id/129.

133   *Thousands of New Yorkers*: Plaskin, *Horowitz*, p. 362.

133   *"one step removed from improvisation"*: Kallberg, "Chopin and the aesthetic of the sketch," p. 420.

134   *"scribbling over paper the whole night"*: Sand to Théodore de Seynes, December 28, 1841, Sand, *Correspondence*, Lubin, ed., Book V, p. 551.

134   *performed parodies of Italian opera*: From a letter of July 9, 1846, by Élise Fournier, of La Rochelle, quoted by the Fryderyk Chopin Institute, https://en.chopin.nifc.pl/chopin/life/calendar/year/1846.

134 *"the voices that had criticized him"*: Franz Liszt, *Revue et gazette musicale de Paris,* May 2, 1841, quoted on Fryderyk Chopin Institute website, Chopin Biography, 1841, https://en.chopin.nifc.pl/chopin/life/calendar/year/1841.

134 *"Ariel of pianists"*: *Gazette Musicale,* February 16, 1848. The review is reproduced by Edouard Ganche in *Frédéric Chopin,* p. 387

134 *"his four maddest children"*: Oshry, "Shifting Modes of Reception," p. 23. This has been variously translated from the German as "wildest," "most unruly," and "maddest."

134 *She complains of his shifting moods*: Sand to Marie de Rozières, July 11, 1841: "The day before yesterday he went the whole day without uttering a single syllable to anyone. . . . The cause I sought in vain," Sand, *Correspondence,* Lubin, ed., Book V, p. 363.

134 *drained the household of laughter and joy*: Sand to Bocage, May 7, 1843, Sand *Correspondence,* Lubin, ed., Book VI, p. 126.

134 *"I cannot hold it against him"*: Sand to Charlotte Marliani from Nohant, July 26, 1844. *Correspondence,* Lubin, ed., book 6, p. 586.

135 *"After the disappointments of my youth"*: Sand, *Story of My Life,* pp. 1103–4.

137 *"I think Chopin must have suffered"*: Cate, pp. 552–53.

137 *"Time will do its work"*: Chopin to Sand, July 24, 1847, Hedley, *Selected Correspondence of Fryderyk Chopin,* p. 293.

137 *"I am entrenching myself"*: Cate, p. 566.

138 *"A week ago"*: Chopin to Solange Clésinger, March 5, 1848, Hedley, p. 308.

139 *"a curious animal"*: Atwood, William G., *The Lioness and the Little One: The Liaison of George Sand and Frédéric Chopin,* New York: Columbia University Press, 1980, p. 45.

139 *tempted to throw a baptismal font*: Baudelaire quoted in Gavoty, *Chopin,* p. 305.

139 *"an immense legal plea"*: Ibid, p. 232.

139 *"lived her truths one at a time"*: Gastone Belotti, quoted in Samson, *Chopin,* pp. 137–38.

139 *"a wandering schoolboy"*: Sand, *Lettres d'un Voyageur, Tome I,* p. 5.

141 *"more Christian than the papacy"*: Sand, *Story of My Life,* pp. 925.

143 *"I can feel neither grief nor joy"*: Chopin to Grzymała, writing from London, end of July 1848, Hedley, *Selected Correspondence of Fryderyk Chopin,* p. 326.

143 *"If no one could tune to Chopin's satisfaction"*: Bellman, "Toward a Well-Tempered Chopin," p. 36.

143 *"took to his bed, and never left it"*: Walker, *Chopin*, p. 613.

143 *"In Europe there are nearly one thousand ladies"*: Nicolas Slonimsky, "Writings on Music," vol. 4, Slonimskyana (New York & London: Routledge, 2005), p. 192.

143 *There were other deathbed myths*: Adam Harasowski describes "the many conflicting and highly coloured accounts" in *The Skein of Legends Around Chopin*, pp. 260–61.

144 *Chopin was not a great reader of literature*: In opening remarks at the Bard College "Chopin and His World" music festival in 2017, Leon Botstein noted that Chopin was "not a great reader."

144 *"clear and concise language"*: Charles Gavard, quoted in Niecks, *Frederick Chopin,* vol. 2, p. 314.

144 *Voltaire began compiling his "Philosophical Dictionary"*: The Enlightenment was a period the Voltaire Foundation has dubbed the "age of the dictionary," a genre of organized thought first popularized by Diderot and d'Alembert's *Encyclopédie*, to which Voltaire contributed. I'm grateful to Gillian Pink at the Voltaire Foundation for her guidance in identifying the 1784 Kehl edition of Voltaire's *Philosophical Dictionary* as likely the edition Chopin owned and from which Gavard read to him.

145 *"with a portion of that spirit"*: Voltaire, "Essay on Taste," from Alexander Gerard, M.A., *An Essay on Taste: With Three Dissertations on the Same Subject* (printed for A. Millar in the Strand, London, 1759), p. 217.

145 *"the simple and natural beauty"*: Voltaire, "Taste," part 2, "On the Taste of Connoisseurs," in *Philosophical Dictionary*, https://ebooks.adelaide.edu.au/v/voltaire/dictionary/chapter440.html.

145 *"Simplicity is everything"*: Eigeldinger, *Chopin: Pianist and Teacher*, p. 54.

145 *"I have always had a great respect"*: Quoted by Grzymała in a letter to Auguste Léo, October 1849, in Hedley, *Selected Correspondence of Fryderyk Chopin*, pp. 374–75.

147 *Members of a national police orchestra*: The full name in French is *L'Orchestre d'Harmonie des Guardiens de la Paix de la Préfecture de Police*. For more, see: https://www.prefecturedepolice.interieur.gouv.fr/Nous-connaitre/Services-et-missions/Service-de-la-memoire-et-des-affaires-culturelles/La-Musique-des-gardiens-de-la-paix.

148 *"Either I am very much mistaken"*: Ochse, *Organists and Organ Playing in Nineteenth-Century France and Belgium*, p. 24.

148 *"the monarch of the church organ"*: H. B. Fabiani, quoted in Rollin Smith, "Lefébure-Wély: 'Prince of Organists,'" in *American Organist*, September 2012, p. 67

148 *Preludes in E minor*: I have a special attachment to the E minor Prelude because it was the first one I learned from the op. 28 collection. It's among Chopin's most popular works, and over the years has been featured in numerous films, television programs, and modern covers from jazz and rock to bossa nova. For me, the most meaningful quotation of the work comes from the fingers of rap artist, Dr. Dre. In the HBO documentary *The Defiant Ones*, Dre is sitting at his piano talking about the pressures of television, explaining why release dates are "the enemies of creativity." They "put a time limit on creativity," he says, "and I don't know if the idea I have today is the good idea. . . . Know what I mean? We're artists, we're just being creative. So it's like: just shut the fuck up and let us do our job. And then we'll give it to you and you can make your money." It's at this moment that he turns away from the camera, back to the piano, and begins playing Chopin's E minor Prelude. Just when this "defiant" modern artist is begging for understanding about the independent, creative process, he instinctively—and intuitively—channels the work of Chopin, a fellow rule-breaker from centuries ago.

148 *"soft and velvety tone"*: From Claude Montal's *L'Art d'accorder soi-même son piano* (Paris: Meissonnier, 1836), quoted in Jean-Jacques Eigeldinger, *Chopin: Pianist and Teacher*, pp. 91–92.

148 *"produced a profound sensation"*: Ochse, *Organists and Organ Playing in Nineteenth-Century France and Belgium*, p. 47.

149 *This "twenty-one year old already knew"*: Ibid, p. 33.

150 *"There is nothing more grotesque"*: Quoted by Rollin Smith in "Édouard Batiste," from an 1839 article in the French periodical *L'Orgue*, titled "Du Vandalisme et du catholicisme dans l'art," *American Organist*, January 2007, p. 70.

151 *"hover and cry"*: quoted in Ganche, *Frédéric Chopin*, p. 420, translation by the author.

152 *they would have heard the now unmistakably heroic work*: There is some disagreement in the literature about when the funeral march was played at the Madeleine. I am relying on musicologist Alan Walker's definitive 2018 biography, *Fryderyk Chopin*, in which he writes that the work was played as "the great doors of the Madeleine Church swung open," pp. 620–21.

152   *"heart-burial"*: "Heart-burial," *Encyclopedia Britannica*, 1911, https://en.wiki source.org/wiki/1911_Encyclopædia_Britannica/Heart-burial.

152   *"[lying] in semi-darkness, slight, gaunt, heartless"*: Tokarczuk, *Flights*, pp. 317, 321–22.

153   *A Nazi music-lover*: details of the story of Chopin's heart are from Walker, *Fryderyk Chopin*, pp. 667–71.

153   *Here a Polish pianist*: Walker, *Chopin*, p. 670.

154   *the piece that was playing on a CD*: Yuki Oda, " 'Nobu' Fever: Japan Falls for a Blind Piano Prodigy," *Time*, November 18, 2009, http://content.time.com/ time/world/article/0,8599,1940215,00.html.

154   *the original autopsy*: Details of Chopin's autopsy and cause of death are from Michał Witt, Artur Szklener, Wojciech Marchwica, and Tadeusz Dobosz, *Journal of Applied Genetics* 59, no. 4 (November 2018), pp 471–431; and Michał Witt, Artur Szklener, Jerzy Kawecki, Witold Rużyłło, Marta Negrusz-Kawecka, Michał Jeleń, Renata Langfort, Wojciech Marchwica, and Tadeusz Dobosz, "A Closer Look at Frederic Chopin's Cause of Death," *American Journal of Medicine* (September 2017), https://doi.org/doi:10.1016/j.amjmed.2017.09.039.

156   *among the hallmarks of his music*: For this insight into the connection between the variants in the Nocturne in E-flat Major, op. 9, no. 2 and Chopin's improvisational instincts, I'm indebted to Eigeldinger's *Chopin: Teacher and Pianist*, p. 123.

156   *"So where is the real Chopin version?"*: Jonathan Bellman, panel discussion, "Chopin's Place in 19th Century Performance Culture," in a presentation "On Chopin's Variant Fioritura," Bard SummerScape festival, "Chopin and His World," August 19, 2017.

Selected Bibliography

Aijón, David Bruno. "Expressive Gesture and Structural Disambiguation in Frédéric Chopin's Fingering Indications: A Preliminary Study Through Selected Etudes." Master's thesis, Cardiff University, 2018.

Ariès, Philippe. *The Hour of Our Death: The Classic History of Western Attitudes Towards Death Over the Last One Thousand Years.* New York: Vintage Books, 2008.

Allard, Sébastien, and Côme Fabre. *Delacroix.* New York: The Metropolitan Museum of Art, 2018. Distributed by Yale University Press.

Bach, C. P. E. *Essay on the True Art of Playing Keyboard Instruments.* New York: W. W. Norton, 1949.

Bellman, Jonathan D. "Toward a Well-Tempered Chopin," *Chopin in Performance: History, Theory, Practice.* Warsaw: Narodowy Instytut Fryderyka Chopina, 2005.

———. "Chopin's Pianism and the Reconstruction of the Ineffable." *Keyboard Perspectives III,* Ithaca: Westfield Center for Historical Keyboard Studies, 2010, pp. 1–21.

Bellman, Jonathan D., and Halina Goldberg, eds. *Chopin and His World.* Princeton: Princeton University Press, 2017.

Bellos, David. *The Novel of the Century: The Extraordinary Adventure of* Les Misérables. New York: Farrar, Straus & Giroux, 2017.

Bernstein, Leonard. *The Unanswered Questions: Six Talks at Harvard (The Charles Eliot Norton Series).* Cambridge, MA: Harvard University Press, 1982.

Selected Bibliography

Biss, Jonathan. "Exploring Beethoven's Piano Sonatas." Curtis Institute of Music, 2017. Https://www.coursera.org/learn/beethoven-piano-sonatas.

Bobrowski, Tadeusz. *Memoir of My Life.* Translated and edited with an introduction by Addison Bross. Boulder: East European Monographs and Lublin: Marie Curie-Skłowska University,2008. Distributed by Columbia University Press.

Boczkowska, Ewelina. "Chopin's Ghosts,"*19th-Century Music,* vol. 35, no. 3, Chopin's Subjects, Spring, 2012, pp. 204–223

Burke, Richard N. "The *marche funèbre* from Beethoven to Mahler." PhD diss., City University of New York. U.M.I. Dissertation Services, Ann Arbor, MI: 1991.

Caruncho, Manuel Vázquez, and Fernández Brañas Franciso Fernández. "The Hallucinations of Frédéric Chopin." *Medical Humanities,* June 2011.

Cate, Curtis. *George Sand: A Biography.* New York: Avon Books, 1975.

Chapin, Miles, and Rodica Prato. *88 Keys: The Making of a Steinway Piano.* New York: Clarkson Potter, 1997.

Chopin, Frédéric. *Selected Correspondence of Fryderyk Chopin*, Translated and Edited with Additional Material and a Commentary by Arthur Hedley. London: Heinemann: 1962.

Chopin, Frédéric. *Chopin's Letters.* Collected by Henryk Opieński. Translated from the Original Polish and French with a Preface and Editorial Notes by E. L. Voynich. New York: Alfred A. Knopf, 1931.

Chopin, Frédéric. *Correspondance de Frédéric Chopin.* Recueillie, révisée, annotée et traduite par Bronislas Édouard Sydow, en collaboration avec Suzanne et Denise Chainaye. Paris: *La Revue Musicale*, Richard Masse, Éditeurs, in collaboration with Suzanne and Denise Chainaye, 1981.

Choussat Hélène, *Souvenirs.* Ed. Gabriel Quetglas Olin. Palma: Institut d'Estudis Baleàrics, 2010.

Corkle, Rachel. "Language and Music in Dialogue." *George Sand Studies,* 31. New York: The George Sand Association and Hofstra University, 2012.

Cortés, Rafael. *A Pianist: Wanderings of the Mind and Spirit, Essays on Music and Life.* 2011.

Custine, Astolphe de. *Letters from Russi.* Edited and with an Introduction by Anka Muhlstein. New York: New York Review of Books, 2002.

Dale, Kathleen. *Nineteenth-Century Piano Music: A Handbook for Pianists.* London: Oxford University Press, 1954.

David, Hans T. and Arthur Mendel, eds. *The New Bach Reader: A Life of Johann Sebastian Bach in Letters and Documents.* New York: W. W. Norton & Co., 1998.

Davies, Norman. *God's Playground: A History of Poland,* vol. 1, revised edition. New York: Columbia University Press, 2005.

———. *Europe: A History.* New York: HarperPerennial, 1998.

Delacroix, Eugène. *The Journal of Eugène Delacroix.* London: Phaidon Press Limited, 1951, 1995.

———. *Selected Letters: 1813–1863.* Edited and translated by Jean Stewart. Boston: MFA Publications, a division of the Museum of Fine Arts, 1970, 2001. Distributed by D.A.P.

Diruta, Girolamo. *Il Transilvano Diologo.* Venice: Appresso Alessandro Vincenti, 1597 and 1695. Accessed at IMSLP Petrucci Music Library, https://imslp.org/wiki/Il_Transilvano_(Diruta,_Girolamo).

Dubal, David. *The Art of the Piano: Its Performers, Literature, and Recordings.* New York: Amadeus Press, 2004.

Dendle, Brian J., and Shelby Thacker. *British Travellers in Mallorca in the Nineteenth Century: An Anthology of Texts.* Newark, DE: Juan de la Cuesta—Hispanic Monographs, 2006.

Eigeldinger, Jean-Jacques. *Chopin: Pianist and Teacher as Seen by His Pupils,* Trans. by Naomi Shohet with Krysia Osostowicz and Roy Howat. Cambridge: Cambridge University Press, 1986.

———. *L'achèvement des Préludes opo. 28 de Chopin, Revue de Musicologie,* T. 75, No. 2, 1989, pp. 229–42. Https://www.jstor.org/stable/928884?seq=1#page_scan_tab_contents

———. *Esquisses pour un méthode de piano.* Textes réunis et présentés par Jean-Jacques Eigeldinger. Paris: Flammarion, 1993.

———. "Chopin and 'La Note Bleue': An Interpretation of the Prelude Op. 45." *Music & Letters* 78, no. 2, May 1997, pp. 233–53, Http://www.jstor.org/stable/737392.

———. "Chopin and Pleyel." *Early Music,* August 2001.

———. *J. S. Bach, Vingt-Quatre Préludes et Fugues.* Annoté par Frédéric Chopin. Commentaire de Jean-Jacques Eigeldinger. Paris: Société Française de Musciologie, 2010.

———. *Autour Des 24 Préludes de Frédéric Chopin.* Valldemossa, Valldemossa: Le Museo Frédéric Chopin y George Sand, Real Cartuja, 2019.

Selected Bibliography

Ferra, Bartomeu. *Chopin and George Sand in Majorca*, Trans. R.D.F. Pring-Mill. Palma: Edicions La Cartoixa, 1961.

Gaines, James R. *Evening in the Palace of Reason: Bach Meets Frederick the Great in the Age of Enlightenmnet.* New York: Harper Perennial, 2005.

Ganche, Édouard. *Frédéric Chopin: Sa Vie et Ses Œuvres, 1810–1849*. Paris: Mercure de France, 1921.

———. *L'Autèntica Cella de Frédéric Chopin a la Cartoixa de Valldemossa.* Valldemossa: Sociedat Quetglas Tous S.L., 1994.

Gavoty, Bernard. *Frederic Chopin*. Trans. Martin Sokolinsky, New York: Charles Scribner's Sons, 1977.

Gerig, Reginald R. *Famous Pianists and Their Technique, New Edition,* with a Foreword by Alan Walker. Bloomington: Indiana University Press, 2007.

Gide, André. *Notes on Chopin,* Trans. Bernard Frechtman. New York: Philosophical Library, 1949.

Goldberg, Halina, Ed. *The Age of Chopin: Interdisciplinary Inquiries.* Bloomington: Indiana University Press, 2004.

———. *Music in Chopin's Warsaw.* Oxford: Oxford University Press, 2008.

Graves, Robert, with Illustrations by Paul Hogarth. *Majorca Observed*. Garden City: Doubleday & Company, Inc., 1954.

Harasowski, Adam. *The Skein of Legends Around Chopin*. Glasgow: William MacLellan & Co., Ltd., 1967.

Henry-Massard, Franck. *Mon Carnet George Sand.* Https://moncarnetgeorgesand.fr.

Hipkins, A. J. *How Chopin Played: From Contemporary Impressions Collected from the Diaries and Note-books of the Late A .J. Hipkins, F.S.A.* London: J. M. Dent & Sons, 1937.

Hoftstadter, Douglas R. *Metamagical Themas: Questing for the Essence of Mind and Pattern.* New York: Basic Books, 1985.

Hugo, Victor. *Les Misérables*. Trans. Charles E. Wilbour. New York: The Modern Library, 1992.

Isacoff, Stuart. *A Natural History of the Piano: The Instrument, the Music, the Musicians—from Mozart to Modern Jazz and Everything in Between.* New York: Alfred A. Knopf, 2011.

Isserlis, Steven. *Robert Schumann's Advice to Young Musicians, Revisited by Steven Isserlis.* Chicago: University of Chicago Press, 2017.

Kallberg, Jeffrey. "Chopin in the Marketplace: Aspects of the International Music

Publishing Industry in the First Half of the Nineteenth Century: Part I: France and England." Music Library Association, *Notes,* Second Series, 39, no. 3, Marc., 1983, pp. 535–69.

———. "The Rhetoric of Genre: Chopin's Nocturne in G Minor." *19th-Century Music,* 2, no. 3, Spring 1988, pp. 238–61.

———. "Chopin and the Aesthetic of the Sketch: A New Prelude in E flat Minor?" *Early Music,* August 2001.

———. "Chopin's March, Chopin's Death." *Nineteenth Century Music,* 25, no. 1, Summer 2001.

Kelly, Thomas Forrest. *Early Music: A Very Short Introduction.* Oxford: Oxford University Press, 2011.

———. *Capturing the Music: The Story of Notation.* New York: W. W. Norton & Co., 2015.

Klein, Michael. "The Mazurka in C# Minor, Op. 30, No. 4." *19th Century Music,* 35, no. 3, Spring 2012, pp. 238–60. Http://www.jstor.org/stable/10.1525/ncm.2012.35.3.238.

Koropeckyj, Roman. *Adam Mickiewicz: The Life of a Romantic.* Ithaca: Cornell University Press, 2008.

Kramer, Lawrence. "Chopin at the Funeral: Episodes in the History of Modern Death." *Journal of the American Musciological Society,* 54, no. 1, Spring 2001, pp. 97–125. Http://www.jstor.org/stable/10.1525/jams.2001.54.1.97.

Laqueur, Thomas W. *The Work of the Dead: A Cultural History of Mortal Remains.* Princeton, NJ: Princeton University Press, 2015.

Leikin, Anatole. "Repeat with Caution: A Dilemma of the First Movement of Chopin's Sonata Op. 35." *The Musical Quarterly,* 85, no. 3, Autumn 2001, pp. 568–82. Http://www.jstor.org/stable/3600997 .

Letellier, Robert Ignatius. *Meyerbeer's Robert le Diable: The Premier Opéra Romantique.* Newcastle upon Tyne: Cambridge Scholars Publishing, 2012.

Liszt, Franz. *Liszt's Chopin.* Trans. Meirion Hughes. Manchester: Manchester University Press, 2011.

Loesser, Arthur. *Men, Women and Pianos: A Social History.* With a New Introduction by Edward Rothstein and a Preface by Jacques Barzun. Mineola, NY: Dover, 1990. First published in 1954 by Fireside.

Lubin, Georges. *La Memoire des Lieux: George Sand en Berry.* Brussels: Editions Complexe, 1992.

Selected Bibliography

Luppé, Marquis de. *Astolphe de Custine*. Monaco: Editions du Rocher, 1957, p. 202.

McCullough, David. *The Greater Journey: Americans in Paris*. New York: Simon & Schuster, 2011.

Miłosz, Czesław. *The History of Polish Literature*. 2nd edition. Berkeley: University of California Press, 1983.

Monelle, Raymond. *The Musical Topic: Hunt, Military and Pastoral*. Bloomington: Indiana University Press, 2006.

Moore, Aubertine Woodward. "Sigismund Thalberg—Prince of the Salon." *The Etude Magazine*, September 1914. Https://etudemagazine.com/etude/1914/09/sigismund-thalberg—prince-of-the-salon.html.

Moran, Michael. *A Country in the Moon: Travels in Search of the Heart of Poland*. London: Granta Books, 2009 .

Moses, Claire Goldberg. *French Feminism in the 19th Century*. Albany, NY: State University of Albany Press, 1984.

Muhlstein, Anka. *A Taste for Freedom: The Life of Astolphe de Custine*. New York: Helen Marx Books, 1999.

Niecks, Frederick. *Frederick Chopin: As a Man and Musician*. Vols. 1 and 2. London: Novello, Ewer & Co., 1888.

Ochse, Orpha. *Organists and Organ Playing in Nineteenth-Century France and Belgium*. Bloomington: Indiana University Press, 1994.

Olivier, Juste. *Paris en 1830*. Chapel Hill: University of North Carolina Studies in the Romance Languages and Literatures, 1951.

Oshry, Jonathan Isaac. "Shifting Modes of Reception: Chopin's Piano Sonata in B Flat Minor, Opus 35," PhD diss., University of Manchester, 1999.

Pabjan, Barbara. "The Reception of Chopin and His Music in Polish Society." *International Review of the Aesthetics and Sociology of Music*, 41, no. 2, December 2010, pp. 343–78. Http://www.jstor.org/stable/41203372.

Paetsch, Annabelle. "Performance Practices in Chopin's Piano Sonatas, Op. 35 and 58: A Critical Study of Nineteenth-Century Manuscript and Printed Sources." PhD diss., University of Western Ontario, Canada, 2001.

Paget, François, and André Duchesne. *Astolphe de Custine, Un Hôte Illustre de Saint-Gratien*. Montmorency: Société d'Histoire de Montmorency et de sa Region, 2016.

Parakilas, James. *Piano Roles: Three Hundred Years of Life with the Piano*. New Haven: Yale University Press, 2002.

————. "Disrupting the Genre: Unforeseen Personifications in Chopin." *19th Century Music*, 35, no. 3, 2012, pp. 165–81.

Parnas, Kornelia. *Maria: Une Idylle d'Amour en Musique, Chopin À Maria Wodzińska*. Paris: Costallat & Cie, 1910.

Parker, June. *Walking in Mallorca: Classic Mountain Walks in Mallorca*. 4th Edition, updated by Paddy Dillon. Cumbria, UK: Cicerone Press, 2006.

Patte, Jean-Yves, *Les étés de Frédéric Chopin à Nohant, 1839–1846*. Paris: Èditions du Patrimoine, Centre des Monuments Nationaux, 2009.

Petty, Wayne. "Chopin and the Ghost of Beethoven." *19th-Century Music*. 22, no. 3, Spring 1999, pp. 281–99. Http://www.jstor.org/stable/746802.

Philip, Robert. *The Classical Music Lover's Companion to Orchestral Music*. New Haven: Yale University Press, 2018.

Plaskin, Glenn. *Horowitz: A Biography*. New York: Quill, 1983.

Pollens, Stewart. *Bartolomeo Cristofori and the Invention of the Piano*. Cambridge: Cambridge University Press, 2017.

Postman, Neil. *Building a Bridge to the Eighteenth Century: How the Past Can Improve Our Future*. New York: Vintage Books, 1999.

Purves, Dale. *Music as Biology: The Tones We Like and Why*. Cambridge: Harvard University Press, 2017.

Reid, Martine. *George Sand*. Trans. Gretchen van Slyke. University Park: Pennsylvania State University Press, 2018.

Rink, John Scott. "The Evolution of Chopin's 'Structural Style' and its Relation to Improvisation." PhD diss. St. John's College, Cambridge, January 1989.

————. and Jim Samson, eds. *Chopin Studies, 2*. Cambridge: Cambridge University Press, 1994.

————. "Frédéric Chopin: Esquisses pour une méthode de piano by Jean-Jacques Eigeldinger." *Music & Letters*, 75, no. 3, August, 1994, pp. 471–75. Https://www.jstor.org/stable/737367.

Ripoll, Luis. *Chopin's Winter in Majorca: 1838–1839*. Trans. Alan Sillitoe. Palma: 1955.

Rosen, Charles. *Sonata Forms*. Revised Edition. New York: W. W. Norton & Co., 1988.

————. "The First Movement of Chopin's Sonata in B flat Minor, Op. 35," *19th-Century Music*, 14, no. 1, Summer 1990, pp. 60–66.

————. *Beethoven's Piano Sonatas: A Short Companion*. New Haven: Yale University Press, 2002.

Rousseau, Jean-Jacques. *Emile, Or On Education.* 1762, quoted in *The Essential Writings of Rousseau*, New York: Modern Library, 2013.

Samson, Jim, ed. *The Cambridge Companion to Chopin.*Cambridge: Cambridge University Press, 1992.

———. *Chopin.* New York: Oxford University Press, 1996.

———. "Chopin, Past and Present." *Early Music,* 29, no. 3, August, 2001, pp. 381–87 Http://www.jstor.org/stable/3519182.

Sand, George. "Préface." *Les Confessions de J.-J. Rousseau.* Paris: Charpentier, Libraire-Éditeur, 1847.

———. *Lettres d'un Voyageur.* Vol. 1. Paris: Michel Lévy Frères, Éditeurs, 1869.

———. *Valentine.* Paris: Michel Lévy Frères, Éditeurs, 1869.

———. *Correspondance: 1812–1876.* Vol. 2, Paris: Ancienne Maison Michel Lévy Frères, Calmann Lévy, Éditeur, 1883.

———. *Letters of George Sand.* Translated and edited by Raphaël Ledos de Beaufort, in 3 volumes. London: Ward & Downey, 1886.

———. *Winter in Majorca.* Translated and annotated by Robert Graves, with a "Historical Summary." Chicago: Academy Chicago Publishers, 1956.

———. *Correspondance: Textes Réunis, Classés et Annotés par George Lubin.* Vols. 5, 6, 7, 9. Paris: Garnier Frères, 1969.

———. *Seven Strings of the Lyre: A Woman's Version of the Faust Legend.* Trans. George A. Kennedy. Chapel Hill, NC, and London: University of North Carolina Press, 1989.

———. *Story of My Life: The Autobiography of George Sand.* A group translation edited by Thelma Jurgrau, Albany: State University of New York Press, 1991.

———. *Lucrezia Floriani.* Trans. Julius Eker. Chicago: Academy of Chicago Press, 1993.

———. *Gabriel.* Trans. Kathleen Robin Hart and Paul Fenouillet. New York: Modern Language Association of America, 2010.

———. *Spiridion.* Trans. Patricia J. F. Worth. Albany: State University of New York Press, 2015.

———. *A Winter in Mallorca.* Trans Sara Wood. Ed. Gabriel Quetglas Olin. Real Cartuja de Valldemossa: Le Museo Frédéric Chopin y George Sand, 2019.

Schiff, Andras. "Piano Sonata in A flat major, Op. 26." Beethoven Lecture-Recitals, Part 4. Wigmore Hall. Https://wigmore-hall.org.uk/podcasts/andras-schiff -beethoven-lecture-recitals.

Siek, Stephen. *A Dictionary for the Modern Pianist*. Lanham, MD: Rowman & Little-field Publishers, 2016.

Smith, Rollin. "Édouard Batiste." *The American Organist*, January 2007, pp. 7074.

———. "Lefébure-Wély: 'Prince of Organists.'" *The American Organist*, September 2012, pp. 62–70.

Tokarczuk, Olga. *Flights*. Trans. Jennifer Croft. New York: Riverhead Books, 2018.

Tomaszewski, Mieczysław. *Fryderyk Chopin: A Diary in Images*. Trans. Rosemary Hunt. Warsaw: Wydawnictwo Arkady and Polskie Wydawnictwo Muzyczne, 1990.

Tommasini, Anthon., *The Indispensable Composers: A Personal Guide*. New York: Penguin Press, 2018.

Tresch, John. "The Prophet and the Pendulum: Sensational Science and Audiovisual Phantasmagoria around 1848." *Grey Room*, 43, Spring 2011, pp. 16–41.

———. *The Romantic Machine: Utopian Science and Technology After Napoleon*. Chicago: University of Chicago Press, 2012.

Voltaire (François-Marie Arouet). "Goût." *Dictionnaire Philosophique*, in *Completes de Voltaire*. Vol. 40. De L'imprimerie de la Société Littéraire-Typographique, 1784, pp. 482–503.

Walker, Alan, ed. *The Chopin Companion: Profiles of the Man and the Musician*. New York: W. W. Norton & Co., Inc., 1966.

———. *Fryderyk Chopin: A Life and Times*. New York: Farrar, Straus and Giroux, 2018.

Wason, Robert W.. "Two Bach Preludes / Two Chopin Preludes, or *Toujours travailler Bach—se sera votre meilleur moyen de progresser*." *Music Theory Spectrum*, 24, no. 1, Spring 2002, pp. 103–20. Http://www.jstor.org/stable/10.1525/mts.2002.24.1.103

Accessed: 03-04-2017 18:24 UTC.

Wharton, Edith, *A Motor-Flight Through France* DeKalb, ILL: Northern Illinois Press, 1991, 2012

White, Craig. "Introduction to Classical Music." Yale University. Https://www.coursera.org/learn/introclassicalmusic/home/info, 2017.

Witt, Michał, Artur Szklener, Jerzy Kawecki, Witold RuzÃáýło, Marta Negrusz-Kawecka, Michał Jeleń, Renata Langfort, Wojciech Marchwica, and

Selected Bibliography

Tadeusz Dobosz. "A Closer Look at Frederic Chopin's Cause of Death." *The American Journal of Medicine*, 2017. Https://doi.org/doi:10.1016/j.amjmed .2017.09.039.

Woodard, Patricia. " 'Flee as a Bird': Mary Dana Shindler's Legacy" *American Music*, 26, no. 1, Spring, 2008, pp. 74–103. Http://www.jstor.org/stable/40071689.

Wolff, Christoph. *Bach: The Learned Musician*. New York: W. W. Norton & Co., 2000.

Index

Page numbers in *italics* refer to illustrations.

Index

Index

Index

Index

jazz, x, xxvi, 12
    Funeral March in the style of, xiv–xv, xx–xxi
Jędrzejewicz, Kalasanty, 153
Jehl, Sylvie, 122, 140
Jérôme (mason), 74
Journal (Delacroix), 119–20
July Revolution (1830), 10, 77, 130, 132

Kahn, Jeremy, xxi
Kallberg, Jeffrey, 129–30
Kawaguchi, Naruhiko, 49
Kleiner Trauermarsch in C Minor, K. 453a (Mozart), 126
Kosz, Mieczysław, xx
Kraków main market square, 5-6
kujawiak (folk dance), 12

Lane, Piers, 156
"Largo in E-flat Major" (Chopin), 80
Laurens, Jean-Joseph Bonaventure, 91
Lefébure-Wély, Louis, 147–48, 149
Leipzig, xxiv
Lemberg, 20, 21
Lento con gran espressione (Chopin), 153
Lenz, Wilhelm von, xxvii, 69
Leroux, Pierre, 27
Letters to a Traveler (Sand), 139
Liszt, Franz, 21, 33, 34, 39, 41, 42–43, 56, 68–69, 97, 116, 134
Llull, Ramon, 180
London, xxiv, 16, 44, 57, 143
Louis XVI, King of France, 74
Louis Philippe, King of France, 10, 25, 26, 130
Lucrezia Floriani (Sand), 135–37
lullabies, xvii, 13, 98, 127, 133

Ma, Yo-Yo, 22
Maffei, Scipione, 32
Maison de George Sand, 142
Majorca, xxiv, xxvi, 72, 79, 83–107, 134
    celda in, 87–96, 98–99, 101–2, 106, 107

Chopin's creative work in, 86, 94, 107, 115, 148
Hermitage de la Trinitat in, 92, 93–94
natural beauty and wildlife of, 87, 91, 93
streets and roads of, 87, 89–90, 91, 92
Valldemossa region of, 87–88, 90–92, 94
Majorca Observed (Graves), 91
Malinowski, Stephen, 104
Mallefille, Félicien, 72
Mallorquin, El (steamship), 83, 88, 109
"Man from Harlem, The" (Calloway), xix–xx
marche funèbre, op. 72, no. 2 (Chopin), 127–28
Marcia Funebre Sulla Morte d'un Eroe (Beethoven), 126
"Marche Lugubre" (Gossec), 125–26
Marliani, Charlotte, 138, 140
Mary II, Queen of England, xx
Maxfield, Rebecca, 113
Mazurka in C-sharp minor, op. 50, no. 3 (Chopin), 48
Mazurka in A-flat minor, op. 17, no. 4 (Chopin), 12
Mazurka in E minor, op. 41, no.1 (Chopin), 86
Mazurka in F minor, op. post. 68, no. 4 (Chopin), 133
mazurkas (Chopin), 12, 48, 86, 133
Mendelssohn, Fanny, 43
Mendelssohn, Felix, 34, 42, 65
Mendizábal, Juan Álvarez, 87
Metropolitan Museum of Art, 30, 118
metronome, and "rule of irregularity," 21
Meyerbeer, Giacomo, 27–28, 53
Mickiewicz, Adam, 9, 10
Mikuli, Karol, 45, 62
Miller, Asher, 118–19
Miłosz, Czeslaw, 8
Misérables, Les (Hugo), 1, 26
Monelle, Raymond, 126
Montal, Claude, 95
Montessori, Maria, 68
Moog synthesizer, 125

Index

Morgan Library and Museum, xxiv–xxv, 57

Morris, Wesley, xix

Morrison, Toni, xix

Morse, Samuel, 27

Morton, Jelly Roll, 185

Moscheles, Ignaz, 14–15, 56

Mozart, Wolfgang Amadeus, 34, 39, 112, 123, 126, 150, 151

Muhlstein, Anka, 75

music:
  as abstract form, ix
  community and, xiii–xiv
  death and, xiii, xiv
  improvisatory, xxi, xxv, 21, 72, 95, 150, 156
  language of, ix, xiii, xxiii, 23
  listening to, ix–x, xiv, 35, 66–67
  mathematics of, ix, 21
  notation of, ix, xxiv, 58
  perception of, x
  performing of, xiii–xiv
  programmatic, 101, 146
  recordings of, x, xi, xiii
  sheet, 34
  tonal intervals in, 30
  writing about, ix

musical staff, 58–59

Music Animation Machine, 104

Music in Chopin's Warsaw (Goldberg), 68

Napoleon I, Emperor of the French, 12, 75, 146, 147, 150

Napoleonic Code, 71

"New Poland," establishment of, 7

Nicholas I, Czar of Russia, 9

Nocturne in D-flat major, op. 27, no. 2 (Chopin), 44

Nocturne in E-flat major, op. 9, no.2 (Chopin), 155–56

Nocturne in G minor, op. 15, no. 3 (Chopin), 12, 69

nocturnes (Chopin), xvi, 12, 44–45, 69, 86

Nocturnes, op. 37 (Chopin), 86

Nohant, xxiv, 114–18, 120–21, 123–24, 128–29, 140

Norma (Bellini), 62–63

Ohlsson, Garrick, 99

Oort, Bart van, 156

opera, 41–42, 61, 81
  bel canto, 31–32, 44, 62, 63, 156

Oratorium (Breuker), xx

orchestras, 43
  increasing size of, xxiii, 39
  period, 49

organs, 28, 104, 147–49

Paderewski, Ignacy Jan, 20–22, 35, 153

Palma, 83, 85, 87, 89, 92

Pape, Jean-Henri, 31

Paris:
  Chopin's life in, xxii, xxiv, 13, 16, 25–28, 39, 40, 69, 129, 143
  Church of the Madeleine in, xxv, 146–52
  Louvre Palace in, 119, 130
  Montmartre, xxv
  Montmartre Cemetery in, 130
  Notre-Dame Cathedral in, xxv
  Père Lachaise Cemetery in, 2, 4, 152, 156–57
  Place de la Bastille in, 130
  Place Vendôme in, 143, 144
  Pleyel House in, 88, 90
  Polish Library in, xxv
  salon audiences in, 44

Parke-Bernet Galleries, 13, 14

Peabody Conservatory of Music, 63–64

Pennsylvania, University of, 28

Pestalozzi, Heinrich, 65–69, 127

photography, x, xxi, 104

Piano Concerto in F minor, op. 21 (Chopin), 49, 159–60

Piano Concertos (Chopin), xxiii, 49

pianoforte, xxiv, 29–30, 39, 104, 151

pianos, xxiv
  Bechstein, 34

Index

Blüthner, 34
Bösendorfer, 34, 37, 47
Brodman, 34
Buchholtz, 40, 48
comparison of modern and nineteenth
  century, x, 37
damper pedals on, 38, 46
Érard, 32–33, 34, 35, 43, 44, 45, 50, 68
golden age of, 36
grand, 42
invention and development of, 28–40, 63
keyboards of, xix, xxiv, 2–3, *3*, 34, 45, 96
Pleyel, xvi, xx, 32–33, 34, 35, 38,
  44–45, 48, 49, 51, 68, 72, 88–90
soundboards of, 33
Steinway, x, xxvi, 34, 35, 37–38, 43, 47,
  49, 50, 51, 99
Streicher, 34, 40
technology of, xxii, 28–29
tuning of, 95, 143
upright, 88, 90
Viennese-style versus English, 32, 36–37
Yamaha, 37, 47
Piano Sonata in A-flat major, op. 26
  (Beethoven), 123–26
Piano Sonata in A-minor, K. 310 (Mozart), 34
Piano Sonata, op. 27 no. 2 *Moonlight*
  (Beethoven), 34, 38
Piano Sonata, op. 106 *Hammerklavier*
  (Beethoven), 96
Picasso, Pablo, 119
Pleyel, Camille, 33, 89, 90
Pleyel, Ignaz, 32, 33, 39
Poland, 5–10, 19
  "captive," 7–8, 25,
  culture of, 6
  first European constitution established
    in, 8–9
  government of, xv
  independence regained in, 45–46
  invasions and occupations of, 6–8,
    10–11, 13, 21, 22
  Law and Justice Party in, 22–23

liberal humanism and religious freedom
  in, 8
national anthem of, 9
1939 Nazi invasion and occupation of,
  6, 22
"Noble Democracy" of, 8
partitions of, 1, 6–7, 9, 46
self-exile of Chopin from, xxii, 4, 10–11,
  12–13, 15, 18, 79
Solidarity movement in, 6
stateless period in, 7–8
Polish army, 10
Polish Consulate in New York City, xv,
  xviii, xxi, 13, 57
Polish language, 57
Polish National Television, 47
Polish Radio, 6, 47, 80, 154
Pollini, Maurizio, 43, 46
Polonaise, op.40, no. 1 "Military"
  (Chopin), 80, 86
Polonaise-Fantaisie, op. 61 (Chopin), 133
Porter, Cole, x, xvi
Preliminary School of Finger Dexterity, The
  (Czerny), 56
Prelude in B minor, op. 28, No. 6
  (Chopin), 148
Prelude in E minor, op. 28, No. 4
  (Chopin), 148
Prelude no. 15, op. 28 "Raindrop" (Chopin),
  45, 86, 95, 96, 98–100, 101–2, 104, 105
Prelude, op. 28, no. 17 "Castle Clock"
  (Chopin), 14–15, 86, 95, 104, 105
preludes (Chopin), xx, 14–15, 44, 45, 88
printing press, 26–27
Projet de Méthode (Chopin), 58–60, 63, 64,
  69–70
Providence, R.I., 113
Prussia, 45–46
Purcell, Henry, funeral march of, xx, 125, 126
Pythagoras, 30

Quadrado, José Maria, 85
Quetglas, Gabriel, 92, 93–94, 95, 98, 99 101

Index

Index

About the Author

Annik LaFarge is author of the award-winning *On the High Line: Exploring America's Most Original Urban Park* and the blog LivinThe HighLine.com. She has contributed articles to numerous publications, including *The New York Times*, *Bark* magazine, and *HuffPost*. Also a photographer, editor, and lecturer, she lives in New York City and Hudson and online at anniklafarge.com.